Technology and Digital Media in the Early Years

A Co-Publication of Routledge and NAEYC

Technology and Digital Media in the Early Years offers early childhood teacher educators, professional development providers, and early childhood educators in preservice, inservice, and continuing education settings a thought-provoking guide to effective, appropriate, and intentional use of technology with young children. This book provides strategies, theoretical frameworks, links to research evidence, descriptions of best practice, and resources to develop essential digital literacy knowledge, skills, and experiences for early childhood educators in the digital age.

Technology and Digital Media in the Early Years puts educators right at the intersections of child development, early learning, developmentally appropriate practice, early childhood teaching practices, children's media research, teacher education, and professional development practices. The book is based on current research, promising programs and practices, and a set of best practices for teaching with technology in early childhood education that are based on the National Association for the Education of Young Children (NAEYC) & Fred Rogers Center joint position statement on Technology and Interactive Media and the Fred Rogers Center Framework for Quality in Children's Digital Media. Pedagogical principles, classroom practices, and teaching strategies are presented in a practical, straightforward way informed by child development theory, developmentally appropriate practice, and research on effective, appropriate, and intentional use of technology in early childhood settings. A companion website provides additional resources and links to further illustrate principles and best practices for teaching and learning in the digital age.

Chip Donohue, PhD, is Dean of Distance Learning and Continuing Education, and Director of TEC Center, Erikson Institute, USA.

Technology and Digital Media in the Early Years

Tools for Teaching and Learning

Edited by Chip Donohue

naeyc®

National Association for the
Education of Young Children
Washington, DC 20005
www.naeyc.org

Routledge
Taylor & Francis Group

NEW YORK AND LONDON

Published simultaneously 2015 by Routledge, 711 Third Avenue, New York, NY 10017 and the National Association for the Education of Young Children, 1313 L Street NW, Suite 500, Washington, DC 20005

Routledge is an imprint of the Taylor & Francis Group, an informa business

Library of Congress Cataloging-in-Publication Data

Technology and digital media in the early years : tools for teaching and
    learning / edited by Chip Donohue.
        pages cm
    Includes bibliographical references and index.
 1. Early childhood education—Computer-assisted instruction.
2. Computers and children.   3. Educational technology.
I. Donohue, Chip.
    LB1139.35.C64T38   2014
    371.33—dc23
    2014005911

ISBN: 978-0-415-72581-1 (hbk)
ISBN: 978-0-415-72582-8 (pbk)
ISBN: 978-1-315-85657-5 (ebk)

NAEYC item # 1123

Typeset in Times New Roman and Gill Sans
by Apex CoVantage, LLC

MIX
Paper from
responsible sources
FSC
www.fsc.org   FSC® C014174

Printed and bound in the United States of America by Sheridan Books, Inc. (a Sheridan Group Company).

Contents

Dedication

Connecting the dots between digital media and early learning

One of the greatest honors in my career was to be named a Senior Fellow at the Fred Rogers Center for Children's Media and Early Learning at Saint Vincent College in Latrobe, Pennsylvania. It has been an incredible opportunity and responsibility to be charged with carrying forward Fred's approach to technology as a tool for supporting healthy growth, development, and learning, and for finding ways for the technology and digital media of today to be an effective tool for social-emotional development and relationships, just as Fred showed us. This book includes contributions by a number of colleagues with close ties to the Fred Rogers Center and the Fred Rogers Company including David Kleeman, Michael Robb, Roberta Schomburg, Hedda Sharapan, Alice Wilder, and me. On our collective behalf, I dedicate this book to the early childhood educators, children's librarians, parents, and media makers who are carrying Fred's message forward into the digital age through their effective, appropriate and intentional use of technology and digital media tools with young children.

Foreword

By Ed Greene

Author Note

Ed Greene, PhD, serves as Senior Director for Educational Outreach and Partnerships at the Hispanic Information Television Network (HITN), Early Learning Collaborative, Brooklyn, New York. Prior to his work at HITN, Ed served for five years as a senior adviser and consultant to Cito USA (a subsidiary of Cito, the Netherlands) and its Piramide Approach to Early Learning. Over his forty-year career, Ed has worked directly with infants, toddlers, preschool children, adolescents, and families, as well as in a variety of roles and capacities in the philanthropic, private, and public sectors and higher education.

> *When the integration of technology and interactive media in early childhood programs is built upon solid developmental foundations, and early childhood professionals are aware of both the challenges and the opportunities, educators are positioned to improve program quality by intentionally leveraging the potential of technology and media for the benefit of every child*

The excerpt from the NAEYC and Fred Rogers Center joint position paper captures what is, for me, the essence of this incredibly important book. The contributors have managed to create multiple pathways to help enlighten, educate, and push our thinking beyond the thoughts that something new is coming. It is clear that the digital age has arrived and is part of a rapidly emerging reality of the 21st century.

As a professional in the field of child development, early learning, and children's digital media for over 40 years, it has been my privilege to work with children and families. I have also been fortunate to work in a variety of settings where teaching, learning, technology and media provided many challenges and opportunities to create educational and instructional resources and tools.

Today, my work is with the Hispanic Information and Telecommunications Network (HITN) in Brooklyn, where we have an exciting early childhood *Ready to Learn* Transmedia project funded by the U.S. Department of Education. As Senior Director of Educational Outreach, I have the pleasure of working with talented producers, game designers, materials developers, and a dedicated team of HITN professionals. The development of digital and non-digital educational materials for 3 to 5 year olds has a focus on the areas of English language development, early literacy, and early math skills to support children on the pathway to readiness for school and for life.

As a practitioner in the field, I strongly recommend this publication as a "must-read." It provides provocative and practical ways to think about creating a blueprint for action *positioned to improve program quality by intentionally leveraging the potential of technology and media for the benefit of every child* (NAEYC & Fred Rogers Center, 2012).

Child development provides a basis for much of what we do in our work with young children and their families. The foundations for this book are strongly rooted in and include:

- NAEYC & Fred Rogers Center Joint Position Statement on Technology and Interactive Media as Tools in Early Childhood Programs Serving Children from Birth through Age 8
- The Fred Rogers Center Framework for Quality in Children's Digital Media.

And although the topic for the book might be *Technology and Digital Media in the Early Years*, you will consistently be brought back to a fundamental point that reiterates why it is critical to know and understand how children grow, development, and learn.

It will also become clear that there is an extremely important thought leader and friend of children who has influenced, nurtured, and guided the thinking of many of the writers in this book about children, technology, and digital media: Fred Rogers.

His words, through various quotations and references throughout the book, remind us about the importance of child development in his own work. He is quoted by one of the chapter authors as saying, "no matter what the machine may be it was people who thought it up and made it, and it's people who make it work."

Fred Roger's tenacity and his unwavering commitment to the healthy development of young children was a trait of persistence. And for those who have concerns about the impact of technology and media, Fred provides thoughtful ways of moving beyond a reaction to pro-action when he is quoted: "I went into television because I hated it so, and I thought there was some way of using this fabulous instrument to be of nurture to those who would watch and listen." (CNN, 2001)

It is not labeled as such, but the book provides the opportunity for you to create a blueprint for action. You must be ready to engage in thoughtful reflection, critical thinking, and the creation of a blueprint for change that will *improve program quality by intentionally leveraging the potential of technology and media for the benefit of every child*, as expressed in the position statement. So, think about each of the 17 chapters of this book as essential elements of a blueprint for actions you can take.

It is to the credit of the editor of this volume, Chip Donohue, that he and this august group of diverse authors came together to produce such an impressive work. These are serious topics that are presented in very user-friendly and sometimes unique ways, including stories of Fred Rogers, data about technology use, and a divining of Marie Montessori's developmental take on the iPad. Chip has brought to this conversation people who can address the issues related to serving the rapidly changing population of language learners in this country and those whose knowledge and research speak to the importance of incorporating Universal Design for Learning principles into more effective approaches to integrating technology into classrooms.

The inclusion of data and research findings are most informative and revelatory, as are the historical reflections that take us back to young children exploring in the age of Seymour Papert's Logo, and the concrete examples of how highly effective tools and technology are used to meet the needs of the young learner. It is also important that social justice and equity issues have been included as an intentional part of a book addressing *Technology and Digital Media in the Early Years*. Included are discussions about the digital divide and the "app gap," as well as the inequalities in access to devices. We are even provided an opportunity to understand how institutions of informal learning such as libraries contribute to and support early learning in the digital age.

This book places the reader at the feet of some of the most gifted, insightful, and sincere contributors to the work being done in child development, early learning, and children's media. The chapter authors are the respected researchers, teachers, and thought leaders to whom we turn for direction, guidance, and hope about technology and interactive media focused on young learners. To each of them, I say congratulations!

The editor, Chip Donohue, is a man who serves as an incredible beacon of hope in the work being done in the field of technology and digital media in the early years. His vision and actions have focused on enhancing learning, improving teaching practices, and providing leadership, vision, and voice to the innovative use of technology and distance-learning methods in teacher education, as well as through the design and development of digital literacy resources and professional development programs for early childhood educators at the TEC Center at Erikson Institute.

I am personally grateful for Chip's contributions to the work in which my colleagues are engaged at the Hispanic Information and Telecommunications Network's Early Learning Collaborative. I thank him for the opportunity to read the manuscript. It is truly a "must-read" and a potential blueprint for action for all who want to *improve program quality by intentionally leveraging the potential of technology and media for the benefit of every child.*

Ed Greene, PhD
Senior Director for Educational Outreach and Partnerships
Hispanic Information Television Network (HITN),
Early Learning Collaborative
Brooklyn, New York

Preface

This book offers early childhood teacher educators, professional development providers, and early childhood educators in preservice, inservice, and continuing education settings a thought-provoking guide to effective, appropriate and intentional use of technology with young children. It provides strategies, theoretical frameworks, links to research evidence, demonstrations and descriptions of best practices, and resources to develop essential digital literacy knowledge, skills, and experiences for early childhood educators in the digital age.

The goal is to help early childhood educators connect the dots between what we know about child development, early learning, developmentally appropriate practice, early childhood teaching practices, children's media research, teacher education, and professional development practices with what we are learning about the appropriate and intentional use of technology tools and digital media with young children. The book highlights current research, promising programs, and approaches, and a set of best practices for teaching with technology in the early years that are based on the National Association for the Education of Young Children (NAEYC) & Fred Rogers Center joint position statement on *Technology and Interactive Media as Tools in Early Childhood Programs Serving Children from Birth through Age 8* and the Fred Rogers Center *Framework for Quality in Children's Digital Media*. Throughout the book, we have linked key concepts, teaching strategies, and technology tools to the principles, guidelines, and key messages of the NAEYC & Fred Rogers Center joint position statement to create a common understanding about what works best for young children at the intersection of digital media and early learning. The pedagogical principles, classroom practices, and teaching strategies, presented are informed by child development theory, developmentally appropriate practice and research on effective, appropriate, and intentional use of technology in early childhood settings.

The editor and chapter authors are all established leaders in early childhood education and thought leaders and innovators in the selection, use, integration, and evaluation of technology and interactive media tools in early childhood teacher preparation and classroom teaching practices. Each chapter includes relevant research, grounds effective teaching practices in child development theory, and developmentally appropriate practice; provides examples of the principles and guidelines of the NAEYC & Fred Rogers Center joint position statement in practice; and includes real-life stories and examples of best practices with technology and media from early childhood educators and settings.

How This Book Is Organized

The book is organized into three parts: Technology and Young Children; Technology in the Classroom; and Technology Beyond the Classroom. Part I, focuses on young children in the digital age with chapters connecting Fred Roger's approach and emphasis on social-emotional development to today's digital media, an overview of technology and digital media as tools for teaching and learning, and tools for teacher education and teacher educators. Chapters 4 and 5 provide a review of theoretical frameworks and how they help us understand and use children's interactive media, and a review of children's media research to identify what we know and what it means to educators, parents, and media makers.

Part II, turns the focus in on the classroom and the teacher with chapters on media literacy, early literacy in the digital age, technology tools to support dual language learners, and a framework for including all children in a technology-supported classroom. It continues with chapters about STEM, simple robotics and programming in early learning, strategies for integrating new technologies into classroom practice, and tips for teachers about innovative practices and emerging technology tools for teachers and teaching.

Part III, moves beyond the classroom with chapters on technology as a tool to strengthen the home-school connection and to strengthen communities, the emerging role of children's librarians at the intersection of digital media and early learning, and strategies for becoming a connected educator and a connected learner to support 21st-century goals for teaching and learning.

Pedagogical Features

There are a number of recurring features that will help you consider your own role at the intersection of digital media and early learning and will provide you with additional resources and links to explore. In most chapters you will find one or more occurrences of the feature, *Position Statement Alignment*, that connects chapter topics and key concepts to the principles, guidelines, and key messages from the Position Statement to help educators reflect on the applications and implications on their use of technology in the early years. At the end of most chapters, you'll find *Teacher Takeaways*, a collection of practical tips, recommendations, and action steps for applying what you've learned in the chapter in your classroom and in your interactions with young children, parents, and families. In addition to a list of references that have been cited in each chapter, there is also a collection of additional resources related to key concepts covered in the chapter including readings, references, links that were mentioned in the chapter, and links to any software, apps, or hardware featured in the chapter in case you want to try them out yourself. The *Learn More . . .* section includes a collection of additional resources and links for those readers who want to dig deeper and learn more about the topics and key concepts of the chapter.

Acknowledgments

An edited volume like this takes a lot of hard work from everyone involved. Thanks to the 23 contributing authors—each one a very busy digital media and early learning thought-leader and innovator—who somehow found time to write, edit, revise, and even write some more if I asked them to. It has been a pleasure to learn with and from you, and to benefit from your generous gifts of time, words, ideas, resources, and best practices that fill every page of this book. I love the idea of adults as media mentors for young children, and it is my pleasure to call you all my media mentors and role models.

My passion and commitment for finding the balance between digital media and child development has been reignited by my role as a Senior Fellow at the Fred Rogers Center for Early Learning and Children's Media at Saint Vincent College. Thanks to everyone there, especially Rita Catalano, Max King, Michael Robb, and Cindy Scarpo.

Roberta Schomburg, another Fred Rogers Center Senior Fellow, shared the responsibility with me of leading the working group that revised and updated the NAEYC & Fred Rogers Center joint position statement on *Technology and Interactive Media as Tools in Early Childhood Programs Serving Children from Birth through Age 8,* that was released in March, 2012. I want to acknowledge Roberta, Madhavi Parikh, and members of the working group for unwavering commitment and leadership during the often contentious 3-year process. The principles and guidelines from the statement you helped shape are integrated throughout this book and are contributing to the field's steadily deepening understanding of effective, appropriate, and intentional use of technology in the early years.

I am deeply indebted to my colleagues at Erikson Institute, especially Amanda Armstrong, Program Coordinator of the TEC Center, who contributed a chapter to the book and keeps the TEC Center going and growing. Thanks to the Distance Learning and Continuing Education Team of Mike Maxse, Mike Paulucci, Erin Silva, and Matthew Zaradich, who put the ideas about technology as a tool for teachers and teaching described in this book into the design, development and delivery of innovative models for early childhood teacher education and professional development.

Thanks to three outstanding educators and classroom technology innovators, Tricia Fuglestad, Maggie Powers, and Erin Stanfill, for sharing stories and best practices with me for the Teacher's Voice segments in Chapter 3 and Chapter 17. You have each inspired the work we do at the TEC Center. If I could go back, I would want to be a child in each of your classrooms, even for a day.

Thanks to Britany Smith, Communications Coordinator at The Fred Rogers Company, and Emily Uhrin, Archivist at the Fred Rogers Center for Early Learning and Children's Media at Saint Vincent College, for helping track down the sources of quotes from Fred Rogers. I also want to thank Bill Isler, Chief Executive Officer, Kevin Morrison, Chief Operating Officer, and Hedda Sharapan, Director of Early Childhood Initiatives and Associate Director of Public Relations at the Fred Rogers Company for giving three Fred Rogers Center Senior Fellows—David Kleeman, Alice Wilder, and myself—permission to include quotes from Fred Rogers in the Introduction, Chapter 1, and Chapter 2. Fred's approach to technology has informed so much of our work and professional lives, and our writing in this book, so we are pleased to be able to share his words of inspiration with our readers and in our own small way join you in making sure the legacy lives on.

I've saved a special thanks for my family, Maria Hill, Sarah Maria Donohue, and Laura Donohue, for their unending support, encouragement, and inspiration—and for understanding why this project had so much meaning to me personally and professionally—here it is.

Chip Donohue

Contributors

Editor

Chip Donohue, PhD, is the Dean of Distance Learning and Continuing Education and Director of the TEC (Technology in Early Childhood) Center at Erikson Institute. He is a Senior Fellow of the Fred Rogers Center for Early Learning and Children's Media at Saint Vincent College, where he co-chaired the working group that revised the 2012 NAEYC & Fred Rogers Center joint position statement on *Technology and Interactive Media as Tools in Early Childhood Programs Serving Children from Birth through Age 8*, and is a founding member of the Alliance for Early Learning in a Digital Age. He is a member of the New Zealand eLearning Guidelines Revision Reference Group and a distance learning advisor to New Zealand Tertiary College. In 2012, he received the first Bammy Award and the Educators Voice Award as Innovator of the Year from the Academy of Education Arts & Sciences.

Chapter Authors

Amanda Armstrong, MS, is the Program Coordinator for the TEC Center. She earned her MS in Child Development with a specialization in Administration from Erikson Institute and has worked with nonprofit organizations focusing on after-school and tutoring programs for children. She has also conducted research for Erikson's Early Math Collaborative and taught at Northwestern University's Leapfrog animation course for third graders. Amanda is currently a leadership team member of ISTE's Early Learning and Technology special interest group and NAEYC's Technology and Young Children interest forum.

Mark Bailey, PhD, is a professor in the College of Education at Pacific University in Forest Grove, Oregon. For the past 25 years, Mark has been exploring the use of pedagogically powerful technological tools to support learning. Mark co-founded the Oregon Technology in Education Network and founded the Early Learning Community (ELC) at Pacific University. The ELC utilizes a synthesis of best practices from a wide range of pedagogical models, and incorporates innovative applications of technology to support its students. He currently serves as the Director of the Pacific University Child Learning and Development Center, and the Campus Director of the School of Learning and Teaching. Recently recognized by Pacific University as a Distinguished University Professor, Mark collaborates with faculty members, K–12 educators, and the teachers in the ELC to refine their use of technologies and pedagogy in support of student-centered learning.

Bonnie Blagojevic, MEd, CAS, is an education consultant and adjunct faculty member at The University of Maine. She is a consulting editor for NAEYC, has co-authored articles for *Teaching Young Children* magazine, and has been an active member of the Technology & Young Children Interest Forum. She is an Apple Distinguished Educator, Class of 2007. She worked with teachers in Maine as part of Early Reading First grants, exploring the use of technology to strengthen early literacy learning. She works with Mano en Mano/Hand in Hand, developing Comienza en Casa/It Starts at Home, a project funded by Maine Migrant Education that incorporates iPads with traditional early learning activities to provide parents with information and materials to promote their child's school readiness in the home. Bonnie is on the Advisory Board for the HITN Early Learning Collaborative, and coordinates pilot testing of apps and materials in Maine for this Ready to Learn funded project.

Craig Blum, PhD, is an associate professor of Special Education, Illinois State University. He has co-authored *Effective RTI Training and Practices: Helping School District Teams Improve Academic Performance and Social Behavior* and *Instructional Technology in Early Childhood Education.* Dr. Blum publishes in peer-reviewed journals and presents nationally and internationally on technology integration in early childhood settings. His primary work focuses on practical technology integration models for early childhood educators with readily-available technology in both special and general education settings. Dr. Blum was part of the Making a Difference with Assistive Technology (MDAT) project, a university partnership with an early childhood education center in central Illinois that worked on professional development through "user groups" and meaningful use of a technology tool kit within the curriculum. He is especially interested in universal design for learning, meaningful use of apps, and other digital technologies in early childhood settings.

Warren Buckleitner, PhD, has a background in child development and the design of children's interactive media. He's been a preschool, elementary and college teacher and has provided testimony to the FTC and the U.S. Congress. He holds a degree in elementary education from Central Michigan University (Cum Laude), an MA in early childhood education from Pacific Oaks College, and a doctorate in educational psychology from Michigan

State University. He coordinates the international Bologna Ragazzi Prize for digital storytelling, and the KAPi (Kids at Play Interactive) Awards and is the founder of the Dust or Magic Institute and the Mediatech Foundation, a nonprofit community technology center housed in his town's public library. He speaks kid's tech at education and library conferences and has covered children's technology for a variety of mainstream publications, including the *New York Times*. He is the editor of *Children's Technology Review*.

Cen Campbell is the founder of LittleeLit.com and the librarian at Bookboard. com. She has driven a bookmobile, managed branch libraries, developed innovative programs for babies, young children, and teens, and now helps other libraries and librarians incorporate digital media into their early literacy programming. She is currently a consultant for the California State Library's Early Learning with Families 2.0 Initiative and serves on the American Library Association's Children & Technology Committee.

Luisa M. Cotto, MEd, is manager of communications and engagement at United Way of Miami-Dade where she provides her expertise in education as a trainer and literacy coach and creates engagement opportunities for families and the community through various projects throughout Miami-Dade County. At the United Way Center for Excellence in Early Education, she serves as advisor on the use of technology in the classrooms and has been trainer and literacy coach for two Early Reading First grants, Project LEER at United Way and LASER CAERS in Tampa. As an advocate for early education and technology, Cotto has published and presented numerous papers and presents at local, state, and national conferences on the importance of planning intentional and appropriate lessons for young children.

Angela Fowler, MA, is on the faculty at Columbia College Chicago, where she is an instructor in the Early Childhood Education Program. She is also the co-founder of Cultivating the Early Years, a Professional Network and Consulting Company that consults on progressive educational approaches to technology, arts integration, math and science, parent engagement, and much more. Angela is currently writing an assessment book based on the *Childfolio* assessment app she created. She is co-chair and organizer for the World Forum Foundation's Children's Rights Working Group and technology track. She has worked in the field of education for more than 25 years and has participated in and coordinated seven study tours to Reggio Emilia, Italy. She is currently completing her PhD in Early Childhood Leadership.

Lisa Guernsey is Director of the Early Education Initiative and Director of the Learning Technologies Project at New America, a nonpartisan think tank in Washington, DC. She focuses on elevating dialogue about early childhood education by contributing to the Ed Central blog, writing papers and commentary on innovations in education, and spotlighting new approaches for helping disadvantaged children succeed. A journalist by training, Lisa has been a technology and education writer at *The New York Times* and *The Chronicle of Higher Education* and has contributed to *Newsweek, Time, The Washington Post,* and *USA TODAY.* Her most recent book is *Screen Time: How Electronic Media—From Baby Videos to Educational Software—Affects Your Young Child.* She won a 2012 gold Eddie magazine award for a School Library Journal article on e-books. A mother of two, she holds a master's degree in English/American Studies and a bachelor's degree in English from the University of Virginia.

Kate Highfield, PhD, is a teacher educator from the Institute of Early Childhood, Macquarie University, in Sydney, Australia. Having taught for many years, Kate now works with educators, student teachers, children, and families. Kate's PhD focused on the use of simple robotics in mathematics learning and examined the key role of metacognition in learning. The focus of her current research and teaching is the use of technologies for learning and play, with a specific focus on how technology can be used as a tool to enhance young children's learning.

Tamara Kaldor, MS, MFA, is a developmental therapist and the founder of Play is Work™, with over a decade of experience supporting Chicago families with children with autism, sensory processing disorder, learning disabilities, and developmental delays. She specializes in working with children and families to find success at home and in school. Tamara is trained in and specializes in using the DIR®/Floortime™ therapy model, providing inclusion support services in the classroom, and using technology to assist in children's social-emotional learning. Tamara also partners and collaborates with parents and teachers to develop tools to help their children grow and move families forward. This happens primarily through her effective and engaging play-based tools for addressing developmental delays, PLAY IS WORK™. Tamara has an MS in Child Development from Erikson Institute and an MFA from the School of the Art Institute of Chicago.

David Kleeman is a strategist, analyst, author, and speaker who leads the children's media industry in developing sustainable, kid-friendly solutions. He is building a unique new global kids and family "think tank" as Senior Vice President of Insights Programs and PlayVangelist for PlayCollective. From 1988–2013, Kleeman was President of the American Center for Children and Media, promoting the exchange of ideas, expertise and information as a means for building quality. He remains advisory board chair to the international children's TV festival (Prix Jeunesse), a 2013 Senior Fellow of the Fred Rogers Center for Early Learning and Children's Media at Saint Vincent College, and a Governor of the Academy of Television Arts & Sciences. In 2014, he received the "Pioneer" Award from Kids @ Play Interactive. Kleeman travels worldwide seeking best practices in children's and family media, technology, and products and writes extensively about quality in children's media.

Carisa Kluver, MSW, has a master's in Social Work from the University of Washington and a bachelor's in Anthropology from UC Berkeley. She worked as a school counselor, health educator, and researcher in maternal and child health for over a decade before founding the app review site Digital-Storytime.com and the blog, The Digital Media Diet. She has reviewed hundreds of enhanced book apps, as well as writing and researching about literacy, kids, and the evolving digital publishing industry.

Alexis R. Lauricella is a lecturer in the department of Communication Studies and the Associate Director of the Center on Media and Human Development at Northwestern University. Dr. Lauricella earned her PhD in Developmental Psychology and her master's in Public Policy from Georgetown University. Her research focuses on children's learning from media and parents' and teachers' attitudes toward and use of media with young children. Recent publications include empirical research articles in *Journal of Applied Developmental Psychology, Computers & Education, Journal of Children and Media, Media Psychology, Merrill Palmer Quarterly* and reports for the Fred Rogers Center and the Center on Media and Human Development. Dr. Lauricella is also the founder of www.PlayLearnParent.com, a website that translates child development research for parents.

Michael H. Levine, PhD, is Founding Director of the Joan Ganz Cooney Center, an independent nonprofit organization based at Sesame Workshop. The center conducts research and builds multi-sector partnerships to scale innovation and investment in promising educational media technologies for children. Prior to joining the Center, Michael served as Vice President for Asia Society, managing the global nonprofit's interactive media and educational initiatives to promote knowledge and understanding of other world regions and cultures. Michael previously oversaw Carnegie Corporation of New York's groundbreaking work in early childhood development, educational media, and primary grades reform and was a senior advisor to the New York City Schools Chancellor. He serves on numerous nonprofit boards, including Classroom, Inc., Forum for Youth Investment, We Are Family Foundation, PBS' Next Generation Learning Media, and Journeys in Film. Michael received his PhD in Social Policy from Brandeis University's Florence Heller School and his BS from Cornell University.

Karen N. Nemeth is an author, consultant and presenter on first and second language development in early childhood education. She is a writer and consulting editor for the National Association for the Education of Young Children (NAEYC) and serves as the co-chair of the national Early Childhood Special Interest Group for the National Association for Bilingual Education (NABE), as steering board member for the International TESOL (Teachers of English to Speakers of Other Languages) Early Education Interest Section, and is on the board of New Jersey Teachers of English to Speakers of

Other Languages/New Jersey Bilingual Educators (NJTESOL/NJBE). She provides resources for teaching young dual language learners at Language Castle LLC and ideas for using developmentally appropriate technology to support learning at the Early Childhood Technology Network.

Howard P. Parette, EdD, is professor in the Department of Special Education at Illinois State University and former Kara Peters Endowed Chair in Assistive Technology and Director of the Special Education Assistive Technology (SEAT) Center. Across four decades, he has published extensively in the area of service delivery to children and disabilities and their families, with particular emphasis on cultural issues and technology decision making. In the past 6 years, his scholarly work has addressed readily available technology integration in early childhood classrooms. He developed and currently teaches a unique university course developed specifically for early childhood majors—*Technology and Young Children with Disabilities*. Experiences from this course provided the foundation for a new co-authored textbook, *Instructional Technology in Early Childhood*, designed to inform and guide 21st-century early childhood practitioners.

Brian Puerling, MS, is a National Board Certified Teacher and author of *Teaching in the Digital Age: Smart Tools for Age 3 to Grade 3*. He is a graduate of Erikson Institute and a former preschool teacher in the Chicago Public Schools. He is currently the Director of Education Technology at the Catherine Cook School in Chicago, on the Board of Directors for the Chicago Metro Association for Education of Young Children, and has worked as an early childhood teacher coach, a curriculum reviewer, and a presenter and consultant for the Chicago Public Schools, the Erikson Institute, United Way Miami-Dade, and the Early Childhood Council of New Zealand, and a guest blogger for the Fred Rogers Center. Brian currently serves on the National Advisory Board for Media Smart Libraries, is a former participant on the Sesame Workshop Teacher Council, and was a recipient of the PBS Innovative Educator Award and PBS Teacher's Choice Award in 2010.

Michael B. Robb, PhD, is Director of Education and Research at the Fred Rogers Center for Early Learning and Children's Media at Saint Vincent College. He leads the development, content, and partnerships for the Fred Rogers Center *Early Learning Environment™*, a website that curates high-quality digital resources in early literacy and digital media literacy for families and educators of children birth to age 5. He has published research and analysis on the impact of digital media on young children's language development, early literacy outcomes, and problem solving in *Child Development, Infant and Child Development*, and the *British Journal of Developmental Psychology*. Dr. Robb holds a PhD in Psychology from the University of California, Riverside.

Faith Rogow, PhD, is co-author of *The Teacher's Guide to Media Literacy: Critical Thinking in a Multimedia World* and is a media literacy education strategist and innovator. She was the founding president of NAMLE, a founding editorial board member of the Journal for Media Literacy Education, a founding advisor to Project Look Sharp and a co-author of NAMLE's seminal document, *Core Principles of Media Literacy Education in the U.S.* In 1996, she started Insighters Educational Consulting to "help people learn from media and one another." Her groundbreaking article, *The ABCs of Media Literacy*, has been widely circulated and she has earned a reputation as one of the few people in the United States advocating for and creating media literacy education that is developmentally appropriate for early childhood. As a professional development specialist, she has taught thousands of teachers, students, administrators, child care professionals, and parents to understand and harness the power of media.

Roberta Schomburg, PhD, is professor and Director of Graduate Studies in Early Childhood at Carlow University in Pittsburgh. She is currently working to establish Carlow University as a satellite for the Carnegie Mellon CREATE Lab to help educators, children, and families develop technological fluency through creative exploration of robotic technologies and socially meaningful innovation. As a Senior Fellow at the Fred Rogers Center for Early Learning and Children's Media at Saint Vincent College, she co-authored the NAEYC & Fred Rogers Center joint position statement *Technology and Interactive Media as Tools in Programs that Serve Young Children from Birth through Age 8.* She has been a consultant with The Fred Rogers Company for the past 30 years where she worked on the *Mister Rogers' Plan and Play Book,* helped design professional development materials for teachers, and is now an advisor for *Daniel Tiger's Neighborhood.*

Hedda Sharapan recently celebrated the start of her 47th year with Fred Rogers and the small nonprofit company that he founded. She was asked to work on his production from the very first day of the *Neighborhood* series in 1966, and served as Assistant Director, Assistant Producer, Associate Producer and currently serves as Director of Early Childhood Initiatives. Continuing to carry on Fred Rogers' legacy, her work includes writing for articles, books, and websites, consulting on scripts for *Daniel Tiger's Neighborhood,* along with creating and presenting professional development materials for early childhood educators. Her monthly professional development newsletter reaches nearly 15,000 subscribers. In 2010, Hedda was named one of two "Heroes on the Horizon" at the NAEYC annual conference, and in 2011, she received a Lifetime Achievement Award from The National Association for Family Child Care. In 2013 she was awarded an Honorary Doctorate in Humane Letters from St. Vincent College in Latrobe, PA.

Alice Wilder is the educational advisor developing the Amazon Originals curriculum for kids and implementing Amazon's unique educational point of view into the development of new series. She also serves as the Chief Content

Officer for *Speakaboos*, a kid-centric, cross-publisher literacy platform and is the co-creator and Executive Producer of *Cha-Ching Money Smart Kids* the "School House Rock" of financial literacy for 7- to 12-year-olds. Her work also includes being the co-creator and head of research and education for *Super Why!* on PBS Kids, and a Producer and the Director of Research and Development for Nick Jr.'s *Blue's Clues*. She is a Senior Fellow at the Fred Rogers Center for Early Learning and Children's Media at Saint Vincent College. Her groundbreaking work in formative research was cited in *The Tipping Point* by Malcolm Gladwell. Alice bases her work on the philosophy that "the only way to understand what children are capable of doing, what appeals to them, and what they know, is to ask them!"

Abbreviations and Acronyms

AAP	American Academy of Pediatrics
ACEI	Association for Childhood Education International
ALA	American Library Association
ALSC	Association for Library Service to Children
AMI	Association Montessori International/USA
ASCD	Association for Supervision and Curriculum Development
CAEP	Council for Accreditation of Educator Preparation
CAST	Center for Applied Special Technology
CCFC	Campaign for a Commercial-Free Childhood
CDA	Child Development Associate
CLDC	Child Learning & Development Center, Pacific University
CMCH	Center on Media and Child Health
CMHD	Center on Media and Human Development
CLASP	Center for Law and Social Policy
COPPA	Children's Online Privacy Protection Act
CSM	Common Sense Media
DAP	Developmentally Appropriate Practice
DLL	Dual Language Learner
ECEtech.net	Early Childhood Technology Network
ELE	Early Learning Environment, Fred Rogers Center
ELL	English Language Learner
ECRR	Every Child Ready to Read
FCTD	Family Center on Technology and Disability
FETC	Florida Educational Technology Conference
Fred Rogers Center	Fred Rogers Center for Early Learning and Children's Media at Saint Vincent College
HFRP	Harvard Family Research Project
HITN ELC	Hispanic Information and Telecommunications Network Early Learning Collaborative
IMLS	Institute of Museum and Library Services

IRA	International Reading Association
ISTE	International Society for Technology in Education
MoMA	Museum of Modern Art
NAECTE	National Association of Early Childhood Teacher Educators
NAEP	National Assessment of Educational Progress
NAEYC	National Association for the Education of Young Children
NAMLE	National Association for Medial Literacy Education
NASBE	National Association of State Boards of Education
NCATE	National Council for Accreditation of Teacher Education
NCFL	National Center for Families Learning
NSF	National Science Foundation
OHS	Office of Head Start
PBS	Public Broadcasting Service
QR code	Quick Response code
SEAT	Special Education Assistive Technology Center
STEM	Science, Technology, Engineering and Mathematics
STEAM	STEM + Art
STREAM	STEAM + Reading
TEC Center	Technology in Early Childhood Center at Erikson Institute
UDL	Universal Design for Learning

Figures and Tables

Figures

Tables

Introduction

Chip Donohue

Setting the Context: From Fred Rogers to the Digital Age

I first became interested in technology and young children in 1983, when an Apple IIe computer found its way into my office and the classrooms at Woodland Montessori School in Madison, Wisconsin, thanks to Patrick Dickson, a parent who became my major professor in the doctoral program at the University of Wisconsin-Madison. Over the 30 years that have followed, I've been interested in technology as a tool for teaching the teachers, for teachers to use in their teaching, and for teaching and learning with young children. I've seen every "next great thing" come and go since then, but like most of us interested in child development and children's media, I knew everything had really changed for young children when the multi-touch interactive iPad arrived in 2010.

At about the same time, I became a Senior Fellow at the Fred Rogers Center for Early Learning and Children's Media at Saint Vincent College and gained a deeper appreciation for how Fred Rogers' approach to technology and children's media focused on the whole child, emphasizing social-emotional development and relationships. I began to understand how he used the technology of his day to support and encourage healthy growth, child development, and early learning for young children and to empower parents and caregivers who worked with or on behalf of young children to do the same.

My primary responsibility as a Fred Rogers Center Senior Fellow was to partner with Roberta Schomburg of Carlow University, also a Senior Fellow who worked with Fred Rogers for many years, to co-chair the working group that revised and updated the NAEYC & Fred Rogers Center joint position statement (2012) on *Technology and Interactive Media as Tools in Early Childhood Programs Serving Children from Birth through Age 8*. The NAEYC technology position statement had last been updated in 1996. In terms of technology tools and how technology was being used in early childhood classrooms, a lot had changed since then. The dawn of the digital age and the arrival of mobile devices, multi-touch screens, tablet computers, and interactive media brought with it new challenges and new opportunities for early childhood educators and parents of young children. What hadn't changed was that effective selection and use of technology with young children in early childhood settings needed to be grounded in the principles of Developmentally Appropriate Practice (Copple & Bredekamp, 2009), would depend on the digital literacy knowledge, skills, and experiences of the teacher, caregiver, or parent, and needed to tap into the affordances of the new digital tools that were quickly changing the way we used technology in our personal and professional lives.

An overview of the position statement and the key message are provided in Chapter 3. Quotes and passages from the NAEYC & Fred Rogers Center joint position statement (2012) are woven throughout this book to connect the principles, guidelines, and key messages with the topics and key concepts presented in each chapter.

While the position statement was being revised, the Fred Rogers Center began meeting with children's media research, media makers, child development specialists, and early childhood educators to develop *A Framework for Quality in Digital Media for Young Children: Considerations for Parents. Educators, and Media Creators* (2012).

The Framework is built around three principles of quality:

> **Principle 1:** Quality digital media should safeguard the health, well-being, and overall development of young children.
> **Principle 2:** Quality in digital media for young children should take into account the child, the content, and the context of use.
> **Principle 3:** Determinations of quality should be grounded in an evidence base that can be used by parents, educators, policymakers, and others to make decisions about the selection and use of particular digital media products, and by media creators to improve the development new products in response to consumer expectations of quality.
>
> (Fred Rogers Center, 2012, pp. 1–2)

A third framework for considering the appropriateness of technology and digital media with young children comes from Lisa Guernsey, Director of the Early Education Initiative and the Learning Technologies Project at New America, and a contributing author to this book, who first described the three *C*s of children's media—Content, Context and the individual Child in the preface to her book, *Screen Time: How Electronic Media—From Baby Videos to Educational Software—Affects Your Young Child* (2007, p. xv).

- **Content:** How does this help children engage, express, imagine, or explore?
- **Context:** How does it complement, and not interrupt, children's natural play?
- **The individual child:** How do we choose the right tech tools and experiences for each child's needs, abilities, interests and development stage?

Each of these frameworks offers a critical lens through which to view and evaluate quality in digital media, and effective practices in the selection, use, integration, and evaluation of digital media by early childhood educators and parents. Taken together, they provide a solid foundation on which to build your digital media knowledge, skills, and philosophy of how you will (and won't) use technology and interactive media as tools with young children in your early childhood program.

Between 2010 and 2012, during this amazing confluence of technology innovation, new principles and guidelines for appropriate and intentional use, emerging classroom practices, and new research on interactive media, it was clear to me that child development specialists, early childhood educators, children's media professionals, and researchers had a lot to learn with and from each other. In the digital age, the pace of technology innovation and the arrival, almost daily, of new technology and interactive media products for young children has the potential to change teaching and learning in the early years. The essential question this book sets out to answer is, will this be for better or worse when it comes to young children's growth, development, and learning? The contributing authors have gathered information, resources, links, and examples of best practice to be sure the answer will be for the better.

I had a wonderful opportunity to learn more about Fred Rogers and his approach to technology as a tool during the three-year process of revising and updating the NAEYC & Fred Rogers Center position statement (2012) and to listen carefully to the cautions, concerns, and excitement expressed by educators and parents. These experiences, coupled with the chance to meet so many children's media professionals, media makers, and app designers who shared a desire to appropriately and intentionally "connect the dots" between child development, early learning, children's media research and design, and best practices for teaching and learning in the digital age was the catalyst for this book and the collection of chapters by thought-leaders from each of these professions and perspectives. And new research on responsive interactions and "socially contingent" language between a toddler and a loving adult via Skype suggests that for language learning, responsiveness is the key in live conversations and on a screen (Roseberry, Hirsch-Pasek, & Golinkoff, 2013)—Good news for families who use Skype to connect young children to parents, grandparents, and other family members and communicate across the miles and generations.

Perhaps it is the blending and balancing of interactive technology and interactions with others that offers the most promise for effective and appropriate uses of technology in the early years—closely connecting Fred Rogers' approach with our emerging understanding of appropriate and intentional use of digital media to support early learning.

About the Book

The book is divided into three parts:

1. Technology and Young Children
2. Technology in the Classroom
3. Technology Beyond the Classroom

The organizations of the chapters and topics allows you to read through from front to back, or to select specific topics of interest to you to read first. Wherever you begin, the topics and key concepts will help enhance your digital literacy and improve your digital age teaching and learning.

As we planned for this book and began writing the content, a simple set of questions with complex answers guided our thinking:

> What do educators know?
> What do educators need to learn?
> What do educators need to be able to do?
> What are the best practices?
> Why does it matter?

The contributing authors offer their unique perspectives on how to answer these fundamental questions in the topics they've chosen to write about and the key concepts they've shared. As you read the chapters, you'll have opportunities to align your thinking and teaching practices with the three frameworks and reflect on your own answers to these questions. Along the way, you'll have opportunities to enhance your digital literacy by learning more about how to appropriately and intentionally connect your goals for children's healthy growth, development, and early learning with principles and practices of effective use, so that you can select, use, integrate, and evaluate technology and digital media for your classroom and for each individual child.

About the Authors

The authors invited to contribute chapters to this book are experts in child development, early childhood education, teacher education, parent engagement, informal learning, research, media literacy, and children's media. Each is an influential thought-leader in the national and international conversations around effective, appropriate, and intentional use of technology in the early years. They bring years of experience and expertise to their writing, and share a commitment to young children and child development first, technology second. Like Fred Rogers, they always keep the child first and consider what is best for the child's development and learning. They share a commitment to using technology as a tool to support relationships, social-emotional development, and pro-social behaviors. You are in very good hands as you read through the chapters, explore the topics and key concepts, and reflect on your own approach to young children and technology.

This quote from Fred Rogers serves as a reminder of what is most important and a perfect stepping off point for your reading, learning, and teaching:

> Computers can be useful machines, especially when they help people communicate in caring ways with each other.
>
> (Rogers, 1996, p. 37)

References

Copple, C., & Bredekamp, S. (Eds.). (2009). *Developmentally appropriate practice in early childhood programs serving children from birth through age 8* (3rd ed.). Washington, DC: NAEYC.

Fred Rogers Center for Early Learning and Children's Media at Saint Vincent College. (2012). *A framework for quality in digital media for children: Considerations for parents, educators, and media creators.* Latrobe, PA: Fred Rogers Center.

Guernsey, L. (2007). *Screen time: How electronic media—from baby videos to educational software—affects your young child.* New York, NY: Basic Books.

National Association for the Education of Young Children & Fred Rogers Center for Early Learning and Children's Media at Saint Vincent College. (2012). *Technology and interactive media as tools in early childhood programs serving children from birth through age 8.* Washington, DC: NAEYC; Latrobe, PA: Fred Rogers Center for Early Learning and Children's Media at Saint Vincent College.

Rogers, F. (1996). *Dear Mister Rogers, Does it ever rain in your neighborhood? Letters to Mr. Rogers.* New York, NY: Penguin Books.

Roseberry, S., Hirsch-Pasek, K., & Golinkoff, R.M. (2013, September). Skype me! Socially contingent interactions help toddlers learn language. *Child Development.* Retrieved from http://dx.doi.org/10.1111/cdev.12166

Resources

• Fred Rogers Center for Early Learning and Children's Media at Saint Vincent College. (2012). *A framework for quality in digital media for children: Considerations for parents, educators, and media creators.* Retrieved from www.fredrogerscenter.org/media/resources/Framework_Statement_2-April_2012-Full_Doc+Exec_Summary.pdf

• Guernsey, L. (2007). *Screen time: How electronic media—from baby videos to educational software—affects your young child.* Retrieved from www.lisaguernsey.com/Screen-Time.htm

• *Key messages of the NAEYC/Fred Rogers Center position statement on technology and interactive media in early childhood programs.* (2012). Retrieved from www.naeyc.org/files/naeyc/12_KeyMessages_Technology.pdf

• National Association for the Education of Young Children & the Fred Rogers Center for Early Learning and Children's Media at Saint Vincent College. (2012). *Technology and interactive media as tools in early childhood programs serving children from birth through age 8* [A joint position statement]. Retrieved from www.naeyc.org/content/technology-and-young-children

Part I

Technology and Young Children

EDITOR'S INTRODUCTION

The book and the chapters in Part I begin with an essay and chapter that connect Fred Rogers' approach to the digital age and to the ideas, resources, and best practices shared throughout the book. Our use of technology and interactive media needs to be as appropriate and intentional as Fred Rogers showed us, if we are to make the most of new technology tools and experiences that support healthy growth, development, and learning, strengthen adult/child interactions, foster relationships, and promote healthy social-emotional development and pro-social behaviors.

David Kleeman and **Alice Wilder** open Part I and begin the book with an essay in response to a question I posed to them about Fred Rogers and the digital age tools and interactive media of today. I asked them to reflect on and respond to the question, "What would Fred Rogers say?" As leaders in the children's media field and Senior Fellows at the Fred Rogers Center for Early Learning and Children's Media at Saint Vincent College, they have closely watched technology and children's media trends and created a few of their own. In this thoughtful reflection, they consider Fred's words and his approach to children's healthy growth, development, and learning as guidance for how he might have made use of these new digital tools, mobile devices, touch-screens and interactive media in his work on behalf of young children, parents, and families. Kleeman and Wilder provide the perfect starting point for the approach we have taken in this book, which is to consider what's best for the child's healthy development first and then look to technology and digital media for tools to achieve these goals.

In Chapter 2, **Hedda Sharapan**, who worked closely with Fred Rogers for many years, explains how his approach to social-emotional development can guide our selection of technology tools and experiences that support interactions, relationships, and pro-social behaviors. She reminds us to remain cautious and continue to ask hard questions about the role of technology in the early years, even as she shares specific strategies and examples from teachers using technology as a tool for social-emotional development.

I step beyond my editor role in Chapter 3 and provide an overview and framework for thinking about technology in the early years, and for the effective, appropriate and intentional use of technology with young children. I discuss both the concerns and the opportunities that have been debated in the field, introduce the principles, guidelines, key messages and key words from the National Association for the Education of Young Children (NAEYC) & Fred Rogers Center joint position statement, and share resources on technology in the early years. Words and ideas from the position statement are integrated throughout the book, so in this chapter, the goal is to introduce the essential ideas and provide necessary resources to build a foundation for understanding and learning from all that follows.

I join **Roberta Schomburg** for Chapter 4 as we talk about three interrelated ways of thinking about technology as a tool: for teaching teachers, for teacher classroom management, and as a tool for teaching and learning with young children in the classroom. We identify new demands on teacher education and teacher educators to prepare early childhood teachers who have the technology confidence, competence, and digital media literacy necessary to select, use, integrate, and evaluate technology for the classroom and for individual children. We examine what teacher preparation standards and organizations are saying and doing about digital media literacy, for teacher educators, preservice, and inservice teachers.

Warren Buckleitner provides a playful and thought-provoking overview of "Child Development Theory 101" and describes how theory can and should inform our selection and use of technology tools with young children. He poses the question, "What would Maria Montessori say about the iPad?" and then looks for answers in the words, philosophy, and approach of Montessori and other famous theorists. He creates an imagined conversation and even invites us to listen in, between Montessori, Piaget, Bruner, and Vygotsky as they play with an iPad and try out some apps. He explores the intersection of multi-touch screens and apps with developmental frameworks. His search for examples of behaviorism, constructivism, and social construction in app design and use helps us see how theory shapes design and practice, and how design and practice demonstrate what we know and understand about child development theory.

Part I closes with a thoughtful and thorough review of children's media research by **Michael B. Robb** and **Alexis R. Lauricella**. Robb and Lauricella identify what we know and what it means from the body of research on children's media, and the emerging research on interactive media and digital devices. They look at what we know about child development in the context of technology by exploring physical development, cognitive development, and language. They look at how what we know from many years of research on television viewing and children's development contributes to our understanding of new digital tools and how the features of effective children's media might be reflected in app design for interactive screens. Throughout the chapter, they distill complex research findings into teacher takeaways and pose questions that connect the research to practice, build a bridge between television-based children's media research and the affordances of new digital tools, and identify questions that remain.

Chapter 1

What Would Fred Rogers Say?

David Kleeman and Alice Wilder

> *"Fred's instinct in the 1950s was to be excited and challenged by new media, never to be afraid or put off by it. It was the potential of new media to play a constructive role in the development and education of young children that inspired him, and he sustained this open-minded and entrepreneurial attitude to media and technology all his life."*
> —Maxwell King and Rita Catalano, Fred Rogers Center for Early Learning and Children's Media (as cited in Buckleitner, 2010)

What Fred Rogers would have thought about today's digital technologies, and their potential for children's healthy development and learning, could be the topic of countless dissertations and endless debates. For the purposes of this chapter, we chose to seek insight in Fred's own words; of course, even that is subject to argument. There are entire books of quotes and an archive full of his wisdom in speech and writing; for any hypothesis we make here, there are surely statements that could contradict our view. In addition to his words, however, we can infer his philosophy and approach by the media he made, the way he lived his life, and the personal experiences of the people whose lives he touched.

Considering these, we believe he would have emphasized that digital play-things and learning aids are simply tools and that their potential lies in the hands of the people who program them, the loving caregivers who choose how and when to use them, and the needs and abilities of specific children. As Fred wrote, "no matter what the machine may be, it was people who thought it up and made it, and it's people who make it work" (Rogers, 1994, p. 64).

Fred admitted, "I went into television because I hated it so, and I thought there was some way of using this fabulous instrument to be of nurture to those who would watch and listen" (CNN, 2001). His mission—in fact, his ministry—was to provide constructive media that puts children first.

"We serve children best," Fred taught, "when we try to find out what their own inner needs are and what their own unique accomplishments are, and help them capitalize on that" (Rogers, 1994, p. 5). With these words, he described perhaps the greatest strength of today's media and technology: flexibility and personal-ization. Fred was gifted at making a mass medium feel personal, talking through the screen as though to an individual child. He surely would have appreciated the capacity for today's interactive media to be "leveled" and marveled at the analytic functions built into games, so that they can adapt on the fly to a player's level of engagement, strengths or weaknesses.

Among the most iconic scenes from *Mister Rogers' Neighborhood* were his interactions with Jeff Erlanger, a wheelchair-bound young man. What made them special was their focus on what made Jeff able, not disabled. Fred wrote, "I really think that everybody, every day, should be able to feel some success" (Rogers, 1994, p. 3). The affordances of mobile media—direct touchscreens, speech recognition, adaptive teaching and learning—appear to hold amazing potential for enabling children with physical, mental, or emotional challenges, and this is a crucial area for continued exploration.

We believe Fred would have been happy about generative, open-ended digital tools for creativity. "Children are not merely vessels into which facts are poured one week, and then when it comes time for exams they turn themselves upside down and let the facts run out," he wrote. "Children bring all of themselves, their feelings and their experiences to the learning" (Rogers, 1994, p. 87).

Digital media can offer a platform and outlet for that creativity—a go-anywhere, use-anytime, bottomless block set or art box, a portable piano, a storytelling tool kit. Make no mistake—digital tools aren't the same as the real thing—kids absolutely need the tactile experience of fresh clay, finger paints, dress-up play, and musical instruments. They're different, a new category of play and self-expression, and we're still learning the contexts in which they're best used.

When discussing the value of any technology, context matters; content is only as good as the user's experience. Tools to record voices, add photos, or otherwise personalize an app help parents and children connect over digital experiences. Other media play patterns allow kids and parents to cooperate toward a game or goal. All these depend, however, on the parent, teacher, or caregiver taking the initiative to create a truly interactive experience, whether within the mediated experience, parallel to it, or afterward.

Currently, the least well-developed area in mobile media is how to use these devices to support children's social and emotional development, so much at the core of Fred Rogers' work. He may have predicted that it would be challenging when he said that "a computer can help you learn to spell 'HUG,' but it can never know the risk or the joy or actually giving or receiving one" (Rogers, 1994, p. 89).

Fred would certainly have cautioned us to know our limits—that we not try to fill children's every moment, or mediate every experience through a screen. He worried that "millions of children of all ages are getting an overdose of mechanical entertainment and suffering a deficiency in healthier forms of play" and said "you rarely have time for everything you want in this life, so you need to make choices" (Rogers, 1994, p. 62).

Mindful of the trust children lend to the stories and characters they see on screen, Fred called the space between the set and the viewer "very holy ground." He spoke of the implicit message children take from their playthings: "here's the kind of world I expect you to build." This applies equally to digital, interactive media: Content creators need to understand, respect, and return children's investment in our offerings to them.

Returning to the quote with which we opened, Fred was not scared or dismissive of new technologies. After all, he said, "each generation, in its turn, is a link between all that has gone before and all that comes after" (Fred Rogers Company, n.d.).

Fred Rogers wrote, "Where would any of us be without teachers—without people who have a passion for their art or their science or their craft and love it right in front of us?" (Rogers, 2005, p. 94). Fred suggested that media had the potential to present children with enthusiastic teachers all the time. It is our responsibility to be the passionate teachers, or at least to bring teaching materials to life via media.

In laying a foundation for the future, it's always important to learn from the past. Fred Rogers used to end public presentations by asking the audience to think silently about someone who had been important to them. Before you go on to read the rest of this book, may we ask you to stop and recall an enthusiastic teacher in your life—someone who sparked your passion for helping children grow in healthy ways. . . . *Now read on!*

References

Buckleitner, W. (2010). Can technology enhance the life of a young child? *Children's Technology Review, 18*(4), 6–7.

CNN. (2001, August 31). Mr. Rogers says goodbye for now. Retrieved from www.cnn.com/2001/SHOWBIZ/TV/08/31/rogers.finale/index.html

Fred Rogers Company. (n.d.). Retrieved from www.fredrogers.org/fred-rogers/legacy/

Rogers, F. (1994). *You are special: Words of wisdom from America's most beloved neighbor*. New York, NY: Penguin Books.

Rogers, F. (2005). *Life's journeys according to Mister Rogers: Things to remember along the way*. New York, NY: Hyperion Books.

Chapter 2

Technology as a Tool for Social-Emotional Development: What We Can Learn From Fred Rogers' Approach

Hedda Sharapan

Fred Rogers' Approach to Technology

From the very first time I met Fred Rogers, I sensed that he had a unique approach to technology. It was 1965, I had just graduated with a bachelor's degree in psychology, and I was considering the possibility of a career in children's television. Someone at WQED, our PBS station, suggested that I go to Fred Rogers for some advice. That was before *Mister Rogers' Neighborhood*, but I knew Fred's name because of *Children's Corner*, a local children's program he worked on in the 1950s at WQED. Even though on *Children's Corner* Fred was behind the scenes as co-producer, puppeteer, composer, and organist, he was well known as an experienced television producer. So I figured he would be giving me helpful advice.

What was Fred's recommendation? It didn't surprise me that he suggested graduate school, but it did surprise me that he wasn't talking about advanced study in television production or communication. Instead, he was encouraging me to pursue a master's degree in child development, and he highly recommended the University of Pittsburgh's graduate program where, at that time, he was continuing his studies and working directly with children. What he most appreciated was that their graduate school was focused not just on theory, but students were given the opportunity to spend a great deal of time with children, observing them, listening and learning what's important for their development. From that first conversation I had with him, I could see that his attention was not on the technology itself, but rather on the other side of the camera—the children. Television was just a tool that helped him offer what he knew was important to his audience.

In fact, Fred saw the potential of television early on to serve the needs of children, even though when he first saw this new technology in 1951 (home on spring break of his senior year at Rollins College where he was studying music composition), he described the children's TV programs as "nonsense" and "pies in faces." He felt children deserved better, and that's why he postponed his studies in the ministry and went instead to NBC in New York to learn about television so that he could find ways to use it as a gift for children and families.

I was fortunate to be able to take Fred's advice and attend the graduate school he recommended. The child development graduate program at the University of Pittsburgh focused on attachment, relationship, play, and social-emotional development. In my second year of grad school there, Fred received funding for *Mister Rogers' Neighborhood*, and he asked me to join the production in part-time evening work as the assistant director. Sitting there in the control room, I could see and hear my graduate studies coming to life in the thematic content, in Fred's words and songs, in his actions, his *Neighborhood of Make-Believe* stories, his conversations with guests, and especially in his relationship with his viewers. While his earlier program *Children's Corner* was more freewheeling fun and for a somewhat older audience, it was obvious that he was now focused on young children and social-emotional development, a major aspect of our graduate work.

It was obvious that Fred knew how to use the "screen" to foster children's healthy growth, especially in the areas of social-emotional development, for example:

- Acknowledging feelings
- Using words to talk about feelings
- Working on self-control
- Encouraging persistence
- Expecting and accepting mistakes as a part of learning
- Developing empathy
- Being able to work through conflicts with friends
- Feeling good about themselves
- Appreciating and respecting others

It's no wonder that over the years we heard from families that, with the help of the *Neighborhood* program, their children were more likely to talk about their feelings, fears, and concerns, as well as what made them feel good, proud of themselves, and more accepting of others.

In the midst of our work on the *Neighborhood* series, we were starting to deal with the new electronic technology of the 1980s. When computers came along, even in our office, I would have to say that Fred was slow to adapt to them. He continued writing scripts with his blue-tip pens on yellow legal pads and corresponding with colleagues with his distinctive handwriting on note cards. (His appreciation for email as a way to connect with friends and colleagues came much later.)

It even seemed to me that Fred had mixed feelings in 1984 when CBS Software asked him to create an activity or game for children to play on a computer. I remember his concern about reports that computer play was isolating. Instead of children spending time talking or doing things with their families or friends, we heard that they were focused on a computer screen. On the other hand, I also remember Fred wishing that technology existed that could give children ways to actively create their own play, especially with his Make-Believe characters.

I worked on that project with Fred, and I saw how he approached this new technology with caution and with deep understanding of children, but also with a sense of excitement about its potential. The activity we created was called "Many Ways to Say I Love You," based on one of Fred's *Neighborhood* songs), and it gave children a way to create an online greeting card for someone in their family. That kind of online sticker-book activity is quite common now, but it was ahead of its time then. Along with stickers of the Make-Believe characters, there were other familiar items (including a car sticker that animated, going away, and then pausing a bit before coming back to help children with separation fears). We also offered a choice of phrases that could help children (and parents) to express their feelings, such as "I need a hug" or "What a day" or "Proud of you."

That's the kind of attention to the real needs of children and families that was important to Fred. This wasn't just technology for the sake of what it can do, but for the sake of how it can help children and their families. It seems that Fred saw computer software as one more tool to help children express their feelings and strengthen family relationships. And after all, isn't that what the word technology means? It's just a fancy word for man-made tool.

Technology has come a long way since then. Here at The Fred Rogers Company, we've developed a number of computer games, activities, and apps for *Mister Rogers' Neighborhood* and *Daniel Tiger's Neighborhood*. As part of our mission of carrying on Fred's legacy, we continue to work on ways to use today's technology to address some of the real needs, feelings, and concerns of young children, particularly in the areas of social and emotional development.

Early Childhood Professionals Who Are Also Approaching Technology as a Tool for Social-Emotional Development

As I was thinking about how Fred used the technology of his day to help children express their feelings in healthy ways and to get along with others, it occurred to me that most people, even in our field, don't generally think about using activities or apps in those ways. It's easier to see that screens could be used for teaching cognitive skills like number recognition and matching. I also think we'd all agree that there are some things about screen activities that can have a negative or even harmful effect. But I've been taking Fred's approach, looking at the potential of technology as a tool that can help children gain skills involved in social-emotional development. By keeping an open mind, I've been hearing from early childhood professionals who are excited by the social-emotional benefits they're seeing from certain screen activities—even benefits they didn't expect, and I'm glad to have this opportunity to share their stories with you.

Finding Ways to Express Feelings

One of Fred's favorite phrases was, "Whatever is mentionable can be more manageable," and he used his television program to help children know that it can help to talk about feelings. I thought about that when I heard from a teacher who told me that when a child in her group is having a difficult time missing "Mommy," she encourages the child to dictate an email to the mother, and then she sends it. She found that it's been reassuring for children to put their feelings into words in an email and to hear from their parents who send an email back, letting them know that even though they're apart right now, "Mommy" or "Daddy" is thinking of them, too.

Many teachers help children talk about feelings by identifying facial expressions. But instead of using books with photos or illustrations, some teachers are giving children a more personal and meaningful way to learn about feelings by making their own photo albums about feelings. They use their smartphones or digital cameras to take photos of the children in their group with facial expressions that match feelings. After having the photos printed, they put them in an album, and children can look through them again and again—as a way to identify their own feelings and to develop empathy for others.

Another variation is to use the technology to make a photo album of the children doing something positive with their mad feelings, something that doesn't hurt others—as Fred suggested in his song, "What Do You Do with the Mad that You Feel?" (©Fred M. Rogers 1968)—like drawing a mad picture, doing a mad dance, pounding some clay, or talking with someone. Those kinds of books, created with the help of technology, can also be made with social stories to encourage children to deal with their own real situations and to find healthy ways to express their feelings.

At the Fred Rogers Company, we've also worked hard to create meaningful activities and apps that can help children talk about their feelings, and we've centered them on our Make-Believe characters. For example, our "Daniel Tiger Play at Home" app includes a way children can create music based on feeling happy, sad, or mad. I have to say, though, that while we're excited about the possibilities, at the same time we're very much aware of the limitations, even with today's more powerful technology. It's easier to create technology that can help children with letters and numbers, matching and making puzzles. It's much more challenging to create technology in the service of social-emotional development.

Developing Self-Control and Dealing With Limits

One of the most important parts of Fred's song "What Do You Do with the Mad that You Feel?" is the ending, with the words "I can stop when I want to . . . stop when I wish . . . and what a good feeling to know that the feeling is really mine." We all know it's hard for children to stop doing something they're engaged in and enjoying, and we give them rules and limits, and we help them build self-control.

I know there are teachers who worry that the electronic devices will create more conflicts and more self-control issues and make it harder to set limits, and that's understandable. They're concerned that children are so mesmerized with what's on the screen that they won't want to turn off the screen or give others a turn.

Yet I've heard teachers say that, as with any other activity, you need to help children know the limits with technology and know that you're going to enforce them. Just as we give additional early warnings to help children who get upset when it's time to come inside from the playground, helping children know that it soon will be time to stop playing on a screen device is not so different. Some teachers find it helpful to use a timer, which children are accustomed to from other activities. I've heard, too, that after a while, the novelty of screen play wears off, and children willingly move on to other activities.

Teachers also tell me that with thoughtful work on limit setting, they find that children learn to discipline themselves with the devices. So we could consider that the new technology gives us another opportunity to help children work on self-control—and gives children another situation to let them know we care about them and how they spend their time and energies.

It also occurred to me that there's another way that some teachers are using technology to help children with self-control, but I don't think they realize it. For example, they bring out a camera or smartphone at cleanup time to help the children who don't want to stop the work they've been doing on an elaborate block structure. Those children tend to be much more willing to stop and put the blocks away if their play can be documented in a photo, especially if they themselves can take the photo. They feel proud to use a camera, a very "grownup" tool, and when you think about it, they have to use a lot of skills to be able to take a good photo. They have to carefully adjust the camera to get the picture in the lens, hold still, and use hand-eye coordination. When you think about it, all of those skills are related to self-control.

Developing Persistence

On the *Neighborhood* program, children watched Fred himself work on trying to learn new things, from hand motions to songs, juggling, or writing Chinese calligraphy. He wanted children to see that some things are hard to learn, even for adults, but we keep on trying.

We all know that persistence is one of the keys to success in school, and I was especially interested to hear from a teacher who found an app that's encouraged persistence, especially with the older preschool boys in her group. She downloaded the Handwriting Without Tears app that lets them practice writing alphabet letters on a digital tablet, and she found that the boys are now engaged and keep on working on writing the letters correctly. She hasn't seen the frustration and humiliation that seemed to trigger difficult and disruptive behaviors around that same task. In fact, she told me it's decreased the challenging behaviors in her group. Working on an electronic tablet seems to elevate the handwriting task and makes it easier (and neater) for them to erase any misplaced lines and try again. That teacher told me that after the boys have mastered using their finger on an electronic tablet, she plans to give them a stylus to write the letters on the screen. Using a stylus as a tool would then help them make the transition to a regular writing tool like a pencil.

There's another aspect of persistence that was always important in the *Neighborhood* series, and that was helping children accept mistakes (and keep on trying). Obviously, game developers have discovered something powerful about intrinsic motivation. They've figured out a way to make a game or activity so motivating that children are willing to keep trying, even though they make mistakes again and again. Somehow their mistakes on electronic games and activities aren't so discouraging. When you think of it, that's one of the best problem-solving experiences we can give children. We want them to *want* to keep trying— and to understand that making mistakes is part of learning.

Inviting Interaction

Fred approached technology as a way to help people connect and interact with each other. What teachers tell me is that they're seeing more interaction and conversation around today's technology than they expected to see. They're even describing the area with the computer or tablet as a "language-rich" place in the room.

There seems to be a lot of social interaction in that area, too. Teachers are finding that children using today's screens are engaged in cooperative play, encouraging each other, exploring, discovering, and problem-solving together. They're surprised to find that electronic tablets and computer screens aren't isolating children. Instead, they tell me that it's the children who are painting at an easel who work in isolation, independently and privately. But when they're creating artwork on a tablet device, they tend to work with others, sharing new "tricks" and effects that they've found or are discovering together.

There seems to also be something about screen activities that encourages children to help each other figure things out when they're stuck. Maybe because the technology has become so intuitive, children (adults, too!) don't use manuals or instructions. I think that's why children enjoy working together to help each other. It's a challenge for them, and they're exploring and discovering together. You might even find that some children you wouldn't expect are becoming leaders because they're more open to persisting at exploring the technology and problem solving.

Enriching Dramatic Play

Part of Fred's intent of building his program around a "neighborhood" theme was to help children understand the value of relationships with family, friends, and others in the community. So it was especially interesting for me to hear about "neighborly" play growing out of children's electronic play. It all started when a very observant and highly creative teacher told me that on two electronic tablets next to each other, she loaded an app, My Play Home, that allows children to have on-screen "dollhouse" play. This particular app offers a home setting with a family (mother, father, children, and a baby) and lots of possible interactions, like pouring juice, swinging on a tire swing, bouncing a basketball into a hoop, putting the baby to bed, etc.

The teacher noticed that two girls were playing side by side, each with her own tablet, making "neighborly" conversation with the families in each other's houses. Watching their social play, the teacher wondered if she could encourage the same kind of neighborly play with dollhouses. Typically there was only one dollhouse in the room, but she decided to set up several dollhouses side by side. She was delighted to see the children continuing their neighborly scenario and to find how much that expanded and enriched their play. The teacher told me that without the experience of observing their play with side-by-side electronic tablets, she wouldn't have thought of putting several dollhouses together. She also had a sense that the children's neighborly experiences with the app played a role in inspiring their rich social play with the real dollhouses.

Another Way for Teachers to Learn About the Children

When Fred was studying child development and working with children, he said that the most important way for him to learn was to "listen." With children's fascination with today's electronic technology, we now have another opportunity to listen to children's ideas, feelings, and thinking processes as they're working on the activities or games.

As with any other activity the children are engaged in, we can learn a lot when we ask open-ended questions about the work they are doing on the electronic devices. And because the technology is so new, even to us, many teachers are asking out of genuine curiosity. For example, teachers are asking, "How did you do that? I'd love to know." And "How did you figure that out?" And "That's really interesting! Show me what you did to make that happen."

Besides learning some things about the technology from the children's strategies, any time you're really listening to a child's ideas, thoughts, and feelings will help strengthen your connection with that child. When you show an interest in what a child is doing and thinking, you're strengthening that relationship, and as Fred Rogers continually reminded us, "It's through relationships that we grow best and learn best."

By engaging in conversation around what children are thinking and how they're problem-solving with the technology, you'll also be giving them a boost for their future learning. The way education is going, children need to do more than just give an answer to a problem; they have to explain *how* they came to that answer. That's *metacognition*, and these days, students have to be able to communicate their thinking process. Elementary school teachers are now asking, "What were you thinking about as you worked on the problem . . . or as you read that story?"

When you listen to the children's ideas, you might be surprised to know how much they're thinking and learning as they work on solving problems on the computer or tablet. And you might be surprised to find that some of the most creative problem-solvers may be the children who exhibit challenging behaviors at other tasks. By strengthening your relationship with them in those conversations around their technology interests, you might even find some of their challenging behaviors decreasing.

Position Statement Alignment

> When used wisely, technology and media can support learning and relationships. Enjoyable and engaging shared experiences that optimize the potential for children's learning and development can support children's relationships both with adults and their peers.
>
> NAEYC & Fred Rogers Center (2012), p. 1

Caution and Collaboration

Even with all the positive uses of technology that I've heard about, I have to admit that I, too, continue to be skeptical. I am concerned about how seductive screens are and how time with them can deprive children of time in rich, open-ended, hands-on play experiences and in face-to-face interaction with others that are essential for success in school and in life.

While I'm struggling along with everyone else to find ways that early childhood professionals can use technology appropriately, I try to keep in mind something else I learned from Fred: "No matter how helpful computers are as tools (and of course they can be very helpful tools), they don't begin to compare in significance to the teacher-child relationship, which is human and mutual. A computer can help you learn to spell "HUG," but it can never know the risk of the joy or actually giving or receiving one. I keep that in mind so I myself don't get so fascinated by what the technology *can do* that I forget *what it can't do*.

I do believe that collaboration will help us. We're all new at this because the technology is growing exponentially every day! And there are many in our early childhood communities who are open to the conversation and want to share what they're finding with others.

If we can stay skeptical, we'll keep on questioning and making thoughtful decisions. As we collaborate, we just might find new and intriguing ways to use screen time, ways that are not only appropriate, but would be what Fred hoped his television program would be—a meaningful gift to help children grow to become competent, caring, and compassionate human beings.

Position Statement Alignment

> Throughout the process of researching and writing this position statement, we have been guided by the legacy of Fred Rogers. By appropriately and intentionally using the technology of his day—broadcast television—to connect with each individual child and with parents and families, Fred Rogers demonstrated the positive potential of using technology and media in ways that are grounded in principles of child development.
>
> NAEYC & Fred Rogers Center (2012), p. 2

Resources

- Daniel Tiger's Neighborhood, www.fredrogers.org/media/daniel-tigers-neighborhood/
- The Fred Rogers Center for Early Learning and Children's Media at Saint Vincent College, www.fredrogerscenter.org
- The Fred Rogers Company, www.fredrogers.org/
- Mister Rogers' *Neighborhood*, www.fredrogers.org/media/mister-rogers-neighborhood/
- Professional Development Newsletter Subscription, www.fredrogers.org/professional/signup/
- Professional Development Resource Library, www.fredrogers.org/professional/video/

Learn More . . .

- Hedda Sharapan. (2012). From STEM to STEAM: How early childhood educators can apply Fred Rogers' approach. *Young Children, 67*(1), 36–40.
- Hedda Sharapan. (2013, March 21). What I learned from Fred Rogers [Fred Rogers Center Blog]. Retrieved from www.fredrogerscenter.org/blog/what-i-learned-from-fred-rogers/
- Hedda Sharapan. (2014). High tech—High touch. The Fred Rogers Company, Professional resources. Retrieved from www.fredrogers.org/professional/video/steam/hightech.php
  Handwriting Without Tears www.hwtears.com/hwt
  My Play Home www.myplayhomeapp.com
- Technology and interactive media as tools in early childhood programs serving children from birth through age 8. A Joint Position statement of the National Association for the Education of Young Children and the Fred Rogers Center for Early Learning and Children's Media at Saint Vincent College (2012). www.naeyc.org/content/technology-and-young-children

Chapter 3

Technology and Digital Media as Tools for Teaching and Learning in the Digital Age

Chip Donohue

Introduction

It's challenging to be an analog adult in the digital world young children are growing up in today. Making effective, appropriate, and intentional choices about the use of technology tools and digital media with young children can be difficult, even overwhelming, for early childhood educators and parents who live in a world full of TVs, computers, tablets, smartphones, handheld digital games, and other mobile devices. In such a screen-saturated world, we need to ask ourselves how best to manage the quality and quantity of technology and media use in children's lives—both how much children watch and what they watch and do when they are using screens.

In early childhood programs, at school, at home, and in informal learning settings like libraries, museums, zoos, and nature centers, we all share a responsibility to be sure children's engagement with screen media supports early learning and the development of the whole child. And to be sure technology and media do not displace active play, time outdoors, hands-on activities with real materials, and creative expression through art, music, and movement. But where to begin?

For early childhood educators teaching in the digital age, there are new resources to turn to including frameworks, guidelines, principles of best practice, and developmentally appropriate practices. And social learning and being a connected educator offers ever-expanding opportunities to learn with and from other educators in communities of practice. Educators who want to learn more about selecting, using, integrating, and evaluating technology and digital media for use in the classroom to support healthy development and early learning have more places to turn and more sources to draw from. In this chapter, the focus is on three essential frameworks that can help you build a foundation for appropriate and intentional choices about technology in the early years.

Three Frameworks = One Foundation

This book is grounded in three frameworks for thinking about and teaching with digital media for early learning:

1. The NAEYC & Fred Rogers Center joint position statement on *Technology and Interactive Media as Tools in Early Childhood Programs Serving Children from Birth through Age 8* (2012)

2. The Fred Rogers Center's *A Framework for Quality in Digital Media for Young Children: Considerations for Parents. Educators and Media Creators* (2012)
3. The three *Cs*—content, context, and the individual child—from Lisa Guernsey's book, *Screen Time: How Electronic Media—From Baby Videos to Educational Software—Affects Your Young Child* (2007)

As described in the Introduction, everyone who has contributed chapters to this book hope that you will take time to access and read the position statement and *Framework for Quality* as you begin to explore the ideas and best practices we share. To understand and appreciate our perspectives, approaches, and practices, it's important to be grounded in the same foundational sources and resources that inform us.

Begin with the Position Statement and a summary of the key messages:

*   When used intentionally and appropriately, technology and interactive media are effective tools to support learning and development.
*   Intentional use requires early childhood teachers and administrators to have information and resources regarding the nature of these tools and the implications of their use with children.
*   Limitations on the use of technology and media are important.
*   Special considerations must be given to the use of technology with infants and toddlers.
*   Attention to digital citizenship and equitable access is essential.
*   Ongoing research and professional development are needed.

                        NAEYC & Fred Rogers Center Joint Position
                                        Statement (2012), pp. 1–2

Learn more about the position statement, key messages, examples of effective practice, and selected resources on technology in early childhood education at www.naeyc.org/content/technology-and-young-children.

Review the *Framework for Quality* guiding principles from The Fred Rogers Center.

*   **Principle 1:** Quality digital media should safeguard the health, well-being, and overall development of young children.
*   **Principle 2:** Quality in digital media for young children should take into account the child, the content, and the context of use.
*   **Principle 3:** Determinations of quality should be grounded in an evidence base that can be used by parents, educators, policymakers, and others to make decisions about the selection and use of particular digital media products, and by media creators to improve and develop new products in response to consumer expectations of quality.

                                Fred Rogers Center (2012), pp. 1–2

Principle one of the *Framework for Quality* (Fred Rogers Center, 2012) is the starting point for any conversation about using technology tools and interactive media with young children, and it reminds us that despite our enthusiasm for new technology tools, we must always think about what is best for the child before we consider whether technology provides the best tool to support development and learning.

- **Principle 1: Quality digital media should safeguard the health, well-being, and overall development of young children.**

  Above all, the use and content of digital media should not harm young children. The healthy cognitive, social, emotional, physical, and linguistic development of the whole child is as important as ever in the digital age. Decades of child development research tells us that healthy development depends upon positive and nurturing social interactions between children and adults, creative play, exposure to language, and exploration. A young child's experience with digital media should not exclude or diminish these critical developmental experiences. Digital media should never be used in ways that are emotionally damaging, physically harmful, disrespectful, degrading, dangerous, exploitative, or intimidating to children. This includes undue exposure to violence or highly sexualized images as well as invasive marketing and over-commercialization. Safety considerations include Internet privacy guidelines for children and adults, child-friendly hardware and mechanical features, and standards for digital citizenship.

  Fred Rogers Center (2012), p. 6

Read the Framework at www.fredrogerscenter.org/media/resources/Framework_Statement_2-April_2012-Full_Doc+Exec_Summary.pdf

Consider the three Cs—Lisa Guernsey writes about the three Cs—content, context and the individual child—and provides a third framework to help educators and parents thoughtfully select and use media with young children.

- *Content*—How does this help children engage, express, imagine, or explore?
- *Context*—How does it complement, and not interrupt, children's natural play?
- The individual *child*—How do we choose the right tech tools and experiences for each child's needs, abilities, interests, and development stage?

Just as these three frameworks can provide a foundation for you, the ideas influenced the development of the others. Guernsey's three Cs approach helped to inform the position statement process and was integrated directly into Principle 2 from the *Framework for Quality* (Fred Rogers Center, 2012) as shown below.

Principle 2: Quality in digital media for young children should take into account the child, the content, and the context of use.

Child: The distinct cognitive abilities, physical abilities, social-emotional needs, aptitudes, and interests of individual children, at different developmental stages, should be considered.

Content: The intent of the content should be clear—to educate, introduce new information, develop particular skills, and/or entertain.

Context: Especially for children age 5 and younger, the media product should encourage joint engagement (e.g., by parents or teachers with children, by children with their siblings or peers). For older children, interactivity and engagement with the media product, including the engagement of children as creators of content, should be a priority.

If relevant, the conduciveness of certain location(s) of use (e.g., homes, classrooms, outdoors, other settings for informal learning) to particular goals for learning, development, communication, and/or entertainment, should be specified.

Context of use should take into account the value-added of product features and affordances.

Fred Rogers Center (2012), pp. 1–2

Understand the keywords. During the a 3-year process of listening, drafting, receiving comments, listening some more, and revising again that led to the final version of the position statement, a list of keywords emerged as both descriptors and values that guided the working group. These words now serve as essential characteristics of effective and appropriate use of technology with young children.

- From the start, we defined technology and media as *tools* to be used alongside other tools and materials commonly found in early childhood environments.
- Being *intentional* is a higher order teaching skill that means you understand if, when, and how to use technology, and more importantly, you know why.
- *Appropriate* grounds the position statement on the well-established principles of developmentally appropriate practice.
- *Effective* refers to the uses of technology and media that advance your learning goals and enhance learning opportunities across the curriculum for each individual child and for all the children in your classroom.
- *Integrated* means thinking about technology across the curriculum, throughout the day—not technology as a separate activity.
- The word *balanced* gets to the heart of our belief that technology should be in addition to, not instead of, essential early childhood experiences. Educators need to find the right balance when integrating technology into the classroom alongside a room already full of invaluable materials and experiences for young children. We recognize that these are valuable tools when used

intentionally with children to extend and support active, hands-on, creative, and authentic engagement with those around them and with their world.

- *Interactive* is an important keyword. While new digital devices can offer children amazing interactive experiences on the screen, we want to be sure that young children have interactions with their peers and caring adults, as well as with appropriate technology tools. It also contrasts with noninteractive or "passive" use of media, where children are placed in front of screens with little or no interaction with the technology or with others.
- *Engaging* speaks to the quality of the technology or media experience as well as engagement with peers and adults—so all three *C*s need to be accounted for—content, context, and the child.
- *Co-engagement or Joint Engagement With Media* is a central idea that places technology as a tool for encouraging adult child and child-to-child interactions and invites a more social and less isolating experience.
- The words *access* and *equity* are professional responsibilities early educators share to be sure that all children have opportunities to experience technology and media and to gain valuable skills for learning and digital media literacy for the 21st century.
- The words *select, use, integrate,* and *evaluate* are action words that describe the role of the teacher and the ongoing and dynamic nature of teaching with technology—and are a constant reminder that it takes knowledge, experience, and digital media literacy for the adult to choose and use technology in appropriate and intentional ways.
- And finally, *professional development* acknowledges the need to support educators as they enhance their digital literacy and strengthen their ability to use technology in intentional and effective ways.

Identify and address the concerns. Some advocates for children, quality early childhood experiences, and childhoods without technology (or with very little), have raised concerns that cannot be ignored. Early childhood educators interested in using technology with young children need to always be aware of these concerns and take them into consideration when making choices for the classroom.

Among the most frequently raised concerns about technology in the early years are the following:

- The need to address access and equity issues so that new digital devices are tools for all children and can help close the achievement gap and the digital divide—not make them worse
- Exposure to inappropriate content and commercial messages targeting children
- Negative impact on social-emotional development due to less socialization and more social isolation and the risk of technology interrupting the adult/child relationship
- The need to emphasize interactive use and interactions with others over passive, noninteractive uses

- The need to monitor and manage screen time and place limits on use—this becomes more complicated when we consider a child's screen exposure throughout the day and across settings in addition to classroom time.
- Displacement—the risk that technology will replace developmentally appropriate and valuable materials and activities
- Negative impact on imaginative and open-ended play, active learning, hands-on learning, and creativity
- Less outdoor time and physical activity leading to more childhood obesity
- Increased sleep disruptions

Position Statement Alignment

> There are concerns about whether young children should have access to technology and screen media in early childhood programs. Several professional and public health organizations and child advocacy groups concerned with child development and health issues such as obesity have recommended that passive, non-interactive technology and screen media not be used in early childhood programs and that there be no screen time for infants and toddlers. NAEYC and the Fred Rogers Center are also concerned about child development and child health issues and have considered them carefully when developing this position statement.
>
> NAEYC & Fred Rogers Center (2012), p. 2

- AAP, American Academy of Pediatrics www.aap.org
- AAP Policy Statement—*Children, Adolescents, and the Media* (2013). http://pediatrics. aappublications.org/content/early/2013/10/24/peds.2013-2656
- *Beyond Remote-Controlled Childhood: Teaching Young Children in the Media Age*, Diane E. Levin www.naeyc.org/store/Beyond-Remote-Controlled-Childhood
- Campaign for a Commercial Free Childhood www.commercialfreechildhood.org
- *Caring for Our Children*, American Academy of Pediatrics, American Public Health Association, National Resource Center for Health and Safety in Child Care and Early Education http://cfoc.nrckids.org
- Center on Media and Child Health www.cmch.tv
- *Facing the Screen Dilemma: Young Children, Technology and Early Education.* Campaign for a Commercial-Free Childhood & Teachers Resisting Unhealthy Children's Entertainment www.commercialfreechildhood.org/sites/default/files/facingthescreendilemma.pdf
- healthychildren.org
- TRUCE, Teachers Resisting Unhealthy Children's Entertainment www.truceteachers. org/

Figure 3.1 Learn More ... About the Cautions and Concerns

Know What Matters. Findings shared by children's media researchers during a research symposium, *Digital Media in Early Learning: What We Know and What We Need to Learn*, cohosted by Lisa Guernsey and New America with the *Alliance for Early Learning in the Digital Age* (Fred Rogers Center, Joan Ganz Cooney Center at Sesame Workshop, the Ounce of Prevention Fund, PBS, Sesame Workshop, and the TEC Center at Erikson), provided evidence-based guidance for educators and parents. Some of my takeaways about what matters most are the following:

- **Relationships matter**—We know that young children learn best in the context of interactions and relationships with tuned-in, responsive, and caring adults, so technology use should support and strengthen adult/child relationships, not interrupt or prevent them.
- **Joint engagement with media matters**—We know that adult/child interactions are key to language learning, and this is also true when using media with children. Reading a book or playing with an app leads to more learning when adults and children share the experience.
- **Content matters**—For screen-based media, the content on the screen really matters, and we're beginning to understand that what children watch on screens can be much more important that how long they watch screen. Content features from children's television that seem to be most important when designing or choosing a media experience for a young child include characters who children build relationships with, an engaging story, elements that promote guided play, and avoidance of distractions.
- **Context matters**—In early childhood education we've long known that children learn best in active environments when they are engaged in meaningful, interactive, and social contexts, and these "essentials" hold true in the digital age with multitouch screen, apps, and interactive experiences.

  Context also includes an understanding of the child's media use at home and how the family uses media. Educators need to consider media use in the context of the child's family, home environment, community, culture language, and experience.
- **Creating media matters**—In the 21st century, it will not be enough to know how to use technology. Those who are capable of creating their own messages and expressing themselves through media—including having control over their own media use and being intrinsically motivated—will progress from consuming media to meaning-making with media to creating media. Teachers who can progress from media consumer to creator will be better able to guide young children along this continuum as well.

Position Statement Alignment

It is the position of NAEYC and the Fred Rogers Center that: Technology and interactive media are tools that can promote effective learning and development when they are used intentionally by early childhood educators, within the framework of developmentally appropriate practice, to support learning goals established for individual children. The framework of developmentally appropriate practice begins with knowledge about what children of the age and developmental status represented in a particular group are typically like. This knowledge provides a general idea of the activities, routines, interactions, and curriculum that should be effective. Each child in the particular group is then considered, both as an individual and within the context of that child's specific family, community, culture, linguistic norms, social group, past experience (including learning and behavior), and current circumstances.

Children's experiences with technology and interactive media are increasingly part of the context of their lives, which must be considered as part of the developmentally appropriate framework.

To make informed decisions regarding the intentional use of technology and interactive media in ways that support children's learning and development, early childhood teachers and staff need information and resources about the nature of these tools and the implications of their use with children.

NAEYC & Fred Rogers Center (2012), p. 5

Emphasize the benefits. When used intentionally and appropriately, technology and interactive media: can be additional tools for learning and development and can enhance children's cognitive and social abilities; support inclusive practice; provide tools to support English language learning; enhance early childhood practice when integrated into the environment, curriculum, and daily routines; and help educators make and sustain home-school connections.

NAEYC & Fred Rogers Center (2012), 5–9

NAEYC and the Fred Rogers Center (2012) summarize the benefits this way,

Effective uses of technology and media are active, hands-on, engaging, and empowering; give the child control; provide adaptive scaffolds to ease the accomplishment of tasks; and are used as one of many options to support children's learning.

NAEYC & Fred Rogers Center, (2012), p. 6

Putting it all together. As you continue to develop your technology knowledge and skills and begin to integrate technology and interactive media tools into your teaching, one of your best resources will be other teachers who are using technology well and can demonstrate what appropriate and intentional use looks like. Here's what three innovative teachers had to say about technology in their classrooms:

Erin says . . . When I introduce technology to my students, I provide ample time for them to freely explore and experiment with the devices. Children need time to explore any new material, and this is also true for

- Center on Media and Human Development http://cmhd.northwestern.edu/
- Children's Technology Review http://childrenstech.com/
- CLDC Best Practices Page, Child Learning & Development Center, Pacific University http://fg.ed.pacificu.edu/cldc/bestpractices.html
- Common Sense Media www.commonsensemedia.org/
- *Digital Media Literacy in Early Childhood Programs*, Pittsburgh Association for the Education of Young Children, PAEYC www.paeyc.org/digital-media-literacy
- Early Childhood Investigations Webinars www.esbyfs.com/early-childhood-investigations-webinars
- Early Learning Environment (*Ele*), Fred Rogers Center www.yourele.org
- ECEtech.net, Early Childhood Technology Network www.ecetech.net/dev/
- edWeb.net, *PreK-3 Digital Learning* www.edweb.net/prek3digitallearning
- Fred Rogers Center for Early Learning and Children's Media at Saint Vincent College www.fredrogerscenter.org
- HITN Early Learning Collaborative http://earlylearningcollaborative.org
- ISTE, International Society for Technology in Education www.iste.org
- Joan Ganz Cooney Center at Sesame Workshop www.joanganzcooneycenter.org/
- NAEYC, National Association for the Education of Young Children www.naeyc.org
- NAMLE, National Association for Media Literacy Education http://namle.net/
- *National Library of Virtual Manipulatives*, Utah State University http://nlvm.usu.edu/en/nav/vlibrary.html
- New America's Early Education Initiative and Learning Technologies Project http://education.newamerica.net
- Pittsburgh Kids + Creativity Network http://remakelearning.org/
- *Results Matter Video Library – iPads in Early Childhood*, Colorado Department of Education www.cde.state.co.us/resultsmatter/rmvideoseries_ipadsinearlychildhood
- TEC Center at Erikson Institute www.teccenter.erikson.edu
- Technology and Young Children Interest Forum www.techandyoungchildren.org/index.shtml

Figure 3.2 Blogs That Focus on Technology in the Early Years

technology. Through exploration, my students are able to get to know the functions of the devices, as well as brainstorm ways they could use them in more purposeful ways. Often students' discoveries through their exploration become a springboard for later learning. For example, my students were taking photographs around the classroom one day. Later, we were reviewing the photographs together on the projector. The students noticed a photo taken of someone's shadow on the wall. Immediately they recognized whom the shadow belonged to, and this jumpstarted a conversation about whether or not they could identify all of their friends by looking at their shadows. This was a provocation for a long-term study of shadows, reflections, and outlines. Open exploration provides children with the possibility to find areas of interest and future discoveries.

Maggie says . . . My best practice with technology in my classroom is using it as a tool to connect and collaborate with other classes around the globe. I use tools like Skype and Wikispaces to facilitate conversations and exchange.

Tricia says . . . We use technology in art education for instruction, art production, exploration, making connections with authentic audiences, and connecting our writing with our images via our online digital art gallery. Students are learning to navigate and participate in the media rich world in my art room as they develop 21st-century skills, practice digital citizenship, and work on creative problem solving.

Maggie adds . . . I view technology as a tool that should be seamlessly integrated into the classroom and one children feel they can choose whenever it will be the best tool for them to express an idea, collaborate with peers, reflect on their learning, or practice a skill. I encourage students to see technology as something they can use for collaboration and creation but also something that they can design and invent. I've learned that technology is often a consumer product at home so I need to help my students understand how they can be more than consumers and empower them to begin collaborating and making or building with technology (e.g., making eBooks, Skyping, creating music, designing robots).

Tricia adds . . . Technology integration is no longer my goal. It's becoming more meshed with best practices for delivering content to my students. I don't try to bring in technology for the sake of technology. I bring it in when it is a better way to teach something or it gives my students a valuable opportunity for learning. I'm finding that when I combine best practices, content knowledge, and technology in meaningful ways for my students that the learning is richer, more engaging, and sometimes transformative.

Thanks to these outstanding teachers and technology innovators for sharing their stories: Tricia Fuglestad, NBCT, K–5 Art Teacher, Dryden Elementary School, Arlington Heights, IL; Maggie Powers, Lower School Technology Coordinator, The Episcopal Academy, Philadelphia, PA, and Erin Stanfill, NBCT, Teacher and Educational Consultant, Burley Elementary, Chicago Public Schools.

Position Statement Alignment

When the integration of technology and interactive media in early childhood programs is built upon solid developmental foundations and early childhood professionals are aware of both the challenges and the opportunities, educators are positioned to improve programs.

NAEYC & Fred Rogers Center (2012), p. 1

Conclusion

Drawing on the big ideas and key concepts from the NAEYC & Fred Rogers Center joint position statement (2012), the Fred Rogers Center *Framework for Quality* (2012) and the three *C*s—content, content, child—from Lisa Guernsey (2007), I've presented an overview and highlights of what educators need to know to be able to use technology thoughtfully and appropriately. What you've read here is a starting point, but do take time to access the position statement and framework and read them carefully before moving on in this book. Having a foundational understanding of these principles and guidelines will serve you well as a learner and as a teacher of young children and help you get the most out of the chapters, topics, and key concepts that follow.

You've taken your first steps toward digital literacy—a journey you'll share with other early childhood educators, teacher educators, professional development providers and trainers, administrators, curriculum coordinators, parents, and media developers who are scrambling to catch up and keep up in the digital age. The adults who work with and on behalf of young children today were not born into the digital age, but the children are growing up in a digital world with new tools that create new opportunities and—if they have digitally literate adult tour guides and media mentors.

What do educators need to be effective tour guides and media mentors?

- Digitally literate teacher educators, professional development providers, and trainers
- Technology integrated into preservice, teacher education, and professional development
- Technology and media knowledge, experience, competency, and fluency leading to digital literacy
- Hands-on opportunities to play with technology before teaching with it
- Confidence to jump in and get started—to use technology to learn how and why to use technology
- Communities of practice and interest where you can access resources and practical information about teaching with technology, exchange ideas, share stories about what works, and ask questions about what doesn't with other educators, and develop your own personal and professional learning network
- Access to evidence-based practices, and examples of effective practice

Take time to check out some of the resources and links that have been shared, and refer back to them often as you move on in the book. In every chapter, you'll gather more resources and links for your journey. The contributing authors and I will do our best to be your tour guides and media mentors.

- *Ask the Mediatrician,* Center on Media and Child Health, Dr. Michael Rich http://cmch.typepad.com/mediatrician/
- *Digital Media Diet,* Carisa Kluver http://digitalmediadiet.com/
- *EdCentral Early Ed,* New America Foundation www.edcentral.org/category/earlyed/
- *Fred Rogers Center* http://www.fredrogerscenter.org
- *Gail Warnings,* Gail Lovely http://gailwarnings.com
- *Joan Ganz Cooney Center* www.joanganzcooneycenter.org/blog/
- *Language Castle Blog,* Karen Nemeth http://languagecastle.com/wordpress/
- *Little eLit,* Cen Campbell http://littleelit.com/
- *PlayLearnParent,* Alexis Lauricella http://playlearnparent.com
- *Teaching like it's 2999,* Jennie Magiera http://teachinglikeits2999.blogspot.com/

Figure 3.3 Online Resources on Effective Practices With Technology in the Early Years

Teacher Takeaways

- **Apply what you know about young children, child development, and appropriate practices.** You already have a solid foundation upon which to base your use of technology and digital media in the classroom.
- **Use the Guidelines.** Review the NAEYC & Fred Rogers Center joint position statement (2012) and the Fred Rogers Center *Framework for Quality* (2012) to understand the principles and guidelines they provide to help educators select, use, integrate, and evaluate technology effectively, appropriately, and intentionally.
- **Know what matters**. For young children and technology that includes relationships, joint engagement with media, the quality of the content, the context for media use, and the opportunity for young children to create media, not just consume it.
- **Consider the three *C*s.** Lisa Guernsey's (2007) content, context, and the individual child provide a framework to help educators and parents thoughtfully select and use media with young children.
- **Promote healthy media habits for young children:**
  - Consider total screen exposure throughout the day and across settings.
  - Shift from "how much" children watch to "what they watch."
  - Use media "with" traditional materials and activities rather than "instead of."
  - Place limits on passive use and avoid inappropriate content.
  - Look for media experiences that are interactive, include positive interactions with, and give the child control.

Facebook pages or groups to like, Pinterest Boards to follow, Twitter usernames to follow, and YouTube channels to subscribe to.

Organization	Site	Social Media Links
Center on Media and Child Health	Facebook	www.facebook.com/centeronmediaand childhealth
	Twitter	@cmch_boston
Children's Technology Review	Facebook	www.facebook.com/groups/dustormagic
	Pinterest	www.pinterest.com/buckleit/dust-or-magic/
	Twitter	@childtech, @dustormagic
	YouTube	www.youtube.com/user/childrenstech
Early Childhood Technology Network	Facebook	www.facebook.com/ECEtechnet
	Pinterest	www.pinterest.com/ecetech/
	Twitter	@ecetech
edWeb.net	Facebook	www.edweb.net/prek3digitallearning
PreK-3 Digital Learning	Pinterest	www.pinterest.com/edwebnet/
	Twitter	@edwebnet
	YouTube	www.youtube.com/user/edwebnet
Fred Rogers Center	Facebook	www.facebook.com/FredRogersCenter
	Pinterest	www.pinterest.com/fredrogersctr/
	Twitter	@FredRogersCtr, @Yourele
	YouTube	www.youtube.com/user/RogersCenter
HITN Early Learning Collaborative	Facebook	www.facebook.com/HITN.ELC
	Pinterest	www.pinterest.com/hitn/
	Twitter	@hitn_elc
Joan Ganz Cooney Center at Sesame Workshop	Facebook	www.facebook.com/CooneyCenter
	Pinterest	www.pinterest.com/cooneycenter/
	Twitter	@CooneyCenter
	YouTube	www.youtube.com/user/CooneyCenter
TEC Center	Facebook	www.facebook.com/teccenter.erikson
	Pinterest	www.pinterest.com/chipdonohue/
	Twitter	@TEC_Center
	YouTube	www.youtube.com/user/eriksonteccenter
Technology and Young Children Interest Forum	Facebook	www.facebook.com/ECETECH
	Listerv	ECETECH-L@lists.maine.edu
	Diigo	http://groups.diigo.com/group/ecetech
	Wiki	http://ecetech.wikispace.com/

Figure 3.4 Learn More . . . About Technology and Young Children on These Social Media Sites

- Emphasize relationships and joint engagement with media.
- Plan for unplugged time—Always ask, "What can we do when we turn off the screen?"
- **Be a positive media role model and mentor:**
    - Remember you are a role model for young children and they are watching how, when, and why you use technology and media.

- Be aware of your own tech behavior, because you have a powerful influence on children's tech attitudes and use.
- Develop your own technology skills and digital media literacy so that you can be a media mentor to young children, parents, and educators.
- Identify trusted sources for resources and recommendations on technology and interactive media.

- **Start a tech playgroup** with other educators and parents to have fun with technology and interactive media, to help guide your digital choices, and to discover new ways of appropriately using technology with young children.

References

Fred Rogers Center for Early Learning and Children's Media at Saint Vincent College. (2012). *A framework for quality in digital media for children: Considerations for parents, educators, and media creators.* Latrobe, PA: Fred Rogers Center.

Guernsey, L. (2007). *Screen time: How electronic media—from baby videos to educational software—affects your young child.* New York, NY: Basic Books.

National Association for the Education of Young Children & Fred Rogers Center for Early Learning and Children's Media at Saint Vincent College. (2012). *Technology and interactive media as tools in early childhood programs serving children from birth through age 8.* Washington, DC: NAEYC; Latrobe, PA: Fred Rogers Center for Early Learning and Children's Media at Saint Vincent College.

Resources

Buckleitner, W. (2009). What should a preschooler know about technology? *Early Childhood Today.* Retrieved from www.scholastic.com/teachers/article/what-should-preschooler-know-about-technology

Clark, L. S. (2013). *The parent app: Understanding families in the digital age.* Oxford, UK: Oxford University Press.

Harvey, S., Goudvia, A., Muhtaris, K., & Ziemke, K. (2013). *Connecting comprehension and technology: Adapt and extend toolkit practices.* Portsmouth, NH: Heinemann

Robb, M., Catalano, R., Smith, T., Polojac, S., Figlar, M., Minzenberg, B., & Schomburg, R. (2013). *Checklist for identifying exemplary uses of technology and interactive media for early learning: The Pennsylvania digital media literacy project.* Latrobe, PA: Fred Rogers Center for Early Learning and Children's Media at Saint Vincent College.

Shillady, A., & Muccio, A. S. (Eds.). (2012). *Spotlight on young children and technology.* Washington, DC: NAEYC.

Skype, www.skype.com/en/

Technology and Young Children Interest Forum. (2008). On our minds: Meaningful technology integration in the early learning environment. *Young Children, 63*(5), 1–3.

Vasquez, V. M., & Felderman, C. B. (2012). *Technology and critical literacy in early childhood.* New York, NY: Routledge.

Learn More . . .

- Center for Digital Media Innovation and Diversity, George Mason University, http://cdmid.gmu.edu/
- Children's Innovation Project, CMU CREATE Lab Journal of Children and Media, www.tandfonline.com/toc/rchm20/current#.UYKLu-CVtNY
- *Learning at Home: Families' Educational Media Use in America,* Joan Ganz Cooney Center, www.joanganzcooneycenter.org/publication/learning-at-home/
- *Q & A with Chip Donohue and Roberta Schomburg,* Fred Rogers Center Blog, www.fredrogerscenter.org/blog/a-qa-with-chip-donohue-and-roberta-schomburg/
- *Parenting in the Age of Digital Technology, A National Survey,* Center on Media and Human Development, Northwestern University, http://vjrconsulting.com/storage/PARENTING_IN_THE_AGE_OF_DIGITAL_TECHNOLOGY.pdf
- *Zero to Eight: Children's Media Use in America 2013,* Common Sense Media, www.commonsensemedia.org/sites/default/files/research/zero-to-eight-2013.pdf

Chapter 4

Teaching With Technology: Preparing Early Childhood Educators for the Digital Age

Chip Donohue and Roberta Schomburg

> It is not what the technology can do that makes it important, it is the way it has reignited passion and ideas in teachers. If these devices are being championed by teachers, listen to what they are saying. These teachers are not just championing the technology, they are celebrating a new way of teaching and learning. Something about these devices has helped many teachers to see the classroom very differently. That should be encouraged, supported and most thoroughly welcomed.
> —Dan Donahoo (2012)

Introduction—Teacher Education and Teacher Educators in the Digital Age

Preparing early childhood educators for teaching in the digital age creates new expectations for teacher preparation programs and places greater demands on those who teach the teachers. Teacher educators, professional development providers, trainers, and others responsible for preservice and inservice training, professional development, and continuing education, must now become digitally literate themselves in order to prepare future early childhood educators to select, use, integrate, and evaluate technology and digital media appropriately and intentionally.

To learn how to effectively integrate technology into the early childhood classroom and across the curriculum, educators need experiences that integrate technology tools and interactive media in the courses they take and the trainings they attend. They need to understand the influence of technology and digital media on young children, parents, families, and communities. They need opportunities to learn with and about technology in order to make informed decisions about how, when, and why to support early learning and healthy development through technology and digital media. They need examples of best practice and hands-on experiences to explore and discover which technology tools are developmentally appropriate for young children and to gain the knowledge, skills, and confidence needed to use technology as a tool. The need to become fluent in the use of technology tools: for their own personal and professional learning; for teaching, assessment, and classroom management; to support young children's learning;

for engaging parents and families; to strengthen the home-school connections; and for enhancing the digital media literacy of parents and children.

Teacher educators, and others who design and deliver preservice and inservice education, need to provide educators with opportunities to reflect on the principles and best practices of early childhood education and identify appropriate ways that technology can support and extend these principles through planning, curriculum, and teaching practices.

Position Statement Alignment

> To make informed decisions regarding the intentional use of technology and interactive media in ways that support children's learning and development, early childhood teachers and staff need information and resources about the nature of these tools and the implications of their use with children.
>
> National Association for the Education of Young Children [NAEYC] & Fred Rogers Center (2012), p. 5

To be adequately prepared to make informed decisions about technology and to support its effective use in learning environments for young children, early childhood educators must be knowledgeable and confident about how to appropriately implement technology to meet the needs of the whole child—social, emotional, physical, and cognitive—and how to steer children toward media and technology experiences that will have a positive influence on their development. Educators also have to be knowledgeable enough to answer parents' questions and to support families as they raise young children in the digital age.

Position Statement

> Teachers and administrators need information and resources to effectively select, use, integrate, and evaluate technology and interactive media tools in intentional and developmentally appropriate ways. They need to stay current regarding the rapid changes in technology and the implications for their use in programs.
>
> Preservice and professional development should include in-depth, hands-on technology experiences, ongoing support, and access to the latest technology and interactive media. Educators need opportunities to play and create using these tools. And, examples of successful integrations of technology and interactive media in early childhood programs should be compiled to provide support and inspiration.
>
> NAEYC & Fred Rogers Center (2012), p. 2

21st-Century Teacher Preparation

What do teacher educators need to effectively, appropriately, and intentionally integrate technology and digital media into teacher education and professional development? They need:

- Technology knowledge, skills, and experiences that result in confidence and competence
- Digital literacy in the context of early childhood teacher preparation
- Tools and methods for teaching with and about technology
- Hands-on opportunities to play with technology
- Opportunities to use technology to learn how and why to use technology
- Examples of effective technology integration in teacher education programs
- Ongoing professional development
- Communities of practice and interest
- Research about effective practices

What do early childhood educators need to effectively, appropriately, and intentionally integrate technology and digital media into teacher education and professional development? They need:

- Digitally literate teacher educators
- Technology knowledge, skills, and experience—confidence and competence
- Digital literacy in the context of early childhood education
- Technology integrated into preservice, teacher education, professional development, and continuing education
- Tools and methods for teaching and for use with young children
- Hands-on opportunities to play with technology
- Opportunities to use technology to learn how to use technology
- Communities of practice and interest
- Evidence-based practices and examples of effective practice

Technology Skills for 21st-Century Teaching

A number of national organizations have recently published reports about how early childhood educators use technology in the classroom and have identified the knowledge, skills, dispositions, digital literacy, and technology fluency needed to teach, work, and learn as a 21st-century teacher. A collaborative survey on early childhood technology use by the Center on Media and Human Development at Northwestern University, the Fred Rogers Center, and NAEYC (Wartella, Blackwell, Lauricella, & Robb, 2013) found that only one-fourth of the respondents were familiar with the NAEYC and Fred Rogers Center joint position statement (2012, p. 5).

In this study, the primary technologies available to early childhood educators were older ones such as digital cameras (92%); computers or laptops (84%); and DVD/TV technology (80%). Tablets were available to 29% of the respondents, and 15% had access to e-readers. Access did not translate into frequent usage, however. While 92% had access to digital cameras, only 61% reported using them frequently (more than once a week). Of the 84% who had computers, only 45% used them at least once a week. A similar study conducted in 2010 revealed that very few early childhood educators were using technology regularly (Wartella, Schomburg, Lauricella, Robb, & Flynn, 2010).

By 2012, teaching practices were beginning to change with increased usage in the classroom and respondents reporting higher levels of confidence using technology in their classrooms as well as more positive attitudes about the role of technology in the classroom, particularly in the role of documenting and individualizing children's learning (Wartella et al., 2013). However, 40% of respondents reported that they did not have the necessary technical assistance to implement technology use in their classrooms. And 60% reported that they did not have the professional development support they needed.

The Early Childhood Technology Today Survey (Simon, Nemeth, & McManis, 2013) explored how technology is being used in early childhood classrooms and identified what technology tools are available, the types of technology activities and experiences offered, and the professional development of teachers. In this study, 95% of the teachers now have desktop or laptop computers in their rooms, 44% are using interactive whiteboards, 37% are using a tablet computer, and less than 20% are using smartpens, e-readers, or smartphones.

Seventy-five percent of survey participants identified that they included technology because the children enjoyed it, while 50% said it was to meet the goals of the program. Extension of concepts and skills, indirectly supporting the introduction of concepts and skills and children learning how to use the technology itself were identified by two-thirds of the survey participants as reasons they include technology in the classroom.

The survey also identified common reasons that early childhood educators do not use technology, including lack of funding or insufficient budget; concerns about developmental appropriateness; program philosophy; teachers didn't see added value; and parental opposition.

In the PBS Learning Media (2013) report on how PK–12 teachers are using technology for learning in their classrooms, *Teachers Embrace Digital Media to Propel Learning*, more than two-thirds of teachers said they wanted more technology in their classrooms, with 90% of classrooms having a personal computer, 59% having interactive whiteboards, 36% using handhelds like cell phones and smartphones, and 35% having tablets and e-readers at the time of the survey. The one-third of teachers using a tablet or e-reader in their classroom was a 20% increase over the year before. Teachers identified key benefits of classroom technology, including opportunities to reinforce and expand content; motivate students to learn; respond to a variety of learning styles; and demonstrate something they can't show in any other way.

Project Tomorrow (2013), compared principal's expectations of technology skills development to the actual experiences of aspiring teachers in teacher preparation programs. In each of these categories, what the principals expect was significantly higher than teachers' actual experiences, including: ability to create and use video, podcasts, and other media; identifying and evaluating quality digital content to use in class; incorporating student owned mobile devices; using social media within instruction with students; and how to teach an online class.

A Framework for Quality in Digital Media for Children: Considerations for Parents, Educators, and Media Creators (Fred Rogers Center, 2012, p. 5) suggests that:

> New models of professional and career development, including the establishment of communities of learning and innovation, within and across sectors, should be explored . . . For educators, teacher education and professional development should include digital media literacy as well as opportunities for exploration and creation using digital media.

The report, *Take a Giant Step: A Blueprint for Teaching Children in a Digital Age* (Barron, Cayton-Hodges, Bofferding, Copple, Darling-Hammond & Levine, 2011), describes the process by which teachers gain essential technology skills:

> Developing the knowledge needed for skilled, meaningful integration of technology in teaching requires teachers to unpack the characteristics of media, software, and other technologies, identify their specific potentials, and consider how to incorporate them into learning experiences. Through this process, teachers must take into account two facets of interactivity: the interactivity inherent in the technology and the interactivity among students, teachers, and technology.
>
> Barron et al. (2011), p. 26

The data from these surveys on how teachers are using technology makes it clear that while the types of technology tools, digital devices, and uses are on the rise, inservice teachers need technology knowledge, skills, experience, ongoing professional development, and technical support to make the most of the technology already in their classroom and new educational technologies to come. Preservice teachers need to learn with and about technology tools and interactive media to be prepared for teaching in the 21st century and digital media literacy to best support the young children, parents, and families they serve.

In *Partnering for Success: A 21st Century Model for Teacher Preparation*, the International Association for K–12 Online Learning calls for 21st-century teacher preparation to support 21st-century teaching and learning in classroom:

> If we are to ensure great teachers are trained, mentored and retained for our students—the programs themselves must emulate 21st century skills for individualized student learning—no matter where or how a student learns best . . . No teacher should start their career with anything less than complete confidence that they have been effectively prepared for Day One.
>
> International Association for K–12 Online Learning (2013), p. 4

Table 4.1 Reports and Recommendations on 21st-Century Teacher Preparation

- *A Framework for Quality in Digital Media for Children: Considerations for Parents, Educators, and Media Creators*. (2013). Fred Rogers Center for Early Learning and Children's Media at Saint Vincent College. www.fredrogerscenter.org/media/resources/ Framework_Statement_2-April_2012-Full_Doc+Exec_Summary.pdf
- *Born in Another Time: Ensuring Education Technology Meets the Needs of Students Today—and Tomorrow*. (2012). National Association of State Boards of Education. www.nasbe.org/wp-content/uploads/Born-in-Another-Time-NASBE-full-report.pdf
- *Learning in the 21st Century: Digital Experiences and Expectations of Tomorrow's Teachers*. Project Tomorrow. www.tomorrow.org/speakup/tomorrowsteachers_ report2013.html
- *Partnering for Success: A 21st Century Model for Teacher Preparation*. (2013). International Association for k-12 Online Learning www.inacol.org/cms/wp-content/ uploads/2013/10/iNACOL-Partnering-for-Success-October-2013.pdf
- *Preparing Tomorrow's Teachers to Use Technology: Perspectives of the Leaders of Twelve National Education Associations*. "(2001)" Contemporary Issues in Technology and Teacher Education. http://editlib.org/d/10740
- *Take a Giant Step: A Blueprint for Teaching Children in a Digital Age*. (2011). The Joan Ganz Cooney Center at Sesame Workshop. www.joanganzcooneycenter.org/ Reports-31.html
- *Teachers Embrace Digital Media to Propel Learning*. (2013). PBS Learning Media. www-tc. pbs.org/about/media/about/cms_page_media/615/PBS%20LearningMedia%20 Digital%20Resources%20Infographic-2-4-13.pdf
- *Transforming Teacher Education Through Clinical Practice: A National Strategy to Prepare Effective Teachers*. (2010). National Council for Accreditation of Teacher Education. www.ncate.org/LinkClick.aspx?fileticket=zzeiB1OoqPk%3D&tabid=715

Position Statement Alignment

Current and future early childhood educators also need positive examples of how technology has been selected, used, integrated, and evaluated successfully in early childhood classrooms and programs.

Educators need access to resources and online links, videos, and a professional community of practice where promising examples and applications of emerging technologies and new media can be demonstrated, shared, and discussed.

NAEYC & Fred Rogers Center (2012), p. 11

21st-Century Teacher Preparation

Teacher preparation standards and the knowledge, skills, disposition, and digital literacy needed to teach, work, and learn as a 21st-century teacher have been identified by a number of national organizations.

The *NAEYC Standards for Initial & Advanced Early Childhood Professional Preparation Programs* address required knowledge and skills for educators:

> Early childhood teachers understand technology and media as important influences on children's development. They use technology as one way of communicating with families and sharing children's work, while recognizing the importance of using other communication methods for families with limited Internet access. Similarly, they use technology in child assessment and as a professional resource with colleagues and for their own professional development.
>
> NAEYC, (2010), p. 25

The *Elementary Education Standards and Supporting Explanation* from the Association for Childhood Education International (ACEI, 2007, p. 15), states that successful teacher education candidates,

> use a variety of resources, including technology and textbooks, and look beyond their classroom to determine how numerous information resources in both print and electronic form might benefit their students. Candidates understand and use appropriate technology to help students become capable technology users through communication; through access, management, analysis and problem solving with information; and through collaborative and self-directed learning.

The new *Accreditation Standards from the Council for Accreditation of Educator Preparation* (Council for Accreditation of Educator Preparation [CAEP], 2013) require that teacher education programs prepare their students to help children "gain access to what technology has to offer." This requires that early childhood educators "become proficient in applications of digital media and technological capabilities," and "have opportunities to develop the skills and dispositions for accessing online research databases, digital media, and tools and to identify research-based practices that can improve their students' learning, engagement, and outcomes." They need to "demonstrate their abilities to design and facilitate digital, or connected, learning, mentoring, and collaboration" and to "help identify digital content and technology tools for students' learning. Candidates should help their students gain access to what technology has to offer" (CAEP, 2013, p. 22).

The *ISTE NETS and Performance Indicators for Teachers* (NETS-T) from the Intentional Society for Technology in Education (2008) identify standards and performance indicators for teachers "as they design, implement and assess learning experiences to engage students and improve learning; enrich professional practices; and provide positive models for students, colleagues and the community" (ISTE, 2008, p. 1).

Five ISTE Standards for Evaluating the Skills and Knowledge of Digital Age Teachers

1. **Facilitate and inspire student learning and creativity**—Teachers use their knowledge of subject matter, teaching and learning, and technology to facilitate experiences that advance student learning, creativity, and innovation in both face-to-face and virtual environments.
2. **Design and develop digital-learning experiences and assessments**—Teachers design, develop, and evaluate authentic learning experiences and assessments incorporating contemporary tools and resources to maximize content learning in context and to develop the knowledge, skills, and attitudes identified in the NETS-S.
3. **Model digital-age work and learning**—Teachers exhibit knowledge, skills, and work processes representative of an innovative professional in a global and digital society.
4. **Promote and model digital-age citizenship and responsibility**—Teachers understand local and global societal issues and responsibilities in an evolving digital culture and exhibit legal and ethical behavior in their professional practices.
5. **Engage in professional growth and leadership**—Teachers continuously improve their professional practice, model lifelong learning, and exhibit leadership in their school and professional community by promoting and demonstrating the effective use of digital tools and resources.

ISTE (2008), p. 2

The TPACK: Technological Pedagogical and Content Knowledge model (Mishra & Koehler, 2006) identifies the nature of knowledge teachers need for technology integration in their teaching. TPACK is an important tool in early childhood teacher preparation and digital literacy because the model attempts to address the complex, multifaceted, and situated nature of teacher knowledge—made up of content and pedagogy—as well as the nature of technology knowledge.

The Center for Digital Education suggests that technology must be integrated well to help students learn. The Center builds on the TPACK model of technology, pedagogy, and content knowledge and identifies four key strategies for effective digital teacher preparation programs that give students a chance to learn about and practice teaching in a supportive environment (Roscorla, 2013).

TPACK Strategies for Effective Digital Teacher Preparation

1. **Balance technology, pedagogy, and content knowledge**—Future teachers need to consider how technology tools, teaching methods, and content areas fit together to reach the teacher's goals for the children and for individual children.
2. **Consider the environment that teachers will work in**—future teachers need to learn basic principles of technology use and integration that can be

applied to whatever classroom environment they end up in, from state-of-the art to just getting started.

3. **Build classroom experiences into the program from the beginning**—Future teachers benefit from early exposure to real classrooms, teachers, and children, and the opportunity to observe strategies for technology use and integration.

4. **Choose the best technology tools for the job**—When future teachers have a chance to integrate technology into their classroom they need to be able to select, use, integrate, and evaluate which technology tools are the most effective and appropriate for the individual child, the content area and the classroom context.

Roscorla (2013)

A national survey of teacher education programs (Kennedy & Archambault, 2012) found that just over 1% were preparing preservice teachers for 21st-century models of teaching, learning, and technology integration. Early childhood teacher educators and teacher education programs need to rethink how the skills, methods, pedagogical approaches, and integration of technology tools prepares future early childhood educators to appropriately and intentionally integrate technology and interactive media as tools for teaching and learning in early childhood classrooms. If we expect early childhood educators to effectively select, use, integrate, and evaluate technology and digital media for young children, we need to model effective selection, use, integration, and evaluation in teacher preparation coursework, hands-on experiences, field experiences, and degree programs.

Position Statement Alignment

> Digitally literate educators who are grounded in child development theory and developmentally appropriate practices have the knowledge, skills, and experience to select and use technology tools and interactive media that suit the ages and developmental levels of the children in their care, and they know when and how to integrate technology into the program effectively. Educators who lack technology skills and digital literacy are at risk of making inappropriate choices and using technology with young children in ways that can negatively impact learning and development.
>
> NAEYC & Fred Rogers Center (2012), p. 4

Aligning Preservice Teacher Education and Professional Development Systems

The rapid expansion of technology and interactive media into the lives and work of early childhood educators requires a comprehensive system for preparing new teachers who are coming into the field at the same time that we provide continuing education and professional development to experienced educators. Integrating technology and digital literacy into teacher preparation programs cannot be

Table 4.2 Early Childhood Teacher Preparation Organizations With Technology Standards

- AACTE, American Association of Colleges for Teacher Education (http://aacte.org/)
- ACCESS Associate Degree Early Childhood Teacher Educators (www.accessece.org/)
- ACEI, Association for Childhood Education International (http://acei.org/)
- CAEP, Council for Accreditation of Educator Preparation (http://caepnet.org/)
- ISTE, International Society for Technology in Education (www.iste.org/)
- NAECTE, National Association of Early Childhood Teacher Educators (www.naecte. org/)
- NAEYC, National Association for the Education of Young Children (www.naeyc.org)
- National Association for Media Literacy Education (http://namle.net/)
- NCATE, National Council for Accreditation of Teacher Education (www.ncate.org/)
- TPACK: Technological Pedagogical and Content Knowledge (www.tpack.org)

accomplished by simply adding another category to the preparation standards. To be effective, these principles and concepts must be infused into all aspects of teacher preparation so that competencies related to technological fluency and digital literacy are evident throughout the standards and guidelines.

The *NAEYC Standards for Initial & Advanced Early Childhood Professional Preparation Programs* (2012) includes six standards that provide the vision for excellence in teacher education.

- **Standard 1: Promoting Child Development and Learning**—Preparation programs and professional development must include information about current research on how technology and interactive media affect children's development and learning. Teacher educators and professional developers must be constantly asking themselves: "What research is available and how credible is the research?" Students in early childhood preparation programs should be reading firsthand research and learning to make judgments on their own about the credibility and validity of studies that make claims about the benefits or risks to child development and the effect on children's learning. There is a need for current research that reflects the ever-changing landscape of technology, interactive media, and digital tools. Graduate students and practicing teachers should be conducting in-classroom action research to study their own practice and begin to identify how children are using technology and digital materials. They should be asking themselves questions about the appropriateness of using any given technology tool as they set goals for learning in their classrooms. The NAEYC & Fred Rogers Center joint position statement (2012), emphasizes the need for intentionality in the selection, use, integration, and evaluation of technology. To accomplish this, 21st-century teachers must be knowledgeable about child development and must stay current with emerging research in this fast-paced digital age.

- **Standard 2: Building Family and Community Partnerships**—

> Early childhood teachers understand technology and media as important influences on children's development. They use technology as one way of communicating with families and sharing children's work, while recognizing the importance of using other communication methods for families with limited Internet access. Similarly, they use technology in child assessment and as a professional resource with colleagues and for their own professional development.
>
> NAEYC (2012), p. 25.

For example, the Early Learning Environment (ELE) at the Fred Rogers Center supports families' efforts to encourage language development and early literacy skills in children while building the digital and media literacy skills of parents. The site aggregates information and activities that parents and educators can use to support language and literacy, including digital books, apps, songs, and suggestions for every-day conversations with children.

Another digital resource is Message from Me, a project of the Pittsburgh Association for the Education of Young Children (PAEYC) and Carnegie Mellon's CREATE Lab to foster better home-school connections and to engage children in age-appropriate use of technology in the classroom. Kiosks are installed in child care centers that allow children to take pictures and record messages that they can send to a family member's cell phone or email to share information about their daily activities. PAEYC provides technical assistance and professional development for early educators who are using the kiosks. An iPad app for Message from Me is being developed and piloted in 2014 with professional development support from PAEYC. These family and community initiatives model ways that educators can use digital resources to connect with families and communities through joint engagement with technology.

- **Standard 3: Observing, Documenting, and Assessing to Support Young Children and Families**—A key element of this standard for candidates is "knowing about and using observation, documentation, and other appropriate assessment tools and approaches, including the use of technology in documentation, assessment and data collection (NAEYC, 2012, p. 32). From capturing video and audio files as evidence of children's learning to using digital prompts on handheld devices that guide teachers through an assessment sequence in language or math, faculty, and students need opportunities to select, use, integrate, and assess the value of these tools in classrooms. Creating spaces where preservice and inservice teachers can explore and playfully engage with materials, software, hardware, apps, and data collection devices is a critical component of professional development. These digital playgrounds bring teachers together to explore, exchange ideas, and learn by doing. The NAEYC & Fred Rogers Center joint position statement (2012), calls for professional communities where teachers can share ideas, explore materials, and playfully learn together about technology.

- **Standard 4: Using Developmentally Effective Approaches**—Applying child development knowledge as well as a knowledge of children's social-cultural background and individual needs and preferences is a critical component of Developmentally Appropriate Practice. It is the ability to use a "broad repertoire of developmentally appropriate teaching/learning approaches" (NAEYC, 2012, p.34). Developmentally Appropriate Practice is at the heart of the NAEYC & Fred Rogers Center joint position statement (2012, p. 5), and the driving force for the selection and integration of technology and interactive media into classrooms for young children. Preservice teachers and experienced teachers alike must take into account the child's age and stage of development, cultural context, and individual needs when selecting technology tools. Developmentally appropriate practice includes a focus on the role of relationships in early learning and the important role of social interactions. Teacher preparation and professional development experiences need to incorporate ways to ensure that technology experiences bring children together rather than isolating them for extended periods of time.

- **Standard 5: Using Content Knowledge to Build a Meaningful Curriculum**—Effective early childhood teachers understand how children learn academic content in language and literacy, mathematics, science and inquiry, social studies, and history. They use their own knowledge of these content areas to select experiences that foster the development of understanding and skill development across the curriculum. Today there is a plethora of online information available to novice and experienced teachers who need a quick refresher about such varied things as different types of triangles, or information about the life cycle of a plant. When adults model for children that learning is fun . . . that even adults like to learn new things . . . children begin to incorporate those attitudes into their own approaches to learning. Preservice professional preparation and inservice professional development must provide resources and opportunities for learners to explore, create, and practice the use of digital tools in the context of academic content and available information for their own learning as well as ideas for integrating content areas in developmentally effective ways into early childhood classrooms.

- **Standard 6: Becoming a Professional**—Technological fluency and digital media literacy is necessary for early childhood professionals to participate in the virtual learning communities of today. Accessing materials online, sharing information, and communicating with other professionals through social media and communities of practice all help to ensure that early childhood educators stay connected to the profession and to the latest ideas and practices. Teachers and teacher candidates need places where they can explore technology and digital resources in a safe environment; a place where they can ask questions and experiment; share ideas and test them out; and where they can learn about technology by using technology.

The infusion of knowledge and competencies about technology and interactive media will be most effective when integrated across systems. Many states have already aligned their professional development systems with the NAEYC standards for early childhood teacher preparation. Additionally, the NAEYC standards have been designed to apply across levels of preparation from the CDA (Child Development Associate) credential through graduate studies in early childhood. Integration of the principles of the NAEYC & Fred Rogers Center joint position statement (2012), across all domains of teacher preparation and professional development will help ensure that each and every early childhood educator will have access to opportunities for professional development. Using a systems approach to professional development is critical to the success of early childhood educators in acquiring the necessary skills and knowledge to select, use, integrate, and evaluate technology and interactive media in their classrooms and programs.

Ideas in Action: Digital Media Literacy in Early Childhood Programs (Pennsylvania)

This newly created initiative is a collaboration of the Pennsylvania Office of Child Development and Early Learning (OCDEL), the Fred Rogers Center (FRC), and the Pittsburgh Association for the Education of Young Children (PAEYC) and supported by The Grable Foundation. The goal of the initiative is to promote digital media literacy in early childhood programs across Pennsylvania by operationalizing the NAEYC & Fred Rogers Center joint position statement (2012), and integrating it into the practice of early childhood education through the training of educators and the dissemination of best practices for promoting digital media literacy. The three-part approach includes the following:

1. Raising awareness of new recommendations and promoting systems change through the statewide professional development system.
2. Identifying exemplars in the use of technology and digital media in high quality programs from across the state.
3. Creating standards-aligned curation of technology and digital media resources for teachers and child care providers.

Technology-Based Professional Development and Continuing Education

Professional development for integrating educational technology needs to occur for three groups: teacher education faculty, pre-service teachers, and in-service teachers. Successful technology integration depends on how a given technology is actually used in the specific learning context.

Barron et al. (2011)

Inservice teachers need professional development opportunities that are available, affordable, and accessible and that provide in-depth training and ongoing support. Educators need to feel secure and competent in using technology themselves, and effective technology training needs to focus on how educators use current and emerging technology personally and professionally, and best practices for integrating technology in early childhood settings as a tool for teaching, learning, communicating with parents and families and strengthening communities.

[P]lanning for technology adoption should support both formal training and informal collegial support . . . Pairing tech savvy teachers with beginners, and providing "technology play time" for teachers are some ideas you may want to consider.

Simon et al. (2013)

Technology-based professional development needs to provide access to the latest technology tools and applications, rather than the out-of-date and obsolete technologies often found in early childhood settings. They need opportunities to see how technology tools can be integrated into the classroom environment and used to enhance teaching and learning with young children. They need practice in selecting technology and curating applications that will best support children's development. And they need opportunities for hands-on play and exploration with technology tools before implementing new tools and digital media into the classroom.

Position Statement Alignment

Teachers must take the time to evaluate and select technology and media for the classroom, carefully observe children's use of the materials to identify opportunities and problems, and then make appropriate adaptations. They must be willing to learn about and become familiar with new technologies as they are introduced and be intentional in the choices they make, including assurances that content is developmentally appropriate and that it communicates anti-bias messages.

NAEYC & Fred Rogers Center (2012), p. 6

Conclusion

The digital age has arrived. Teacher educators, teachers, parents, and young children are already using digital devices in new ways, and for adults, the gap between personal and professional use has narrowed as these new tools become an indispensable part of life in the 21st century. But for many early childhood teacher educators and teachers of young children, the digital age feels like it is moving faster than they can respond to or keep up with. The risk of being left behind and left out of the new ways of teaching, learning, communicating, and collaborating is real.

Early childhood educators in the 21st century now have a very real responsibility to gain the technology knowledge, competencies, and experiences needed in their work and in their interactions with parents and young children. Digital media literacy is an essential new literacy for those who teach the teachers, and those who teach young children.

These new tools hold great promise for teaching and learning, but only when they are used effectively, appropriately and intentionally. The knowledge and experience needed to select, use, integrate, and evaluate technology and interactive media as tools in early childhood settings is at the heart of what it means to be a 21st-century educator.

Teacher Takeaways

* Recognize digital media literacy as an essential 21st-century literacy for teacher educators and teachers of young children.
* Gain the technology knowledge, skills, and experience you need by exploring and using technology tools for teaching, learning, communicating, and collaborating with other educators, with parents and families and with young children.
* Use the principles and guidelines from the NAEYC & Fred Rogers Center joint position statement (2012) to guide the appropriate and intentional selection, use, integration, and evaluation of technology with young children.
* Use the Developmentally Appropriate Practice framework to guide decisions about if, when, where, how, and why to include technology in the classroom and as tool for young children's learning.
* Find examples of effective practice, observe other teachers in action, attend conferences, and participate in professional development experiences focused on the appropriate use of technology with young children.
* Become a connected educator by participating in social media, joining a community of interest or practice, learning with and from other educators, and sharing what you're doing and learning with other educators.

References

Association for Childhood Education International. (2007). *Elementary education standards and supporting explanation.* Washington, DC: Author.

Barron, B., Cayton-Hodges, G., Bofferding, L., Copple, C., Darling-Hammond, L., & Levine, M. (2011). *Take a giant step: A blueprint for teaching children in a digital age.* New York, NY: The Joan Ganz Cooney Center.

Council for Accreditation of Educator Preparation. (2013). *CAEP accreditation standards.* Washington, DC: Author.

Donahoo, D. (2012, November 5). Why tablets are important for educating our children. Retrieved from http://archive.wired.com/geekdad/2012/11/tablet-edtech-rewind/

Fred Rogers Center for Early Learning and Children's Media at Saint Vincent College. (2012). *A framework for quality in digital media for children: Considerations for parents, educators, and media creators*. Latrobe, PA: Fred Rogers Center.

International Association for K–12 Online Learning. (2013). *Partnering for success: A 21st century model for teacher preparation*. Vienna, VA: Author.

International Society for Technology in Education. (2008). *The standards for teachers*. Washington, DC: Author.

Kennedy, K., & Archambault, L. (2012). Offering pre-service teachers field experiences in K–12 online learning: A national survey of teacher education programs. *Journal of Teacher Education, 63*(3), 185–200. doi: 10.1177/0022487111433651

Mishra, P., & Koehler, M. J. (2006). Technological pedagogical content knowledge: A framework for teacher knowledge. *Teachers College Record, 108*(6), 1017–1054.

National Association for the Education of Young Children. (2012). *2010 NAEYC standards for initial & advanced early childhood professional preparation programs*. Washington, DC: Author.

National Association for the Education of Young Children, & Fred Rogers Center for Early Learning and Children's Media at Saint Vincent College. (2012). *Technology and interactive media as tools in early childhood programs serving children from birth through age 8*. Washington, DC: NAEYC; Latrobe, PA: Fred Rogers Center for Early Learning and Children's Media at Saint Vincent College.

PBS Learning Media. (2013). *Teachers embrace digital media to propel learning*. Washington, DC: PBS.

Project Tomorrow. (2013). *Learning in the 21st century: Digital experiences and expectations of tomorrow's teachers*. Irvine, CA: Author.

Roscorla, T. (2013, July 8). How to prepare teachers for digital education [Web log post]. Retrieved from www.centerdigitaled.com/news/How-to-Prepare-Teachers-for-Digital-Education.html

Simon, F., Nemeth, K., & McManis, D. (2013). Technology in ECE classrooms: Results of a new survey and implications for the field. *Exchange*, 68–75.

Wartella, E., Schomburg, R. L., Lauricella, A. R., Robb, M., & Flynn, R. (2010). *Technology in the lives of teachers and classrooms: Survey of classroom teachers and family child care providers*. Latrobe, PA: Fred Rogers Center for Early Learning and Children's Media at Saint Vincent College.

Wartella, E., Blackwell, C. K., Lauricella, A. R., & Robb, M. B. (2013). *Technology in the lives of educators and early childhood programs*. Latrobe, PA: Fred Rogers Center for Early Learning and Children's Media at Saint Vincent College.

Resources

Additional Readings on Technology in Early Childhood Teacher Preparation

Bell, L. (Ed.). (2001). Preparing tomorrow's teachers to use technology: Perspectives of the leaders of twelve national education associations. *Contemporary Issues in Technology and Teacher Education* [Online Serial], *1*(4), 517–534. Retrieved from http://editlib.org/d/10740

Campbell, A., & Scotellaro, G. (2009). Learning with technology for pre-service early childhood teachers. *Australasian Journal of Early Childhood, 34*(2), 11–18.

David, J., Lennox, S., Walker, S., & Walsh, K. (2007). Exploring staff perceptions: Early childhood teacher educators examine online teaching and learning challenges and dilemmas. *International Journal for the Scholarship of Teaching and Learning, 1*(2), 1–15.

Donohue, C. & Fox, S. (2012). Lessons learned, innovative practices and emerging trends: Technology for teacher education and professional development. *Exchange*, 74–82.

Downer, J.T., Pianta, R.C., Fan, X., Hamre, B.K., Mashburn, A., & Justice, L. (2011). Effects of web-mediated teacher professional development on the language and literacy skills of children enrolled in prekindergarten programs. *NHSA Dialog, 14*(4), 189–212.

Ertmer, P.A., & Ottenbreit-Leftwich, A.T., Sadik, O., Sendurur, E., & Sendurur, P. (2012). Teacher beliefs and technology integration practices: A critical relationship. *Computers & Education, 59*, 423–435.

Fox, S., & Donohue, C. (2006). Trends and promising practices in early childhood teacher education online: The view from New Zealand. *He Kupu, 29–34.

Guernsey, L. (2011, November 17). EdTech for the younger ones? Not without trained teachers. Retrieved from www.huffingtonpost.com/lisa-guernsey/edtech-for-the-play dough-_b_1097277.html

Hong, S.B., & Trepanier-Street, M. (2004.). Technology: A tool for knowledge construction in a Reggio Emilia inspired teacher education program. *Early Childhood Education Journal, 32*(2), 87–94.

Lutton, A. (2011). *Advancing the early childhood profession: NAEYC standards and guidelines for professional development.* Washington, DC: National Association for the Education of Young Children.

National Association for Media Literacy Education. (2007). Core principles of media literacy education in the United States. Cherry Hill, NJ: Author.

National Association for the Education of Young Children. (2009). *NAEYC standards for early childhood professional preparation programs: A position statement of the national association for the education of young children.* Washington, DC: Author.

National Association of Early Childhood Teacher Educators. (2008). *NAECTE position statement on early childhood certification for teachers of children 6 years old and younger in public school.* Briarcliff Manor, NY: Author.

National Association of State Boards of Education. (2012). *Born in another time: Ensuring education technology meets the needs of students today—and tomorrow.* Arlington, VA: Author.

National Council for Accreditation of Teacher Education. (2010). *Transforming teacher education through clinical practice: A national strategy to prepare effective teachers.* Washington, DC: Author.

Olsen, H., Donaldson, A.J., & Hudson, S.D. (2010). Online professional development: Choices for early childhood educators. *Dimensions of Early Childhood, 38*(1), 12–18.

Pressey, B. (2013). *Comparative analysis of national teacher surveys.* New York, NY: Jon Ganz Cooney Center.

Rogow, F. (2012). *The case for digital media literacy in early childhood education.* Ithaca, NY: Insighters Education Consulting.

Rosen, D.B., & Jaruszewicz, C. (2009). Developmentally appropriate technology use and early childhood teacher education. *Journal of Early Childhood Teacher Education, 30*(2), 162–171.

Scheibe, C. L., & Rogow, F. (2011). *The teacher's guide to media literacy: Critical thinking in a multimedia world.* Thousand Oaks, CA: Corwin.

Simon, F., & Donohue, C. (2012, November/December). The source of leadership for early childhood technology integration: You! *Exchange*, 79–85.

Snider, S., & Hirschy, S. (2009). A self-reflection framework for technology use by classroom teachers of young learners. *He Kupu, 2*(1), 30–34.

Washington, V. (2013). CDA 2.0: Supporting people and advancing the field. *Young Children, 68*(4), 68–70.

Learn More . . .

- Carnegie Mellon CREATE Lab, www.cmucreatelab.org/
- Center for Digital Education, www.centerdigitaled.com/
- CREATE Lab Children's Innovation Project in the Pittsburgh Public Schools, http://cippgh.org/site/
- Digital Media Literacy in Early Childhood Programs (Pennsylvania), www.paeyc.org/digital-media-literacy
- Fred Rogers Center Early Learning Environment, *Ele,* http://ele.fredrogerscenter.org
- Message from Me, www.cmucreatelab.org/projects/Message_from_Me

What Would Maria Montessori Say About the iPad? Theoretical Frameworks for Children's Interactive Media

Warren Buckleitner

Introduction

On the evening of December 8, 1913, a 43-year-old Maria Montessori gave a talk in New York City following a 14-day trans-Atlantic journey by ship.

She set foot on U.S. soil as a celebrity, in part because of the translation of her book *The Montessori Method,* first published in the United States in 1912 by Frederick A. Stokes Company (Montessori, 1964). According to the *New York Times* coverage of her visit, 1000 people were turned away from Carnegie Hall, where she was introduced by John Dewey. In her closing remarks, she said she was seeking nothing less than the perfection of the human race (*New York Times*, 1913).

Today, the same trip takes just 9 hours and there is no fear of icebergs. Transportation technology has certainly changed in this 100-year period. What about pedagogical tools? It is important to consider the historical context of Montessori's work and this particular visit. She came by invitation of Thomas Edison and Alexander Graham Bell, who had already used technology to make a mark on the new 20th century. American educators were concerned more with delivering measured doses of curriculum and measuring progress, so Montessori's child-centric methods must have seemed as radical as the light bulb, telephone, or airplane.

Looking back, we know that Montessori's methods were simply applied theory—the theory coming from Froebel and Pestalozzi—and they were having remarkable success with the hardest to teach "idiot" children from the slums of Rome. These ideas were easy to contrast with America's behaviorism-steeped curriculum that was strongly influenced by Pavlov, Watson, and especially Edward Thorndike. We no longer call children with learning problems "idiots," but there still is no shortage of hard-to-teach children who, in Montessori's words "have not lived up to their genetic potential." In 1913, a cultural shift was in full swing, from agricultural to industrial. As with that time, we now find ourselves in a cultural shift; from industrial to information, marked by social media and touch screens. The inventions of Edison and Bell have served us well. We're now dealing with the likes of Jobs, Bezos, Page, Brin, and Zuckerberg.

Figure 5.1 What would Montessori, Piaget, Skinner, and Vygotsky say? A Theoretical
Dream Panel, Discussing a Tablet

Illustrations by Jenna Buckleitner

Under this new cultural shift are the same stable theories of learning that guided Montessori 100 years ago as she tried to reach the underserved children of Rome. As the field of early childhood education begins to adapt, guided in part by the recent technology position statement from National Association for the Education of Young Children (NAEYC) and the Fred Rogers Center (2012), these theoretical frameworks can provide welcome traction in the slippery discourse surrounding technology and young children. This chapter explores digital play and learning in the context of three theoretical frameworks. This is only a preliminary exploration of some select theories.

What Would This "Dream Panel" of Theorists Say About the iPad?

Imagine that Maria Montessori, Jean Piaget, and B.F. Skinner walked into the speaker ready room before their panel at the NAEYC annual conference. Montessori is angry. "I typed my last name into iTunes and came up with 500 apps! Some are good, but others are merely low-rate flash cards." "Really though, what's the harm with an occasional flash card, as long as it's used with a reward?" asks Skinner. Montessori's cheeks are flushed with emotion. "Some of these apps don't go deeper than lowest level ideas—shapes, colors, letters, and numbers. Take 'Approach to Montessori—Numbers HD Free Lite' [Brain Counts, 2012]," she says. "It combines my name with noisy pedagogy and free offers, and uses my own words for marketing . . . 'prepare for greatness'!!!'" (see Figure 5.2).

Piaget nods in the direction of Skinner. "She has reason to be angry, B. F. Some of these apps imply the acceleration of development, even for infants. We should all be concerned with app quality." Lev Vygotsky, who has been sitting quietly nearby, speaks up. "Isn't the quality you speak of in itself an artifact of culture?" Piaget takes a long, thoughtful puff of his pipe. "Yes, Lev, but we have other concerns. I've noticed that my own daughters now prefer their iPads to the observation of mollusks! But I've been observing them as they play and I'm pleased to report that my stage theory maps well to this digital medium."

"The hands are the instruments of man's intelligence, Jean." reminds Montessori. A glass screen is abstract and symbolic, which must be considered when dealing with preschoolers . . ."

Piaget waves a finger, ". . . but that won't influence the developmental sequence. A child born 100 years ago developed in much the same way as a child born this year. What is different in 2013 are the experiences due to

Figure 5.2 Screen Capture From *Approach to Montessori*, Numbers HD Free Lite

the technology. Candlelight can be provided by LEDs. But we still have the choice of real candles. Parents have genetic screening, antibiotics, and their babies can have bedtime stories read by grandparents who lives half a continent or half a world away." Vygotsky quietly adds, "Mobile devices help ideas flow across geographic and economic chasms. Services like Google, Facebook, YouTube, and Twitter can move ideas from Leningrad to San Francisco at the speed of light." He starts getting very excited. "The knowledge elite could dissolve. Every teacher could have a virtual mentor and unlimited professional development. That, my friends, is worth getting excited about."

Piaget has been intently puffing on his pipe, which has creating a cloud around the group, and cleared the nonsmoking room. "And these devices have cameras . . . electronic eyes that can instantly bridge the concrete and the symbolic. But I must agree with Maria—and the recent NAEYC & Fred Rogers Center (2012) position statement on young children and technology— it can never replace the touch of a butterfly wing."

Skinner chimes in over his game of Candy Crush (King.com Limited, 2013), ". . . and mankind still manages to use incredibly powerful technology for extremely unpowerful activities; like this game. My first teaching machine was cobbled together with plywood and punch cards. These tablets let us deliver the most sophisticated programmed instruction at a low cost. Friends, we can now mass-produce the perfect curriculum and deliver it to every child, and accurately measure the results! No child will be forgotten."

Montessori's iPad is now on reserve power, but she's stumbled on an app called The Human Body (TinyBop, 2013). She's been watching a single blood cell move through a maze of heart valves, as she speeds and slows the heart (See Figure 5.3). Skinner takes a turn as the others watch, amazed. "I would've loved this app as a child," she says quietly. "I believe there are apps for each of us . . . we just have to know what we're looking for."

The Dramatic Digitization of Theory

There are now 24 platforms for children's interactive media, although all but eight are largely extinct. These include Android 4.4 (called KitKat), the Kindle Fire OS (called Fire OS, which is a platform based on Android), Microsoft's Windows Phone 8 for touch screens; Windows 8 for computers and Laptops, and Mac OS Mavericks (10.9.1) for non-touch-screen Macintosh computers. Video game platforms include the Microsoft Xbox, Sony PlayStation, Nintendo Wii, and DS. But the leader by a wide margin is Apple's mobile operating system, called iOS. Children's products, called apps, were first introduced for the iPod and iPhone in 2007. The first children's apps were limited in function and by a small screen size, but they cut the ties with the mouse and keyboard, and introduced many children to their first multi-touch capacitive screens. In the spring of 2010, Steve Jobs introduced the iPad, with a larger screen and 10 hour batteries that created the perfect storm for children's digital content.

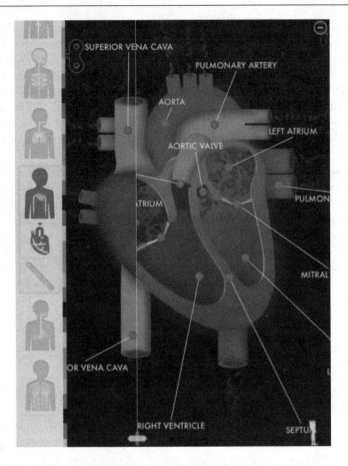

Figure 5.3 Screen Capture From *The Human Body,* TinyBop

In 2007, there were fewer than 10,000 children's interactive media products for children produced between 1984 and 2007. For 2013, that number is the total number of new products in just 1 year, for Apple iOS products alone. Apple reports that there are "over 1,000,000 apps" for both small and large screen iOS devices (T. Miller, personal communication, December 8, 2013). Of these, 475,000 run on the iPad, as the fall of 2013 (Apple, 2013). The next task involved with counting children's apps requires a definition for what a children's app is. A rough solution is to use a smaller sample; in this case, the 200 best-selling apps. At *Children's Technology Review,* we tagged 20 of these apps as being "specifically designed for children." If you use this 10% amount as a conservative estimate, there are about 47,500 iPad apps for children. Keep in mind this is just one subset of one platform (see Figure 5.4).

Each individual app is in itself a human artifact—a bundle of ideas from a team with ideas about how a child should play or learn. At *Children's Technology*

Number of Children's Apps for iPad as of December 2013

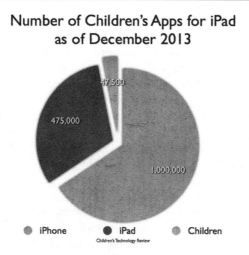

47,500

475,000

1,000,000

● iPhone   ● iPad   ● Children

Children's Technology Review

Figure 5.4 Source: Children's Technology Review

Review, we skim a subset of these products—607 in 2013—selected for being newsworthy, for review.

When Glacier-Like Theories Meet Rivers of Apps

Imagine this panel at the next NAEYC annual conference: "Technology and Young Children: A Discussion by Piaget, Skinner, Montessori, Bruner, and Vygotsky." And while we're at it, we'll invite Fred Rogers to be the moderator. Each panelist will be asked to discuss the strengths and weaknesses of using technology with young children and bring examples of apps to support their theories. What would they say, and which apps would they demonstrate?

This fictional exercise asks you to layer new media across existing frameworks, which is, at best, an interpretive art. In reality, many apps are an eclectic mix of theories that are, in themselves, continually adapting and not cast in stone. In trying to play out this scenario, I'm well aware that I'm glossing over just a few key theories.

Behaviorism

B. F. Skinner (1904–1990) might have described behaviorism's view of a child starting life with a blank slate, prepped for a future of knowledge and skills. The key to a good outcome is careful preparation and results that can be accurately measured. A lesson can be repeated if necessary, and the child's behaviors can be shaped toward mastery. The positive, desired behaviors should be encouraged; the undesirable behaviors are negatively reinforced and extinguished. Many have contributed to Behaviorism's core ideas. Ivan Pavlov (1849–1946) showed that he could condition a dog to salivate with the sound of a bell through association. In the 1900s at Columbia University, John Watson (1878–1958) conducted stimulus-response experiments, and Edward Thorndike (1874–1949) worked to infuse the U.S. curriculum with rewards and consequences and pedagogy designed to be broken into small parts that could be mastered and measured. The move to automate this type of instruction started at Ohio State when Sidney Pressey (1888–1979) began working on a teaching machine, and B. F. Skinner took the entire idea up a notch by documenting responses to stimuli and rewards in both children and animals. He tried to bring a commercial teaching machine to market in the late 1950s. Some attributes of behaviorism in children's apps might include:

- *A token economy.* Any game that uses collectible items such as coins, stars, or jellybeans is reinforcing a desired behavior. In LEGO Star Wars, you collect thousands of studs—the little bumps found on LEGO blocks that can be used to rebuild the machines you need to get to the next level. Disney's Club Penguin (Disney's Interactive, 2013) lets you play games to earn coins to purchase new items for your igloo.
- *Intermittent events.* Conditioning stimuli including intermittent reinforcements are used in apps like Candy Crush or Bejeweled. One of the best-known examples, Angry Birds (Rovio Entertainment, 2009) is a physics game that applies this technique masterfully. You first launch a bird, which is a game of chance. Sometimes you get a huge payoff, but not always. Your big reward might happen any time, and the effect is intoxicating. Skinner could point to many examples of negative reinforcements commonly used in video games either intentionally, such as making a child replay a level, or making a child wait while an activity loads.
- *Mastery Learning.* Edward Thorndike might have liked the individual tracking and scoring system in Moose Math (Duck Duck Moose, 2013). The better you do, the more levels you can unlock, as your progress is remembered, like a bookmark. In addition, the app can keep progress for different children. You can find some excellent examples of mastery learning in Bugs and Buttons 2 (Little Bit Studio, 2013) with 18 math and logic activities with careful challenge leveling mixed with management features.

Constructivism

The constructivism framework has cast a wide net over teaching, learning, and app design. It is well named—a child "constructs" his or her own knowledge internally throughout the lifecycle. The core ideas go back to Switzerland, where Johann Pestalozzi (1746–1827) and his student Friedrich Fröbel (1782–1852)—who coined the word *kindergarten*—cleared the theoretical brush so that Maria Montessori's (1874–1952) could begin designing classroom techniques. The giant of constructivism, however, was Jean Piaget (1896–1980), who defined different stages of development, along with the notions of assimilation, accommodation, and equilibration. These ideas heavily influenced the open classrooms of the 1970s, and such ideas as whole language, LOGO, Scratch, and the Maker movement today. Some examples of constructivism in children's interactive media might include the following:

- *Apple's concept of the Home key.* This single control mechanism may be the biggest contribution to technology-based constructivism, because of the control it offers a child or an adult. It makes it possible for a child to get out of whatever he or she gets into.
- *Linking forms of language.* Piaget and Vygotsky both wrote a great deal about language as a vehicle for packaging knowledge and would undoubtedly have a lot to say about word/object association techniques used in apps like ABC Actions (Peapod Labs, 2013) that pairs words with still, clear photos and videos of meaningful objects. It is possible to toggle from Spanish to English at any time. Other Peapod apps with a similar design, cover topics such as underwater life, bugs, the farm, transportation, and music.
- *Self-correcting problems that dynamically adjust.* Both Thorndike and Piaget would've liked Motion Math: Hungry Guppy (Motion Math Games, 2012); a bottomless pitcher of finger driven, self-correcting math manipulatives. The better you do, the harder the challenge, which is evidence of the eclectic design of apps.
- *Instant formative feedback.* Montessori wrote about automatic or autodidactic materials that provide instant feedback to a child. She might have liked the way LetterSchool (Sanoma Media Netherlands B.V., 2012) quietly directs a child toward the correct result, in a way that is driven by the child's initiative.
- *Programming.* Sometimes interactive media experiences can allow a child to control a screen, rather than the other way around; representing an embodiment of constructivism ideals. One of the first programming languages specifically adapted for children was Logo, which was created at the Massachusetts Institute of Technology (MIT) by a team led by one of Piaget's coworkers, Seymour Papert. More recently, Scratch 2.0 (Maloney, Resnick, Rusk, Silverman & Eastmond, 2010) and Hopscotch (Hopscotch Technologies, 2013), a Scratch-like programming experience for the iPad, let children "code" using jigsaw-puzzle like commands, routines, and subroutines. Papert coined the phrase *constructionism* around the idea that children can also construct cognitive models outside the head.

Social Constructivism

Lev Vygotsky (1896–1934) might have agreed with Piaget that learning takes place "inside the head" through active learning. But he'd argue that external, social forces are at play as well. The Russian psychologist and philosopher was born in 1896, the same year as Piaget, but he died much younger at 37. However, his short but prolific career has indelibly influenced the field of educational psychology and app design. His ideas were inspired by the social changes and challenges in the Soviet Union, and he emphasized the influences of cultural and social contexts in learning and supported a discovery model of learning. Vygotsky believed that learning and development is both internal and external. The internal processes were documented in his book, *Thought and Language*, published in 1962, which had a great deal of overlap with Piaget's major ideas. But he also framed this individual development in a larger societal context. Social video games with leader boards, shared reviews, blogging, all play a role in this cross-cultural transmission of knowledge. Vygotsky's concept of the "zone of proximal development" is a useful idea for interactive media developers. This "zone" has been defined as the distance between a child's independent problem solving and his or her capabilities of problem solving while under adult guidance or the guidance of more capable peers. App designers today can construct help mechanisms to give a child support along with increased challenges. Evidence of social constructivism in the app store might include the following:

- *Cross-cultural communication.* Social media, such as Facebook, Skype, Twitter, Google Docs, and YouTube each provide forums for transmitting ideas across geographic, social, and socio-economic boundaries. YouTube for example, posts thousands of videos of "more capable others" showing how to solve math problems, play a musical instrument or win at a video game. Sharing apps like Kindoma (Kindoma, 2013) make it possible for two people to share the same story from any location, as if they are sitting in the same room.
- *Cross-cultural cognition.* Programming and group creativity experiences like Scratch 2.0 (MIT, 2013) encourages sharing of bits of programs. Not only can programs be commented on, but key ideas can be freely copied and pasted into new programs. A game like Minecraft (Mojang, 2011) is a collaborative problem solving game that provides spatial thinking opportunities and mixes thinking that has no regard to boundary.
- *Putting significant others inside an app.* The Human Body (TinyBop, 2013) lets children explore the wonders of the human body without embarrassment. Of particular note are the working models of the human eye and ear that incorporate the features of the iPad camera and microphone to let children play with the function, as if they were inside the body. The more capable other comes into play, when you can create individual profile for your child, and leave a recorded message for the child. So a teacher could explain the function of the heart in a personal way. Oceanhouse Media apps (Oceanhouse Media, 2013) are a series of e-books that let you add and save your own soundtracks. So a child can hear a favorite Dr. Seuss story like "Green Eggs and Ham" (Oceanhouse Media, 2013), narrated by his or her choice of a grandmother, grandfather, uncle, or friend.

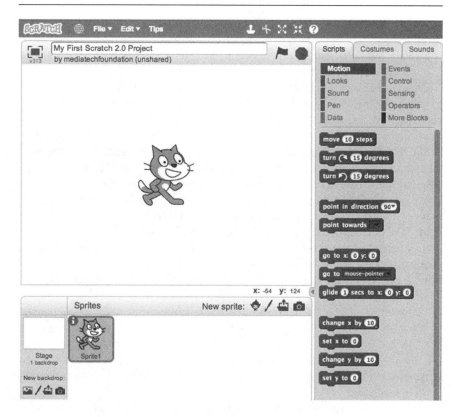

Figure 5.5 Screen Capture From *Scratch 2.0,* MIT

Position Statement Alignment

> Early childhood educators are the decision makers in whether, how, what, when, and why technology and media are implemented through applying their expertise and knowledge of child development and learning, individual children's interests and readiness, and the social and cultural contexts in which children live.
>
> NAEYC & Fred Rogers Center (2012), p. 6

So What Would Montessori Say About the iPad?

If one could revisit Carnegie Hall 100 years ago and ask Maria Montessori about the digital revolution to come, what would she say? Would she condemn digital media as being overly commercialized and abstract? Or would she embrace it, recommending the purchase of tablets for use in the programs that now bear her name? Probably both.

Among Montessori groups, the use of technology-based materials like the iPad continues to be debated. One Montessorian who doesn't seem afraid of the tablets is Virginia McHugh Goodwin, the Executive Director of the Association Montessori International/USA. She told me in a phone interview that "Montessori would appreciate the deep, intuitive connection the iPad fosters between content and user, taking working with knowledge to another level."

Other clues can be derived from Montessori's book, "The Montessori Method." You'll find plenty of evidence that Montessori was a bit of a geek. She wrote about the promise of Roentgen Rays (later renamed X-rays) in 1912 and accurately predicted "wonderful things from the Marconi Telegraph" (aka the radio).

She was also a consummate maker, or game maker, constantly fiddling with innovative materials like sand paper to perfect a new self-teaching gadget. Because she'd always put a child's interests ahead of any formal curriculum, it's a safe bet that she would've encouraged young Sergey Brin's (Google cofounder) play with a Commodore 64. Said Goodwin, "Maria Montessori would view the iPad—and devices like it—as a tool for tomorrow's mind."

So when Montessori wrote that education was "seeking the release of human potentialities," it is easy to imagine her including a tablet, loaded with some carefully designed apps, in her materials. Let me recap the "pro-tablet" reasons:

- *Montessori was a scientist who was future-centric.* She understood that she was living in a changing time and that children needed to be exposed to modern materials. She was in the business of preparing children for their future, to live to their full human potential, so she would've wanted them to embrace and feel empowered by every element of their environment, including technology.
- *She would be discriminating about the types of apps she loaded on her tablets.* She'd look for noncommercial apps that promote active learning, are self-correcting, are multi-leveling, don't talk too much, and empower children. Another word Montessori used frequently was "didactic" as in "didactic materials," or working toward one right answer; a feature found in many better-designed apps.
- *In designing apps, she'd compensate for the iPad's sensory limitation of just sight and sound, using apps in concert with real, concrete experiences.* She would use the iPad to supplement and extend traditional experiences rather than to replace them. A field trip to an apple orchard would include the chance to pick the apples from the trees; perhaps followed by apple tasting; where each child can have their own apple, to hold, smell, and taste. Only then would she read a story from a book about the apples, or let them "pick" the abstract apples on a multi-touch screen. Too often, Montessori might argue, this concrete to abstract process is reversed.

Position Statement Alignment

Technology and interactive media are tools that can promote effective learning and development when they are used intentionally by early childhood educators, within the framework of developmentally appropriate practice to support learning goals established for individual children.

NAEYC & Fred Rogers Center (2012), p. 5

Montessori's Influence on Google, Amazon, and The Sims

Four of today's most successful technology innovators and leaders attribute a Montessori-inspired education to their formative development. Google cofounder Sergey Brin attended Paint Branch Montessori School in Adelphi, Maryland, and talks about his Montessori education. Brin later tried unsuccessfully to get into MIT and went to Stanford instead, where, in 1995, he got into a 2-day argument with another younger student who was visiting Stanford from the University of Michigan, named Larry Page (Google cofounder). Larry Page, son of Carl Victor Page (Michigan State University computer science professor), attended Okemos Montessori School (now called Montessori Radmoor) from 1975 to 1979. He also attended Interlochen Academy and the University of Michigan; taking a class from Elliot Soloway. Will Wright, the designer of *The Sims* and cofounder of Maxis had a "brief, intense" elementary Montessori experience in Atlanta, GA, until sixth grade (Crecente, 2009). Amazon.com founder Jeffrey Bezos took his crib apart with a screwdriver. By his mother's account, the young Bezos got so engrossed in the details of activities at his Montessori school that teachers had to pick him up in his chair to move him to new tasks (Hof, 2009).

Before attributing such technological and financial success to a Montessori education or any other specific curriculum, it is important to consider that Montessori schools are often private, expensive, and cater to parents who themselves may be highly educated or may have large incomes. In the case of both Brin and Page, both had parents who were college professors. Other factors, besides exposure to Montessori ideals, could be associated with a future successful career of a child.

But you have to wonder what would Maria Montessori have to say about the success of these former Montessori School students.

Position Statement Alignment

The challenge for early childhood educators is to make informed choices that maximize learning opportunities for children while managing screen time and mediating the potential for misuse and overuse of screen media, even as these devices offer new interfaces that increase their appeal and use to young children.

NAEYC & Fred Rogers Center (2012), p. 3

Words of Caution

Before you rush out and purchase every child a tablet, consider these words of caution, again extrapolated from Montessori's ideas:

- *Keep an open mind about this issue.* Tablets are like chameleons—they take the form of the app they are running. Some apps match a child and your learning philosophy; others don't. Like anything new, it must be observed and studied to maximize the strengths and minimize downsides. As a scientist, Montessori was trained to systematically study various techniques, use what works, and discard the rest.

- *Keep things in balance.* She'd urge modern parents not to upset the balance of diet, exercise, and the development of the senses through exposure to water, wood, sounds, and sand. Technology-based experiences can supplement this mix. For example, the camera on most iPod Touch is an ideal tool for capturing observations on a field trip.
- *Screens are inherently abstract.* Said Goodwin "She'd (Montessori) remind us that any screen is an abstract, two-dimensional object that is removed from reality." In other words, the movements of a virtual fish in the Koi Pond HD app (The Blimp Pilots, 2011), might fool your cat, but one sniff tells you they're not real. What app could replace the smells and sounds of a marsh pond on a spring day?
- *Technology tends to be expensive and quickly becomes obsolete.* You can buy a lot of chromatic silk frames and sandpaper letters for $500, and anyone knows that next generation iPad will be "newer, better, faster, and cheaper."
- *Don't sugar coat the learning.* She'd like apps that are simple and stripped "of all that is not absolute truth," sans licensed characters, long musical introductions, or links that steer a child toward a shopping cart. Because she frowned on the notion of shaping a child's behavior with external prizes and punishments, she'd recommend apps where the process, in itself, is rewarding. She might ask, "What type of society exposes its young to manipulative tricks with commercial motives?" Montessori would probably insist that every children's app should have a "no candy lane" mode, which perhaps costs a few Euros more.

In the century since Maria Montessori gave her famous Carnegie Hall address, a lot has changed. But a lot is still the same. We still have many of hard-to-teach children with limitless potential, and the job of creating environments where they can thrive is expensive and challenging. But today, it's nice to think that we have better materials.

Teacher Takeaways

Now that you know what I think Montessori might have said about multi-touch screens, what do you think? Here are some ways to apply the key concepts in this chapter:

- Try the Theoretician role-play game.
- Together with a small group, start a popular app, and make sure each person is familiar with what it does and how it works.

- Put the names of five theories on index cards, and have each person draw a theory, at random.
- Next, have them choose a theorist to represent the theory (Behaviorism, John Watson; Cognitive Science, Jerome Bruner; and so on).
- Use Wikipedia and other Web resources if you need a quick refresher on the theories.

References

Apple. (2013). Apple announces iPad Air—Dramatically thinner, lighter & more powerful iPad [Press release]. Retrieved from www.apple.com/pr/library/2013/10/23Apple-Announces-iPad-Air-Dramatically-Thinner-Lighter-More-Powerful-iPad.html

The Blimp Pilots, LLC. (2011). Koi pond HD [Mobile application software]. Retrieved from http://itunes.apple.com

Brain Counts. (2012). Approach to Montessori—Numbers HD free lite [Mobile application software]. Retrieved from http://itunes.apple.com

Crecente, B. (2009, March 29). Maria Montessori: The 138-year-old inspiration behind Spore [Blog post]. Retrieved from www.kotaku.com.au/2009/03/maria_montessori_the_138yearold_inspiration_behind_spore-2/

Disney Interactive. (2013). Club penguin [Mobile application software]. Retrieved from http://itunes.apple.com

Duck Duck Moose. (2013). Moose math [Mobile application software]. Retrieved from http://itunes.apple.com

Hof, R. (2009). Jeff Bezos: The wizard of Web retailing. *Business Week*. Retrieved December 29, 2009, from www.businessweek.com/stories/2004–12–19/jeff-bezos-the-wizard-of-web-retailing

Hopscotch. (2013). Hopscotch [Mobile application software]. Retrieved from http://itunes.apple.com

Kindoma. (2013). Kindoma [Mobile application software]. Retrieved from http://itunes.apple.com

King.com Limited. (2013). Candy Crush Saga [Mobile application software]. Retrieved from http://itunes.apple.com

Little Bit Studio. (2013). Bugs and buttons [Mobile application software]. Retrieved from http://itunes.apple.com

Mojang. (2011). Minecraft [Mobile application software]. Retrieved from http://itunes.apple.com

Maloney, J., Resnick, M., Rusk, N., Silverman, B., & Eastmond, E. (2010, November). The scratch programming language and environment. *ACM Trans. Comput. Educ. 10*, 4. http://doi.acm.org/10.1145/1868358.1868363

MIT Media Lab (2013). Scratch 2.0 [Mobile application software]. Retrieved from http://scratch.mit.edu

Montessori, M. (1964). *Montessori method.* New York, NY: Schocken Books, Inc. Retrieved from www.randomhouse.com/book/116206/montessori-method-by-maria-montessori

Motion Math. (2012). Hungry guppy [Mobile application software]. Retrieved from http://itunes.apple.com

National Association for the Education of Young Children & Fred Rogers Center for Early Learning and Children's Media at Saint Vincent College. (2012). *Technology and interactive media as tools in early childhood programs serving children from birth through age 8*. Washington, DC: NAEYC; Latrobe, PA: Fred Rogers Center for Early Learning and Children's Media at Saint Vincent College.

New York Times. (1913, December 9). Dr. Montessori's aim; She tells great audience that she seeks perfection of the race. Retrieved December 30, 2013, from http://query.nytimes.com/mem/archive-free/pdf?res=9D06E6DE1F3BE633A2575AC0A9649D946296D6CF

Oceanhouse Media (2013). Green eggs and ham [Mobile application software]. Retrieved from http://itunes.apple.com

Peapod Labs. (2013). ABC Actions [Mobile application software]. Retrieved from http://itunes.apple.com

Rovio Entertainment. (2009). Angry birds [Mobile application software]. Retrieved from http://itunes.apple.com

Sanoma Media Netherlands B.V. (2012). Letter School [Mobile application software]. Retrieved from www.letterschool.com

TinyBop. (2013). The human body [Mobile application software]. Retrieved from http://itunes.apple.com

Touch Press (2013). Disney Animated [Mobile application software]. Retrieved from http://itunes.apple.com

Resources

Books and Journals

Bloom, B.S. (Ed.). (1956). *Taxonomy of educational objectives: The classification of educational goals: Handbook I, Cognitive domain*. New York, NY/Toronto, Canada: Longmans, Green.

Buckleitner, W. (1991). *High-scope survey of early childhood software*. Ypsilanti, MI: High/Scope Press.

Buckleitner, W. (2010). Sergey Brin's first computer, and his Montessori education [Video file]. Retrieved from http://youtu.be/3OCAdXjlLBA

Ginsburg, H.P., & Opper, S. (1988). *Piaget's theory of intellectual development*. Englewood Cliffs, NJ: Prentice-Hall.

Montessori, M. (1912). *The Montessori method*. New York, NY: Frederick A. Stokes Company. Retrieved from www.gutenberg.org/files/39863/39863-h/39863-h.htm

Pavlov, I.P. (1927).*Conditioned reflexes*. Mineola, NY: Dover Publications.

Pressey, S.L. (1927). A machine for automatic teaching of drill material. *School and Society*, *25*(645), 549–552.

Skinner, B.F. (1958). Teaching machines. *Science,128*(3330), 969–977.

Standing, E.M. (1984). *Maria Montessori: Her life and work* [Rev. ed.]. New York, NY: New American Library.

Thorndike, E.L. (1912). *Education: A first book*. New York, NY: The MacMillan Company.

Vygotsky, L.L.S. (1978). *Mind in society: The development of higher psychological processes*. Cambridge, MA: Harvard University Press.

Apps

- *ABC Actions*, Peapod Labs, http://peapodlabs.com
- *Angry Birds*, Rovio Entertainment, www.rovio.com
- *Bejeweled,* PopCap Games, www.popcap.com/bejeweled-games
- *Bugs and Buttons*, Little Bit Studio, www.littlebitstudio.com
- *Candy Crush Saga*, King.com Limited, https://king.com
- *Club Penguin*, Disney Interactive, www.clubpenguin.com
- *Disney Animated,* Touch Press, www.touchpress.com
- Facebook, www.facebook.com
- Google, www.google.com/
- *Green Eggs and Ham*, Oceanhouse Media, www.oceanhousemedia.com
- *The Human Body*, TinyBop, www.tinybop.com
- *Hungry Guppy*, Motion Math, http://motionmathgames.com
- *Kindoma*, Kindoma, http://kindoma.com
- *Koi Pond HD*, The Blimp Pilots, LLC, www.theblimppilots.com
- *LEGO Star Wars*, LEGO, www.lego.com/en-us/starwars
- *LetterSchool*, Sanoma Media Netherlands B.V., www.letterschool.com
- *Logo*, MIT, http://el.media.mit.edu/logo-foundation/logo/
- *Minecraft*, Mojang, https://mojang.com
- *Moose Math*, Duck Duck Moose, www.duckduckmoose.com
- Oceanhouse Media, www.oceanhousemedia.com
- *Scratch 2.0*, MIT, http://scratch.mit.edu
- Skype, www.skype.com/en/
- Twitter, https://twitter.com
- YouTube, www.youtube.com

Learn More . . .

- AMI, Association Montessori International/USA, www.amiusa.org
- *Children's Technology Review,* http://childrenstech.com and www.youtube.com/user/childrenstech
- Dust or Magic, http://dustormagic.com
- NAEYC & Fred Rogers Center Joint Position Statement (2012), www.naeyc.org/content/technology-and-young-children
- *Three Words for Digital-Age Parents: Access Balance, and Support*, Warren Buckleitner, Fred Rogers Center Blog, www.fredrogerscenter.org/blog/three-words-for-digital-age-parents-access-balance-and-support/
- Wikipedia, www.wikipedia.org

Chapter 6

Connecting Child Development and Technology: What We Know and What It Means

Michael B. Robb and Alexis R. Lauricella

Introduction

Children are growing up in a constantly changing and fast-evolving digital world. There are televisions in doctor's offices, touch screens in taxicabs, and tablet cases with teething rings for infants. Technology and interactive media are already present in children's and educators' personal lives and have begun to make inroads into both the home and classroom experiences of young children. At home, almost two-thirds of parents of young children own a smartphone, 42% own a tablet device, and 35% of parents own both types of mobile device (Wartella, Rideout, Lauricella, & Connell, 2013). Nearly all (99%) homes with young children own a TV, and almost half (45%) of these families have a TV that is connected to the Internet (Wartella Rideout, et al., 2013). Beyond accessing media in their homes, young children are also accessing and using media technology at school or child care centers. Almost all providers have access to digital cameras (92%), computers (84%), and TVs/DVDs (80%), although access to newer technologies is still below that of these more traditional technologies with just 29% having tablet computers (Wartella, Blackwell, Lauricella, & Robb, 2013).

With decades of research and scientific understanding of child development and more than 40 years of science and study of children's television use, a research literature has been established around the intersections of child development and traditional media technology. However, with the introduction of new technologies, digital devices, and applications, questions about developmentally appropriate usage of technology arise frequently, especially when it comes to use with younger children. A joint position statement of the National Association for the Education of Young Children (NAEYC) and the Fred Rogers Center for Early Learning and Children's Media at Saint Vincent College (2012) acknowledges the many issues surrounding the use of technology and interactive media in early childhood programs as well as the potential opportunities. While serving as a starting point for guiding the developmentally appropriate integration of digital tools in early childhood programs, the statement notes that more research is needed on the impact of technology, especially newer technologies, on children's learning and development, but there are ways in which educators can utilize what is known about more traditional media platforms to make smart media choices regarding new media devices.

Position Statement Alignment

> Educators must be knowledgeable and prepared to make informed decisions about how and when to appropriately select, use, integrate, and evaluate technology and media to meet the cognitive, social, emotional, physical, and linguistic needs of young children. Educators also need to be knowledgeable enough to answer parents' questions and steer children to technology and media experiences that have the potential to exert a positive influence on their development.
>
> NAEYC & Fred Rogers Center (2012), pp. 10–11

What We Know About Child Development in the Context of Technology

Understanding how children learn, grow, and develop is crucial for understanding the ways in which children use, learn, and interact with technology. Children's age and developmental level, including their cognitive, social, motor, language, and emotional skills, play a significant role in how they can use and learn from technology. Below is a snapshot of the ways in which different areas of child development play a role in children's interactions with technology.

Physical Development

Physical development plays an important role in the way in which young children can use and manipulate technology. During the infant and toddler years, children develop the ability to reach, grasp, and pick up small objects (Feldman, 2001). Their gross motor skills, including the control of moving their arms and legs, also develop during their early years of infancy. In the preschool years, between 3 and 6, both fine and gross motor skills improve quickly, but children still struggle with fine motor skills that require the manipulation of very small objects like buttons and writing. Given young children's fine motor skill development, some types of technology are very challenging for them to operate. Young children struggle to successfully point and click with a computer mouse (Lauricella, Barr, & Calvert, 2009), but anecdotal evidence demonstrates that infants are capable of manipulating touch-screen devices (e.g., Chang, Rakowsky, & Clark, 2013). Teachers must be aware of the physical abilities of the young children in their classrooms when deciding whether and which technology to use in the classrooms.

Cognitive Development and Language

During infancy and toddlerhood, children are exploring and learning to understand the world around them through touch and manual manipulation and enjoy cause-and-effect toys (Feldman, 2001). Interactions with technology may revolve around pressing buttons to see what happens, and exploring the immediate responsiveness of certain actions. There is a developmental progression for digital tools that mirrors children's use of physical tools. Children need a chance to explore and experiment with technology tools before they can be expected to master them and use them effectively (NAEYC & Fred Rogers Center, 2012). Experimentation and play with digital technology serves many of the same purposes as experimentation and play with traditional toys and objects during the early years.

During the preschool years, around ages 4 to 5, children exhibit egocentric thinking (Feldman, 2001). Their memory, attention, and symbolic thinking skills have improved but are still developing. Young children have limited cognitive capacity (Fisch, 2000), meaning that media use can consume cognitive resources that could otherwise be used for learning, especially infants, toddlers, and preschoolers. It is important to take advantage of ways to lower the cognitive load placed on young children when they are engaging with media. When the cognitive demands are minimized, it is easier for a child to focus on the most important aspects of media presentation. One way to decrease the cognitive demands of young children is to repeat content (e.g., Barr, Chavez, Fujimoto, Garcia, & Muentener, 2007).

As children get older, their ability to cognitively process information improves, making learning from media easier (Fisch, 2000). Media that requires children to process multiple storylines or narratives at once may be particularly cognitively challenging for young children, potentially inhibiting their ability to learn from the content. Older children have better memories, attention, and language skills, and more experience with the world and media, which may improve their understanding of media content.

Young children's language skills improve rapidly; during the preschool years, they are able speak in complete sentences and understand grammar and syntax rules of language. Children are also better able to follow rules and can play simple games (Feldman, 2001). Many technologies require and rely on language to present information. As young children's language skills improve, they are better able to follow storylines and understand the content presented to them.

What We Know About Technology and Young Children

Academic Learning From Television

Considerable research has demonstrated that preschool children can learn from purposefully created educational television (Ball & Bogatz, 1970), and watching can have positive outcomes on a range of academic skills (Anderson, Huston, Schmitt, Linebarger, & Wright, 2001; Huston, Anderson, Wright, Linebarger, & Schmitt, 2001). Research over the past 40 years on *Sesame Street* has demonstrated that when television programs are created with an age-appropriate learning curriculum, children do learn from watching (Fisch & Truglio, 2001).

Programs like *Dora the Explorer* and *Blue's Clues* have utilized a similar research and curriculum based model, and preschoolers who watch these programs have demonstrated improvements in many school readiness related skills (Crawley, Anderson, Wilder, Williams, & Santomero, 1999; Schmidt & Anderson, 2007). Other reviews of the research on educational television programs have documented the effectiveness of well-designed programs on literacy, math and numeracy, science, and social-emotional skills (e.g., Fisch, 2004a; Kirkorian, Wartella, & Anderson, 2008).

Teacher Takeaway

The NAEYC & Fred Rogers Center joint position statement (2012) notes that technology and media can plan an important role in supporting children's cognitive and social abilities, if they are used in appropriate ways.

- Consider the learning goals you are trying to achieve before selecting any tools, including technology, and make sure media content is developmentally appropriate for students.
- Use technology to extend learning just as you do with other traditional early childhood materials (blocks, art materials, books, etc.).

Remaining Questions

We know children can learn a range of academic skills from media, but questions remain.

- How do the capabilities and affordances of different technologies and interactive media lend themselves to specific learning areas, including literacy, STEM, health, and social-emotional development?
- How can the intentional use of specific technologies, such as tablet computers and interactive whiteboards, at different ages contribute to children's learning?
- How can technology and digital media content be used to support children's play and creativity?

The Role of Formal Features

Much of what we know about how young children learn from media comes from television research that examines how well children comprehend what's on the screen, and how they understand the "formal features" of the medium (visual cues, sound effects, pacing, zooms, cuts, montage, etc.). Used judiciously, formal features can help children pay attention to important ideas or concepts. Specifically, research has shown that certain auditory cues and formal features can help cue children's attention to key parts of the children's program (Calvert, Huston,

Watkins, & Wright, 1982). However, young children may have difficulty comprehending the entirety of television programs if they do not understand the purpose or use of techniques like zooms, cuts, or montage.

Research on new digital media, such as e-books, has begun to explore how features such as "hotspots" impact learning. Hotspots are opportunities for children to interact with an onscreen object. For example, clicking or pressing on an image of a bird could make it fly around the screen and tweet. Research shows that in some instances e-books can help to support literacy skills (e.g., Korat & Shamir, 2008). However, hotspots can either enhance learning when they are congruent and central to the storyline (e.g., Chera & Wood, 2003; de Jong & Bus, 2004; Korat & Shamir, 2007) or can hinder learning when they are distracting (e.g., Labbo & Kuhn, 2000; Ricci & Beal, 2002; Trushell, Burrell, & Maitland, 2001). Other research has begun to compare e-books to traditional print books, but again, the findings are far from clear. Some studies find that children comprehend the story better from a traditional storybook than an enhanced e-book (Chiong, Ree, & Takeuchi, 2012) or a nonenhanced e-book (Krcmar & Cingel, in press), while others find that children can learn equally well from interactive and print books (Robb, 2010).

Teacher Takeaway

As adults, we have had many years of practice to understand the formal features of media presentations. We understand that film can "cut" from one scene to another and that the second scene may or may not be directly related to the first. This is very challenging for young children.

- Pay extra attention to the way material is presented when selecting media for young children—overuse of cuts between scenes, or jumps in time or to different locations, may impair children's ability to comprehend content.
- Look for formal features that are used in ways to support comprehension—for example, zooms and pans help guide children's attention and help them to understand the transition of what is happening.
- Be careful of media where sound effects, visual touches, or other formal features are attractive to children, but pull their attention away from the primary content and focus of the media—young children are particularly drawn to loud sounds and flashy movements.
- Consider the content as well as the way in which the content is presented when using touch-screen devices or e-books in the classroom.

Like traditional media technology, the content should support and extend upon the curriculum in the classrooms. Too many distracting hotspots, games, and other interactive features may seem exciting for young children, but depending on how they are integrated in the game, they may be distracting and could interfere with learning. Sound and visual effects should help guide the child's attention to important parts of the storyline or content.

Remaining Questions

The work on formal features has almost exclusively been done with television. We know very little about children's understanding of the formal features related to interactive technologies.

- How do children understand the mechanics and formal features that occur in interactive media?
- How do audio cues on websites or online games influence children's attention and comprehension of the content?
- How could hotspots be effectively used to support children's early literacy skills, including phonemic awareness, comprehension, and word fluency?

Social Relevancy

Children learn very effectively from social partners, especially at very young ages. Research suggests that infants and toddlers learn better from a live person than from a televised demonstration, an effect commonly called the "video deficit" (Anderson & Pempek, 2005). Additionally, even in the preschool years, social factors play a role in how young children understand and learn from screen media (Reeves & Nass, 1996; Strommen, 2003). In order to learn from social factors, young children have to learn who or what provides dependable information. Research shows that preschool children in many situations are able to discriminate between people who do and do not provide reliable information (Harris, 2007). This ability may extend to particular children's television shows and characters. For example, certain characters may be seen as providing more relevant information about the outside world, and children may be more likely to learn from shows or characters they believe to be "trustworthy" or socially relevant. For example, children learn information better from an on-screen character they know (Gola, Richards, Lauricella, & Calvert, 2013), such as Elmo (Lauricella, Gola, & Calvert, 2011) or their own mother (Krcmar, 2010), compared to characters that are unknown. Beyond knowing and trusting the characters, children are more emotionally involved with programs that feature characters similar to them, along characteristics such as sex, race, class, interests, etc., and thus more likely to attend to the screen (Fisch, 2004b). It also helps if characters are seen as helpful, competent, and smart (Fisch, 2004b).

There is some suggestion that preschoolers' learning from screens is influenced by their parasocial relationships with characters (Gola et al., 2013; Lauricella et al., 2011; Richert, Robb, & Smith, 2011). Parasocial relationships describe the ways in which children respond to on-screen figures as they would to live partners in typical social interactions, such as through identification with characters or empathizing with characters' situations or feelings, even though there is no social contingency (Giles, 2002). Some programs try to replicate real-world social interaction by having characters talk directly to the audience and pause for a response. Programs such as *Dora the Explorer, Super Why, Daniel Tiger's Neighborhood,* and *Blue's Clues* use this technique to elicit participation.

When the viewing experience is made more socially relevant (e.g., Gola et al., 2013; Krcmar, 2010; Lauricella et al., 2011; Troseth, 2003), learning from a screen presentation can be improved. Providing toddlers with experiences in which they use video technology (cameras and television screens) to see themselves live on the TV screen helped children to learn from information presented on a screen (Troseth, 2003). Other research has found that repetition of a video presentation (Barr et al., 2007) and interaction with the program via using a computer content (Lauricella, Pempek, Barr, & Calvert, 2010) helps infants and toddlers overcome the video deficit. The ways in which information is presented to a child on a screen play a role on the young child's ability to learn, especially as compared to learning with a live adult teacher.

Teacher Takeaway

- Select media that features characters of different genders, ethnicities, socio-economic backgrounds, living situations, clothing styles, and other salient characteristics to help children identify with and relate to media content.
- Provide children with platforms, characters, and game play structures that they are familiar with to decrease the cognitive load placed on children, and make it easier to learn new things.
- Look for content where children's responses to a character's prompts are related to the learning goals, in addition to encouraging participation—children may be engaged by television shows where characters address viewers directly, and pause for responses, giving the sense that there is a real social interaction occurring.

Remaining Questions

While television can only create the illusion of a back-and-forth interaction, interactive media actually depends on users' actions to advance. Also, there are many possible ways to increase the social relevancy of interactive media, but we need to know more about how effective they are. For example, some e-books allow children to include pictures of themselves or family members. Other interactive media allows users to customize on-screen characters to their liking. Children may also identify more with characters they control, especially when they have opportunities to interact with other characters.

- What kinds of interactivity are best used in the service of learning goals?
- How can the increased social relevancy of these types of features improve learning?
- Does an increased emergence as an active player, and any increased salience of the activity itself, contribute to improved learning outcomes, or point to opportunities for integrating educational content?

Co-viewing and Adult Influence

Years of research on co-viewing speak to the importance of parental presence and engagement in facilitating children's learning from media. Co-viewing is the parental act of watching television and video content with children and can range from very high involvement to very low involvement. For example, parents viewing with their children and not attempting to engage them in interactions about what is on the screen would be on the low end of the interactive and involvement spectrum. On the other end of the spectrum, parents can help make content assessable in a manner sensitive to their children's needs and developmental level and could include behaviors such as talking about what is on the screen, imitating actions (like singing or dancing), or labeling on-screen objects (Valkenburg, Krcmar, Peeters, & Marseille, 1999). Not all co-viewing is equal.

Rice and colleagues (1990) found that children learned letters and numbers better when parents co-view the television program and ask children to name the letters and numbers during the program. The effect was not found when parents themselves named the letters and numbers while co-viewing (Reiser, Tessmer, & Phelps, 1984; Reiser, Williamson, & Suzuki, 1988). Using dialogic reading techniques, such as asking open-ended questions and asking children to retell the story they viewed after multiple viewings was related to better story understanding and vocabulary learning compared to parents who just pointed out what was happening on-screen (Strouse, O'Doherty, & Troseth, 2013).

In addition, a teacher or parent who treats media content as an educational experience, rather than simply entertainment or a diversion, can prime children to learn. In one study, children who saw a televised program in which they were expected to learn from the show were better able to remember what they watched (Salomon, 1981). A study of 4- to 5-year old children's learning from e-books found that children who used an e-book with a parent remembered story content better than children who used an e-book alone, regardless of what parents said during the reading (Robb, 2010).

With broadband Internet, co-viewing and co-play can also occur across physical locations. By combining a live video feed with a print book using a special interface, researchers were able to support a dialogic reading interaction that engaged caregivers and children in different locations (Raffle et al., 2010). Other research has demonstrated that social interaction via video chat can help toddlers learn language in a similar fashion as live adult (Roseberry, Hirsh-Pasek, & Golinkoff, 2013).

Teacher Takeaway

- Use technology and digital media that encourage adult-child interaction and language-rich exchanges to facilitate learning of new concepts—young children, and especially children birth to 2, learn best with human partners.
- Provide important scaffolding experiences with all media, just like you do with traditional media like books.

- Look for resources that provide suggestions and tips on how to use digital media with young children. For example, the Fred Rogers Center Early Learning Environment provides questions and conversation starters around digital materials.
- Use technology to facilitate co-play or co-reading for adults and children dealing with time zone differences, busy schedules, or other barriers to interaction.
- Help children break down what they are seeing on screen or provide tips or scaffolds to help them complete a challenging portion of a game on a touch-screen device.
- Encourage children to work together and to ask each other questions when using media in the classroom.
- Don't assume that a child is going to automatically learn from watching a television program or using an app.
- Help direct children in advance about what they should be paying attention to while engaging with media and what they can expect to learn.

Remaining Questions

Less is known about the role of parents or teachers in using technology and digital media with children. Interactive features meant to engage a child might also be useful in providing a context for adults to interact with their children in a more comfortable fashion. For example, a parent with limited reading skills might have difficulty fully engaging in a print book with a child, but an e-book might be able to scaffold print reading, allowing the parent to interact with a child around other parts of the book.

- How do parents with different attitudes toward learning, educational backgrounds, and skills sets interact with children around digital media?
- What features of digital media impact parent-child interaction?

While adult interaction during technology use with children can scaffold the learning experience, there are still many questions about the impact of sibling and peer co-use. Both at home and in schools, children use media together.

- How does this co-use among siblings and peers influence learning?
- Are there ways to optimize co-use experiences among children of different ages and developmental levels?

Newer Digital Media

Over the years, new technologies have entered the classroom in similar ways in which they have entered the home. Research on computer use in preschools has demonstrated potential benefits. For example, preschool-age children from low-income families in an urban Head Start centers who received daily access to computers displayed more positive attitudes toward learning, improved self-esteem and self-confidence, and increases in kindergarten readiness skills (Primavera, Wiederlight, & DiGiacomo, 2001). In the same study, children who received additional weekly trainings improved even more than their peers who only had access. Although some critics fear that technology isolates users and reduces social communication, studies of classroom use have indicated the opposite result. Children using computers frequently talk to each other and the teacher, sharing information, discussing what's happening on screen, and helping each to find solutions to problems (Clements & Samara, 2003; Heft & Swaminathan, 2002; Muller & Perlmutter, 1985; Wang & Carter Ching, 2003). Children using educational software have also been observed using more complex speech patterns (Davidson & Wright, 1994) and narrating their actions when interacting with objects within programs (Bredekamp & Rosegrant, 1994).

More recently, a range of newer technologies are being integrated into classrooms. Touch-screen tablets, like iPads, are being introduced in early education settings around the United States, but the effects of these technologies in the classroom are largely unknown. This is partially due to the novel nature of these products but also due to the nature of the platform itself and the content that can be used via the device. Unlike television, but more like computers, new touch-screen devices can provide children with a range of content delivered via apps. Children can use tablet computers to read e-books, play games, take photographs, write notes, and record videos, making it challenging to assess usage outcomes.

Research specifically on apps has only recently begun, and points to the importance of knowing an individual child's developmental level. Children between the ages of 3 to 7 who played a Martha Speaks: Dog Party (WGBH Educational Foundation, 2009) app made gains on a vocabulary posttest (Chiong & Shuler, 2010). However, 5-year old children outperformed children in other groups; developmentally, they were more ready to acquire new words and their meanings and were also less likely than older children to already know the vocabulary words at the pretest. Similarly, 3-year-olds who played a Super Why app made greater gains on a vocabulary posttest than children between 4 to 7 years old, presumably because the app content was better matched to their developmental needs. The older children in the study had already mastered many of the skills that the app was supporting, minimizing any potential gains. Another study of children in a fifth-grade classroom found that children who played Motion Math HD—Fractions (2010), an iPad fractions game for 20 minutes daily for 5 days increased their fractions knowledge an average of 15% (Riconscente, 2011). The same study reported that children rated the fractions app as fun and noted that all the participants wanted to play it more.

Studies of widespread applications of tablet devices in classrooms are only beginning; one study found that on average, children who used iPads in a kindergarten classroom improved on a measure of phonemic awareness and the ability to represent sound with letters (Bebell, Dorris, & Muir, 2012). However, the same study did not find any differences between children who did and did not use an iPad on nine other early literacy measures.

Teacher Takeaway

- Be careful of marketers' claims about the educational effectiveness of products.
- Use professional judgment when deciding what devices and digital media content support learning goals.
- Do not assume that simply giving a child a device will lead to learning.
- Consider how technology may be used cooperatively—learning can occur during discussions between children who are trying to solve a problem on a tablet together, or during guided digital technology play with educators and children.
- Remember that digital tools may have different impacts depending on children's background—what may be a valuable tool for children with no other means of technology access may be less beneficial for children who already have access to a wide array of learning resources.

Remaining Questions

Given the relative newness of touchscreen tablet devices, many of the questions posed with more traditional technologies need to be replicated on touchscreen devices. Educators also need information and trusted resources to find and select quality, age-appropriate apps for children.

- What are the formal features that are used on apps?
- How socially relevant are the apps?
- How are learning goals embedded within the content of the app?
- What does co-use look like with touchscreen devices?
- How can co-use be enhanced when using touchscreen devices?
- What are the strategies to best use different technologies in a range of programs and classrooms, with diverse groups of children?

Conclusion

The digital world of technology and media that surrounds young children today is one that is vastly different from what we have known and scientifically studied in the past. As a result, we have to rely on what is already known about child development in general and use the existing research on other types of technology to make educated decisions about the ways in which we use media technology with young children. The good news is that we already know a considerable amount about connecting child development and technology. We have more than 40 years on educational television programs like *Sesame Street* that have consistently demonstrated that young children can learn academic content from quality television viewing experiences (e.g., Ball & Bogatz, 1970; Fisch & Truglio, 2001). We know the formal features used in television and video production can enhance learning, even as we recognize concerns for how and when these features may pull attention away from learning. We know that learning is aided when embedded in social experiences and thus the social relevancy of the characters on a screen and the social interactions around the screen can powerfully influence learning opportunities. Finally, we are beginning to learn about new media technologies and the ways in which use of these devices is similar to the use of traditional technologies. The affordances of new technologies may support or improve learning in ways that traditional media cannot. Although we know a lot about child development and technology, there are still many questions that remain.

Even as research on children and technology catches up, there are things that educators can do in the absence of research evidence. Educators have experience working with young children and expertise in education. Educators must use their professional judgment when evaluating how to select, use, integrate, and evaluate technology and digital media in their programs (NAEYC & Fred Rogers Center, 2012). Decision making on what will be effective in a classroom will depend on a combination of factors including the developmental level, interests, abilities, linguistic background, and needs of the children in their care. Having a clear educational goal in mind before using an app, website, digital camera, or other digital tool can help educators to use technology appropriately.

Position Statement Alignment

> Research is needed to better understand how young children use and learn with technology and interactive media and also to better understand any short- and long-term effects.
>
> As multi-touch technologies and other emerging user interface possibilities become more affordable and available, new research is needed on what young children are able to do and how these tools and media can be integrated in a classroom.
>
> Research-based evidence about what constitutes quality technology and interactive media for young children is needed to guide policy and inform practice, and to ensure that technology and media tools are used in effective, engaging, and appropriate ways in early childhood programs.
>
> NAEYC & Fred Rogers Center (2012), p. 11

References

Anderson, D. R., Huston, A. C., Schmitt, K. L., Linebarger, D. L., & Wright, J. C. (2001). Early childhood television viewing and adolescent behavior: The recontact study. *Monographs of the Society for Research in Child Development, 66*(1).

Anderson, D. R., & Pempek, T. A. (2005). Television and very young children. *American Behavioral Scientist, 48*(5), 505–522.

Ball, S., & Bogatz, G. (1970). *A summary of the major findings in the first year of Sesame Street: An evaluation.* Princeton, NJ: Educational Testing Service.

Barr, R., Chavez, V., Fujimoto, M., Garcia, A., & Muentener, P. (2007). The effect of repetition on imitation from television during infancy. *Developmental Science, 49*(2), 196–207.

Bebell, D., Dorris, S., & Muir, M. (2012). *Emerging results from the nation's first kindergarten implementation of iPads.* Auburn, ME: Auburn School District. Retrieved from https://s3.amazonaws.com/hackedu/Adv2014_ResearchSum120216.pdf

Bredekamp, S., & Rosegrant, T. (1994). Learning and teaching with technology. In J. Wright & J. Shade (Eds.), *Young children: Active learners in a technological age* (pp. 53–61). Washington, DC: National Association for the Education of Young Children.

Calvert, S. L., Huston, A. C., Watkins, B. A., & Wright, J. C. (1982). The relation between selective attention to television forms and children's comprehension of content. *Child Development, 53*(3), 601. doi:10.2307/1129371

Chang, J., Rakowsky, C., & Clark, D. (2013, June). Toddlers and tablets: Way of the future? *ABC News.* Retrieved from http://abcnews.go.com/Technology/toddlers-tablets-future/story?id=19332916

Chera, P., & Wood, C. (2003). Animated multimedia 'talking books' can promote phonological awareness in children beginning to read. *Learning and Instruction, 13*(1), 33–52.

Chiong, C., Ree, J., & Takeuchi, L. (2012). *QuickReport: Print books vs e-books.* New York, NY: The Joan Ganz Cooney Center at Sesame Workshop.

Chiong, C., & Shuler, C. (2010). *Learning: Is there an app for that?* New York, NY: The Joan Ganz Cooney Center at Sesame Workshop.

Clements, D. H., & Samara, J. (2003). Young children and technology: What does the research say? *Young Children, 58*(6), 34–40.

Crawley, A. M., Anderson, D. R., Wilder, A., Williams, M., & Santomero, A. (1999). Effects of repeated exposures to a single episode of the television program Blue's Clues on the viewing behaviors and comprehension of preschool children. *Journal of Educational Psychology, 91*(4), 630–637. doi:10.1037/0022–0663.91.4.630

Davidson, J., & Wright, J. (1994). The potential of the microcomputer in the early childhood classroom. In J. Wright & J. Shade (Eds.), *Young children: Active learners in a technological age* (pp. 77–91). Washington, DC: National Association for the Education of Young Children.

De Jong, M. T., & Bus, A. G. (2004). The efficacy of electronic books in fostering kindergarten children's emergent story understanding. *Reading Research Quarterly, 39*(4), 378–393. doi: 10.1598/RRQ.39.4.2

Feldman, R. S. (2001). *Child Development.* Upper Saddle River, NJ: Prentice Hall.

Fisch, S. M. (2000). A capacity model of children's comprehension of educational content on television. *Media Psychology, 2*(1), 63–91. doi:10.1207/S1532785XMEP0201_4

Fisch, S. M. (2004a). *Children's learning from educational television: Sesame Street and beyond.* Mahwah, NJ: Lawrence Erlbaum.

Fisch, S. M. (2004b). Characteristics of effective materials for informal education: A cross-media comparison of television, magazines, and interactive media. In F. C. Blumberg, H. T. Everson, & M. Rabinowitz (Eds.), *The design of instruction and evaluation: Affordances of using media and technology.* Mahwah, NJ: Lawrence Erlbaum.

Fisch, S. M., & Truglio, R. T. (2001). *"G" if for growing: Thirty years of research on children and Sesame Street*. Mahwah, NJ: Lawrence Erlbaum.

Giles, D. (2002). Parasocial interaction: A review of the literature and a model for future research. *Media Psychology, 4*, 279–305.

Gola, A. A. H., Richards, M. N., Lauricella, A. R., & Calvert, S. L. (2013). Building meaningful parasocial relationships between toddlers and media characters to teach early mathematical skills. *Media Psychology*. doi: 10.1080/15213269.2013.783774

Harris, P. L. (2007). Trust. *Developmental Science, 10*(1), 135–138. doi:10.1111/j.1467-7687.2007.00575.x

Heft, T. M., & Swaminathan, S. (2002). The effects of computers on the social behavior of preschoolers. *Journal of Research in Childhood Education, 16*(2), 162–174. doi:10.1080/02568540209594982

Huston, A. C., Anderson, D. R., Wright, J. C., Linebarger, D. L., & Schmitt, K. L. (2001). Sesame Street viewers as adolescents: The recontact study. In *"G" is for "growing": Thirty years of research on children and Sesame Street*. Mahwah, NJ: Lawrence Erlbaum Associates.

Kirkorian, H. L., Wartella, E. A., & Anderson, D. R. (2008). Media and young children's learning. *The Future of Children, 18*(1), 39–61.

Korat, O., & Shamir, A. (2007). Electronic books versus adult readers: Effects on children's emergent literacy as a function of social class. *Journal of Computer Assisted Learning, 23*, 248–259. doi: 10.1111/j.1365–2729.2006.00213.x.

Korat, O., & Shamir, A. (2008). The educational electronic book as a tool for supporting children's emergent literacy in low versus middle SES groups. *Computers & Education, 50*(1), 110–124.

Krcmar, M. (2010). Can social meaningfulness and repeat exposure help infants and toddlers overcome the video deficit? *Media Psychology, 13*(1), 31–53. doi:10.1080/15213260903562917

Krmcar, M., & Cingel, D. P. (in press). Parent-child joint reading in traditional and electronic formats. *Media Psychology*.

Labbo, L. D., & Kuhn, M. R. (2000). Weaving chains of affect and cognition: A young child's understanding of CD-ROM talking books. *Journal of Literacy Research, 32*(2), 187–210.

Lauricella, A. R., Barr, R. F., & Calvert, S. L. (2009). Emerging computer skills. *Journal of Children and Media, 3*(3), 217–233. doi:10.1080/17482790902999892

Lauricella, A. R., Gola, A. A. H., & Calvert, S. L. (2011). Toddlers' learning from socially meaningful video characters. *Media Psychology, 14*(2), 216–232. doi:10.1080/15213269.2011.573465

Lauricella, A. R., Pempek, T. A., Barr, R., & Calvert, S. L. (2010). Contingent computer interactions for young children's object retrieval success. *Journal of Applied Developmental Psychology, 31*(5), 362–369. doi: 10.1016/j.appdev.2010.06.002

Motion Math. (2010). Motion Math HD—Fractions [Mobile application software]. Retrieved from http://itunes.apple.com

Muller, A. A., & Perlmutter, M. (1985).Preschool children's problem-solving interactions at computers and jigsaw puzzles. *Journal of Applied Developmental Psychology, 6*(2–3), 173–186. doi:10.1016/0193-3973(85)90058-9

National Association for the Education of Young Children, & Fred Rogers Center for Early Learning and Children's Media at Saint Vincent College. (2012). *Technology and interactive media as tools in early childhood programs serving children from birth through age 8*. Washington, DC: NAEYC; Latrobe, PA: Fred Rogers Center for Early Learning and Children's Media at Saint Vincent College.

Primavera, J., Wiederlight, P. P., & DiGiacomo, T. M. (2001). Technology access for low-income preschoolers: Bridging the digital divide. In *Annual Meeting of the American Psychological Association*. San Francisco, CA.

Raffle, H., Ballagas, R., Revelle, G., Horii, H., Follmer, S., Go, J., … Spasojevic, M. (2010). Family story play: Reading with young children (and Elmo) over a distance. In *Proceedings of the SIGCHI Conference on Human Factors in Computing Systems* (pp. 1583–1592). New York, NY: ACM. doi:10.1145/1753326.1753563

Reeves, B., & Nass, C. (1996). *The media equation: How people treat computers, television, and new media like real people and places*. New York, NY: Cambridge University Press.

Reiser, R. A., Tessmer, M., & Phelps, P. (1984). Adult-child interaction in children's learning from "Sesame Street." *Educational Technology Research and Development, 32*(4), 217–223.

Reiser, R. A., Williamson, N., & Suzuki, K. (1988). Using "Sesame Street" to facilitate children's recognition of letters and numbers. *Educational Technology Research and Development, 36*(1), 15–21.

Ricci, C. M., & Beal, C. R. (2002). The effect of interactive media on children's story memory. *Journal of Educational Psychology, 94*(1), 138–144.

Rice, M., Huston, A. C., Truglio, R., & Wright, J. C. (1990). Words from Sesame Street: Learning vocabulary while viewing. *Developmental Psychology, 26,* 421–428.

Richert, R., Robb, M. B., & Smith, E. (2011). Media as social partners: The social nature of young children's learning from screen media. *Child Development, 82*(1), 82–95.

Riconscente, M. (2011). *Mobile learning improves 5th graders' fractions knowledge and attitudes*. Los Angeles, CA: GameDesk Institute.

Robb, M. B. (2010). *New ways of reading: The impact of an interactive book on young children's story comprehension and parent-child dialogic reading behaviors*. University of California, Riverside, Riverside, CA. Retrieved from http://escholarship.org/uc/item/5xm8n8xk

Roseberry, S., Hirsh-Pasek, K., & Golinkoff, R. M. (2013). Skype me! Socially contingent interactions help toddlers learn language. *Child Development, 1*–15. DOI: 10.1111/cdev.12166

Salomon, G. (1981). Introducing AIME: The assessment of children's mental involvement with television. *New Directions for Child and Adolescent Development, 1981*(13), 89–102. doi:10.1002/cd.23219811308

Schmidt, M. E., & Anderson, D. R. (2007). The impact of television on cognitive development and educational attainment. In *Children and television: Fifty years of research*. Mahwah, NJ: Lawrence Erlbaum.

Strommen, E. F. (2003). Interacting with people versus interacting with machines: Is there a meaningful difference from the point of view of theory? Presented at the Biennial Meeting of the Society for Research in Child Development, Tampa, FL.

Strouse, G. A., O'Doherty, K., & Troseth, G. L. (2013). Effective coviewing: Preschoolers' learning from video after a dialogic questioning intervention. *Developmental Psychology, 49*(12), 2368–2382. doi:10.1037/a0032463

Troseth, G. L. (2003). TV guide: Two-year-old children learn to use video as a source of information. *Developmental Psychology, 39*(1), 140–150. doi:10.1037/0012-1649.39.1.140

Trushell, J., Burrell, C., & Maitland, A. (2001). Year 5 pupils reading an "Interactive Storybook" on CD-ROM: Losing the plot? *British Journal of Educational Technology*, *32*(4), 389–401. doi:10.1111/1467-8535.00209

Valkenburg, P.M., Krcmar, M., Peeters, A.L., & Marseille, N.M. (1999). Developing a scale to assess three styles of television mediation: "Instructive mediation," "restrictive mediation," and "social coviewing." *Journal of Broadcasting and Electronic Media*, *43*, 52–66.

Wang, X.C., & Carter Ching, C. (2003). Social construction of computer experience in a first-grade classroom: Social processes and mediating artifacts. *Early Education & Development*, *14*(3), 335–362. doi:10.1207/s15566935eed1403_4

Wartella, E.A., Blackwell, C.K., Lauricella, A., & Robb, M.B. (2013). *Technology in the lives of educators and early childhood programs*. Latrobe, PA: Fred Rogers Center for Early Learning and Children's Media at Saint Vincent College.

Wartella, E.A., Rideout, V.J., Lauricella, A., & Connell, S. (2013). *Parenting in the age of digital technology*. Chicago, IL: Center on Media and Human Development, School of Communication, Northwestern University.

WGBH Educational Foundation. (2009). Martha speaks: Dog party [Mobile application software]. Retrieved from http://itunes.apple.com

Resources

- *Blue's Clues*, Nick Jr., www.nickjr.com/blues-clues/
- *Daniel Tiger's Neighborhood*, PBS, http://pbskids.org/daniel/
- *Dora the Explorer*, Nick Jr., www.nickjr.com/dora-the-explorer/
- *Martha Speaks*, PBS, http://pbskids.org/martha/
- Motion Math, http://motionmathgames.com
- *Sesame Street*, Sesame Workshop, www.sesamestreet.org
- *Super Why*, PBS, http://pbskids.org/superwhy/

Learn More . . .

- Center on Media and Child Health, CMCH Database, *What Research Is Available?*, www.cmch.tv/SearchAdvanced2.aspx
- Center on Media and Human Development, http://cmhd.northwestern.edu
- Common Sense Media, *Graphite,* www.graphite.org/
- Common Sense Media, *Zero to Eight: Children's Media Use in America 2013,* www.commonsensemedia.org/sites/default/files/research/zero-to-eight-2013.pdf
- Fred Rogers Center, www.fredrogerscenter.org
- Fred Rogers Center Early Learning Environment™ (*Ele*), www.yourele.org
- *How Early Childhood Educators Use Technology in the Classroom,* Michael Robb, Fred Rogers Center Blog, www.fredrogerscenter.org/blog/how-early-childhood-educators-use-technology-in-the-classroom/
- NAEYC & Fred Rogers Center Joint Position Statement, www.naeyc.org/content/technology-and-young-children
- PBS Learning Media, www.pbslearningmedia.org

Part II

Technology in the Classroom

EDITOR'S INTRODUCTION

In Part I, the focus is on broad issues and opportunities with technology and young children, including how technology and digital media can be tools for teaching and learning; implications for teacher education and teacher educators in the digital age; connecting child development theory to practice; and connecting research to practice. Now in the seven chapters that make up Part II, the focus is on technology in the classroom. The contributing authors offer a variety of perspectives on how technology can and should be used to support media literacy; early literacy; dual language learners; inclusive approaches for all children; STEM and simple robotics; the opportunities new technologies offer; and technology tools for teachers and teaching.

Media literacy education strategist, **Faith Rogow**, opens Part II and Chapter 7, with a discussion of what media literacy is, the purpose of media literacy education, what it means in early childhood education, and how teachers can support media literacy for children and parents, while strengthening their own along the way. Rogow says, "To put it another way, media literacy is about helping children develop the life skills they need to become thinkers and makers in the multimedia environment that is their reality." She identifies and describes competencies and outcomes—the skills we all need to be literate in a digital world—and offers strategies for supporting emergent media literacy in developmentally appropriate ways and creating a classroom culture of inquiry.

In Chapter 8, **Lisa Guernsey** and **Michael H. Levine** share lessons learned, innovative and promising practices, and the challenges of improving literacy in a digital age from their report, *Pioneering Literacy in the Digital Wild West*, part of the national Campaign for Grade-Level Reading. The say that "we are at an opportune moment for harnessing digital media to support parents, educators and children in building the next generation's reading skills" and offer examples and next steps for moving from pioneering to common literacy practices. They discuss the role technology can play when it compliments the work of trained teachers and parents, while acknowledging the challenges early childhood educators face.

Technology tools and teaching strategies to support dual language learners are the subjects of Chapter 9, by **Karen N. Nemeth**. She points out the rapid rise in linguistic diversity in early childhood classrooms at the same time as the rapid proliferation of technology tools and supports for teachers. Her goal is to inform educators about new and emerging technology options and to provide tips and strategies that increase their feelings of confidence and competence in selecting, using, integrating, and evaluating technology and digital media for dual language learners. She provides information about who dual language learners are and what they need and connects that to the affordances and advantages of using appropriate technology tools in intentional ways.

In Chapter 10, **Howard P. Parette** and **Craig Blum** address the obstacles and opportunities of including all young children in the technology-supported curriculum. They describe a UDL (Universal Design for Learning) technology integration framework that teachers can use to be sure the environment and activities are inclusive and the use of technology supports classroom goals while providing tools and supports for individual children. They define and describe UDL principles including: Multiple means of representation; Action and expression; and Engagement. They present a technology integration framework grounded in UDL principles that offers teachers a way of thinking about and acting on what they are observing, what the needs of the children are, and their goals for each child. They explain and provide examples of the EXPECT IT-PLAN IT-TEACH IT-SOLVE IT framework in action and discuss its potential as a useful approach for integrating technology.

Stepping into STEM (Science, Technology, Engineering, Mathematics) is the topic of Chapter 11, by **Kate Highfield**, from Macquarie University in Australia. She provides a description of and rationale for STEM in the early years and discusses how simple, affordable, and programmable toys and robotics have a long history in early childhood education, back to the Logo Turtle more than 30 years ago. The concept is not new, but the tools for engaging children in exploring with technology have come a long way. She reviews a research project, "The Robots are at Kindy" to illustrate how programming and robotics can fit into the developmentally appropriate framework, encourage hands-on investigations and experimentation, and allow for integration of STEM concepts across the curriculum.

"Innovate, educate, and empower" are the calls to action in Chapter 12, based on the collaboration between **Mark Bailey** and **Bonnie Blagojevic**. The authors begin with the assumption that early childhood educators are always seeking the most effective tools available for the children in their classrooms. They connect that ongoing interest with new opportunities and new tools available to teachers and for young children, and talk about the importance of having traditional materials alongside digital tools. They highlight the power of new digital tools to transform the nature of learning with young children when used thoughtfully. Digital cameras, digital microscopes, tablets, and open-ended apps for storytelling, documentation and communication are highlighted, including specific classroom examples and best practices. As Bailey and Blagojevic say, "These are exciting times to be an early childhood educator. As quality digital tools continue to be developed, they can support new opportunities to inspire young learners."

Chapter 13, by **Brian Puerling** and **Angela Fowler**, is the seventh and final chapter in Part II. They focus on innovative practice and engaging technologies as they discuss tools for teachers and teaching. In an almost conversational style, they switch back and forth sharing their stories and describing best practice. They identify a wide range of technology tools that teachers can integrate into the classrooms and use to enhance their teaching; improve communication, and strengthen connections between home and school; enable sharing of classroom moments with parents electronically using digital cameras and video; support inquiry-learning and problem solving; conduct assessments, and more. They describe technology tools that let children explore, develop, and share their creativity with others, and they share tips and tools for supporting children's music, art, and storytelling. They end the chapter and Section II with words of encouragement for teachers to always see themselves as learners in the digital age.

Chapter 7

Media Literacy in Early Childhood Education: Inquiry-Based Technology Integration

Faith Rogow

Introduction

Like pencils, digital technologies are tools. And like pencils, knowing how to use digital devices is an important part of being literate, but it isn't enough. Technology now places at our fingertips access to unimaginable amounts of information and a nearly limitless audience. In this world, we need to expand the traditional "three *R*s" to include reasoning and reflection. And we need to do so in ways that foster curiosity, creativity, and collaboration. That's where media literacy education comes in.

Nurturing Thinkers and Makers: The Purposes of Media Literacy Education

For something that often wears the label "21st-century literacy," the goals of media literacy education are surprisingly traditional: Give children all the power and benefits that come with being literate. The National Association for Media Literacy Education (NAMLE) phrased it this way: "The purpose of media literacy education is to develop the habits of inquiry and skills of expression needed to be critical thinkers, effective communicators, and active citizens in today's world" (NAMLE, 2007). To put it another way, media literacy is about helping children develop the life skills they need to become thinkers and makers in the multimedia environment that is their reality.

This doesn't mean abandoning books in favor of electronics. It's not a competition. After all, books are a media technology and a quick visit to a few websites makes it clear that one cannot be media literate without being print literate. But the reality of living in a digital culture is different enough from our recent analog/print-dominant past to compel an expansion of what we think of as literacy. Here are just a few of the changes that shape media literacy education:

- Digital devices now give us easy access to nearly unlimited amounts of information. People who don't have the skills to navigate through that sea of data and transform it into usable knowledge will quickly lose their way.

- In the digital world, even traditional "print" sources routinely combine text with images and audio. Just look at a current newspaper or a text book. People who only attend to the printed words miss a considerable amount of the available information.
- In the digital world, media are converged. Old arguments pitting television against computers or books against screens are irrelevant in a world where smartphones, laptops, and tablets function as music and video players and recorders, maps, magazines, textbooks, social networking hubs, games, clocks, cameras, and so much more. Children who have access to one thing have access to everything.
- Unlike their analog predecessors, digital cameras are cheap, provide immediate results, and make it is easy to create, reproduce, modify, and share pictures. This makes them accessible and developmentally appropriate for very young users in ways that older cameras were not.
- Important aspects of our lives now take place in the digital commons. The Web's participatory culture includes college courses, social networking and dating, political activism, fundraising, job applications, all manner of entertainment, research, collaborative classroom projects, commerce, and so much more (Jenkins, Clinton, Purushotma, Robison, & Weigel, 2006). If, as education visionary Paulo Freire proposed, literate people are able to engage with the *world* as well as the *word*, then literacy now requires the ability to use interactive online technologies.

Competencies and Outcomes

So what new skills does a person need to be literate in the digital world? If it has ever taken you several days to learn how to use a new phone, you understand the limits of simply teaching children how to use gadgets. Interfaces change so quickly that whatever young children learn now about using particular tools is likely to be outdated by the time they enter adulthood (or middle school!). So, simply using technology to teach, or encouraging children to use specific programs or devices won't guarantee future literacy. That's why media literacy education focuses on evergreen core competencies that apply across technologies (Scheibe & Rogow, 2012). These include:

- *Access*—Having physical access to high quality media technologies and content, and knowing how to use those resources effectively
- *Understanding*—Comprehending basic, explicit media messages
- *Awareness*—Taking note of the presence of media messages and their role in one's life
- *Analysis*—Decoding media messages in order to think critically and independently about them
- *Evaluation*—Making informed, reasoned judgments about the value or utility of media for specific purposes

- *Creation*—Making media messages for particular purposes using multiple media formats
- *Reflection*—Contemplating how personal experiences and values influence reactions to and production of media messages; assessing the full range of potential effects of one's production choices on oneself and others
- *Participation*—Initiating or joining in collaborative activities that are enabled by interactive media technologies
- *Action*—Taking meaningful steps to act on one's insights about media messages

These competencies are infused with the same spirit of inquiry that early childhood expert Ellen Galinsky described in *Mind in the Making* (2010) when she named critical thinking as an essential life skill. They extend well beyond equipping children to use technology; they prepare children to succeed as lifelong learners in a technology-rich world.

They also extend beyond nominal "media literacy" initiatives or activities designed for the explicit purpose of reducing screen time, reforming media, or mitigating negative media effects. Media literacy education may produce these results, but they aren't the goal. That distinction is important, because it changes what we actually do with children.

Shifting Paradigms

For many early childhood professionals, integrating media literacy education will require a paradigm shift. In the United States, the dominant paradigm governing the use of technology in early childhood education has been a medical one. Screen time is described using the language of addiction or disease, with warnings about "exposure" and pathologized outcomes like "play deficit disorder" (Levin, 2013). In this approach, the primary goal of interventions is safety.

Of course, safety is a bottom line for all early childhood professionals and because we're all committed to the well-being of children, it would be inappropriate to completely abandon a medical paradigm. But for curriculum designers, this medical-based framing creates a pedagogical conundrum. When we design lessons or curriculum by "backwards mapping" (Wiggins & McTighe, 2005) using safety as our objective, we invariably end up with screen time limits as the primary strategy, and often not much else. Case in point are the widely used child care licensing guidelines, *Caring for Our Children* (American Academy of Pediatrics, American Public Health Association, & National Resource Center for Health and Safety in Child Care and Early Education, 2011), that define as poor practice any screen time greater than 30 minutes per week, irrespective of how screens are being used (Standard 2.2.0.3).

Media literacy educators share many of the concerns about media effects that are the basis for such recommendations. But as *educators*, we also know that just as you can't help children become print literate by keeping them away from books, you can't help them acquire the skills they need to become media literate by keeping them away from screens. It's not about championing the use of technology for its own sake, but rather, about recognizing that in an educational environment, the basis for technology integration should be sound pedagogy, not clock management. To put it another way, we can't accomplish complex *educational* goals using only a *medical* model.

So while not ignoring health and safety concerns, curriculum designers use a different springboard. Rather than starting with the question "How do we keep children safe?" media literacy educators step outside the boundaries of a harm-or-not paradigm to ask, "How can we help children become literate in a digital world?" Because this question focuses on learning rather than risk avoidance, it opens up the rich array of strategies and activities that we typically associate with high-quality literacy instruction.

Emergent Media Literacy

For the same reasons that it is important to lay a foundation for print literacy starting at birth, it makes sense to begin media literacy as early as possible. On the surface, media literacy competencies might seem too sophisticated for infants and toddlers or even preschoolers. But like traditional literacy, we can establish an "ABCs" of media literacy—foundational skills and knowledge that are the building blocks for the complex capabilities we want children to develop as they grow (Rogow, 2002).

The six outcomes below are developmentally appropriate and achievable, even while remaining vigilant about the downsides of some media and technology. Media literate 5-year-olds can do the following:

1. Routinely ask relevant questions about ideas and information and use at least two different strategies for finding credible answers
2. Exhibit the habit of linking answers to specific evidence
3. Demonstrate knowledge that media are made by people who make choices about what to include and what to leave out (i.e., that all media messages are "constructed")
4. Choose appropriate pictures to accompany a story or report they have created and provide a basic explanation for their choice
5. Create and share original stories and reports using images, sounds, and words
6. Identify media technologies as tools that people use for learning, communication, and persuasion, and that (with permission) they can use, too

Using NAMLE's "habits of inquiry" and "skills of expression" as touchstones, we can craft educational practice that guides children toward mastery of these objectives. The pillars of that practice will be

• Modeling
• Questioning

- Decision making
- Integration

Some pillars will offer more suitable opportunities than others for working with children at particular developmental stages. For example, basic modeling—that is, paying attention to what children see us do with media technologies—will be an especially important strategy in infant and toddler care, while decision-making activities mostly match the developmental stages of 4- to 8-year-olds.

Modeling: What They See Is What They Learn Modeling is more than just making consistently healthy or intentional choices about when and where we use media technologies—though as the 2012 joint position statement on technology from NAEYC and the Fred Rogers Center underscores, this is an important starting place (NAEYC & Fred Rogers Center, 2012). Just as native speakers don't learn everything they need to know about language from listening to others, so-called digital natives (Prensky, 2006) don't automatically learn everything they need to know about technology from their environment. So as we model, it's important to explain what we're doing.

For example, say that children notice an interesting bird outside the window and want to know more. A teacher who was concerned primarily about limiting screen time might do research herself and come back to children with the answers she found. But that robs children of the opportunity to engage in the research process and learn how technology can be used productively as a part of that process. That's why a teacher employing media literacy education methods might kick off the inquiry process by making a list of children's questions about the bird, and then asking, "How could we find out the answers to our questions?" Prompt the children to come up with a number of options (e.g., asking a parent, calling the zoo, looking in a library book) and then help them pursue as many of their ideas as possible. Later you can talk through which sources were most helpful and why.

If children don't already include the Internet as one of their sources, you can add it to the list: "We can also use the Internet to find out more about that bird." Then describe what you do as you do it: "I'll use my laptop to log on. What question should I type into the search engine?" Or "I'll use my tablet to take a picture and then we'll do an image search to see if we can find out what type of bird it is. I start by tapping this icon with the camera on it to take the picture and then touch this button to send the picture to our smart board. Next time you see something interesting, you can use the camera that is on the shelf in the play area to take your own picture and I'll help you send it to the computer . . ."

Verbal play-by-play introduces key vocabulary and helps children see tablets and computers as tools that offer more than games or videos. It also provides opportunities to engage children in the practice of asking relevant questions.

Once you've keyed in a question or search term, explain the criteria you use to choose a particular source. As you scroll down the list of results, you can point and say, "Look at all the places that have answers! I'm going to look at the Audubon Society's answer because they have been bird experts for a long time and their scientists work to protect birds." Explaining how we choose trusted sources models the discernment children will eventually need to find credible sources themselves.

Questioning: Creating a Culture of Inquiry. Media literacy education builds on children's natural curiosity, encouraging their questions, helping them learn how to find credible answers, and also expanding the types of questions that they routinely ask about media messages. Of course, ultimately inquiry isn't just about asking questions, it's about asking *relevant* questions, which is why, in the last three decades, media literacy educators have developed question sets designed specifically to foster critical thinking about media messages.

The grid in Figure 7.1 provides one such question set that suggests categories of inquiry. The temptation is to pose these questions only when children encounter media with value messages we find objectionable. And, in fact, they can work quite well to help children look at such media with a more critical eye. For example, Ithaca College's Project Look Sharp has created an inquiry-based nutrition unit that helps youngsters question cereal ads.

However, children get ideas about the world from all sorts of media, not just from commercial or screen media. If the goal is to instill inquiry as a *habit*, then we need to engage children in asking questions about all types of media—including books.

One way to add inquiry to read-alouds without taking a lot of extra time is to follow a predictive question with a question about evidence. After asking "What do you think is going to happen next?" or looking at a book cover and asking "What do you think this book is about?" follow children's answers with "How do you know?" or "What makes you say that?"

For the youngest children, the answers are less important than simply establishing the expectation that their answers will be based on evidence. When children know that they are going to be asked for explanations, they attend to media differently (Rogow, 2011).

With preschoolers, we can also add vocabulary-distinguishing types of evidence. So we might point out to a youngster who provides a prediction based on having previously read the book, "You're using *evidence* based on *your experience*." Or we might say to a child whose answer is based on the book's cover illustration, "So your answer is based on *observation* and what you *noticed* in the picture." Careful observation and evidence-based answers link media literacy to science and prime children for higher-order thinking skills. Such links are possible because we are using a literacy-based approach rather than an inoculation approach.

Another way to develop the routine of asking questions is to plan regular opportunities to look at the media in children's environment. A few times a week, choose one media example—a toy or food package, an ad for a movie that children have been asking to see, a t-shirt, a painting, a restaurant menu, a favorite app—anything that children are already encountering. Then play a game in which children try to generate as many questions as they can think of about the example.

KEY QUESTIONS TO ASK WHEN ANALYZING MEDIA MESSAGES
Adaptations for Early Childhood Education

USING THIS GRID—Media literate people routinely ASK QUESTIONS IN EVERY CATEGORY—the middle column—as they navigate the media world. Occasionally a category will not apply to a particular message, but in general, sophisticated "close reading" requires exploring the full range of issues covered by the ten categories. • The specific questions listed here are suggestions; adapt them or add your own to match your learning goals and children's developmental level. • Encourage children to recognize that many questions will have more than one answer (which is why the categories are in plural form). • To help children develop the habit of giving evidence-based answers, nearly every question should be followed with a probe for evidence: HOW DO YOU KNOW? WHAT MAKES YOU SAY THAT? • Help children expand their thinking by asking questions like WHAT ELSE DO YOU NOTICE? • And remember that the ultimate goal is for children to learn to ask questions for themselves.

		SAMPLE QUESTIONS
AUTHORS & AUDIENCES	**AUTHORSHIP**	Who created this? or Who made up this story?
	PURPOSES	What does this want me to do? Who are they talking to? or Who is this for?
	ECONOMICS	Who paid for this? Who makes money from it?
	EFFECTS	What does the storyteller want me to remember? Is this good for me or people like me? Is it good for people who aren't like me?
	RESPONSES	How does this make me feel? What could I do about [insert topic or message]? What else do I want to know and how could I find out?
MESSAGES & MEANINGS	**CONTENT**	What does this want me to think (or think about)? What is this? What does this tell me about [insert topic]?
	TECHNIQUES	What do they want me to notice? How do they get me to notice what they want?
	INTERPRETATIONS	What might someone think about this who is [insert a type of person, e.g., older than me, from a farm, a teacher, a pet owner, etc.]?
REPRESENTATIONS & REALITY	**CONTEXT**	When was this made? Is it from a long time ago or now?
	CREDIBILITY	How do they know [what they are saying is true]? What is the evidence? Can I trust this source to tell me the truth about this topic? Is this fact, opinion, a little of both, or neither?

Figure 7.1 Key Questions to Ask When Analyzing Media Messages: Adaptations for Early Childhood Education

Courtesy of Faith Rogow

Questions can be silly or serious. Expand their thinking by offering one or two of your own questions (perhaps from the categories on the Key Questions grid). With older children, you might choose one of the questions and brainstorm ways to find answers.

The more we model asking probative questions, the more likely it is that children will begin to copy us and ask questions themselves. With enough reinforcement, the questioning becomes a habit that they apply to both the media they use and the media they create.

Decision Making: Let's Give 'Em Something to Talk About. For very young children, whose limited vocabulary and fine motor skills can inhibit complex communication, the highly accessible nature of digital media technologies opens up a world of rich expression. Carefully scaffolded opportunities to create media help children see tech devices as tools that can help them accomplish specific objectives.

Making media also happens to be one of the best ways to help people internalize the notion that all media are "constructed"—the concept from which all media analysis flows. In order for young children to gain an understanding of constructedness, we need to pair the use of technology with decision-making opportunities and conversations. Typical early childhood education settings are filled with such opportunities. For example:

- Invite children to label their own cubbies by asking, "What kind of picture would tell everyone that this is your cubby?" Help them take photographs—perhaps "selfies" or something else that would represent them. As children post their photos, let them share with one another their explanations for why their picture is a good self-representation. It is the sharing that will help children learn about themselves and the efficacy of their choices. For instance, the child who chooses a picture of Spiderman may find that he is one of many who love the superhero, so that might not work very well as a cubby identifier. Instead, he'll need to find something about himself that is unique. Reflecting on how best to represent themselves lays the groundwork for later years when children will be establishing a digital footprint and making decisions about what to post on their social networks.
- When children make their own stories into books, help them reflect on their choices for the cover. Ask, "Why did you pick this picture (or title)? How does it help people know what's in your book?" or "How does it make people interested in reading your book?" Then help children connect the lessons from making their own media to the media they use: "Just like you made choices about what to include on your book cover, the person who made this video/website/game/poster, etc., made choices. Why do you think they chose _____?"
- Help children better remember the details of their experiences and engage in perspective taking by providing cameras to document a special event, field trip, or neighborhood walk. Add a decision-making component by providing a prompt like "Take pictures of anything you find interesting and also one picture of something that would be interesting to _____. Fill in the blank according to your needs. For example, if children are having issues with gender stereotyping, the prompt might encourage them to consider what

would be of interest to a boy or a girl (which would then be followed up with a conversation that could help them expand their thinking). Or you could encourage imagination by asking children to look at the world from the perspective of a favorite superhero or book/game/film/TV character (very much like they do when they take on roles during free play). Or make the prompt more concrete by asking children to "take at least one picture that is from the point of view of a dog." Follow up with a guessing game to pick out which photos were through the dog's eyes. If needed, use your own photos to provide examples of how a subject appears when you're standing up or you are only a few inches from the ground. Alternatively, use scenes from a video with obviously tall and short characters (*Clifford, The Big Red Dog* works well). You can also use the photographs to practice sequencing, sorting, or as prompts for storytelling, reporting, or sharing the experience with families.

• Encourage family conversations by making a camera available to children so they can take photos at will about something important or interesting they did that day. Send the photo to the phone of the person who picks up the child so instead of asking, "What did you do today?" (which is too general for many young children to answer), a family member can "pass back" their phone and ask, "Tell me about this picture? What was happening?"

• To prepare for Family Day or Open House, involve children in making short videos about what happens on a typical day (Rogow, 2011). Engage them in conversations about what to shoot, as well as whether it is more truthful to simply record what happens on a given day, even if the day was unusual, or to re-enact events from their normal routine, even though it didn't actually happen that day. Let them know that the decisions they are making are just like the ones that news reporters make, and help them notice the things during their day that they left out. Once they are aware of their own production choices, they can begin to understand that people who make the media they use also decide what to include or leave out.

• Combine language development with a lesson on production choices and diversity by having children record a retelling of a familiar story. Invite them to think about what various characters sound like. Is a mouse's voice higher pitched than an elephant's voice? Why would that be? Do the heroes speak with the same accent as the people in your family or community? How about the villains? What about nonhuman sounds? Would the rooster say "cock-a-doodle-do" if it lived in the Philippines or France? (Hint: the answer is no). How could children create sound effects for things that happen in the story like a car going by or an insect flying? It is possible to do this kind of storytelling without technology, but recording the performance makes for a richer learning experience because it provides motivation, invites experimentation and sustained attention (because it is possible to return to the work later and make revisions), and makes it easier to share the finished product.

• Use an image search to gather diverse pictures related to a topic that children are exploring. Then have the group choose one that would be the best illustration for a summary of their work and ask them to explain their choice. Do they want a realistic photograph because it shows what they've actually learned, or perhaps a funny cartoon because people will want to know more about something that made them laugh? Any reasonable explanation is fine. At this age, it's less about the answers than engaging children in the decision-making process.

• Teach media production vocabulary and concepts by engaging children in conversations about their drawings. Ask questions like, "If I was standing in your picture, what would I see if I looked up or to the side? What's outside your *frame*?"

You can reinforce lessons about framing by connecting a video camera to a monitor and letting children move the camera to capture different parts of the room. If a camera isn't available, cut a rectangle in an index card and have children hold it a few inches from their faces and look through the hole. Invite them to notice what is and isn't included as they move their frame from side to side or closer to their eyes. The things they can see are in the "frame." Encourage children to notice that the things outside their frame are still in the room—they are just choosing not to include them. Point out that media makers do the same thing.

Alternatively, you can have children use their full bodies to make frames. Teacher John Landis tapes a line on the floor and designates one side as "inside the frame" and the other as "outside the frame." Then the class plays Simon Says with the leader directing players to place various body parts inside or outside the "frame." He follows up with a game of hokey pokey with hands and feet in or outside the "frame" of the circle (Hobbs & Moore, 2013).

You can also use drawings to have conversations about sound: "If I was standing in your picture, what would I hear? Would I be able to guess the sounds from the things you included in your drawing?" Or, with older children, even about props: "How would I know that this is your mom and not someone else's mom? What props could you include in your picture to show that this is your mom?" This kind of conversation not only introduces production vocabulary, but also sharpens observational skills as children reflect on the information conveyed by the objects that they include in their drawings.

When we put technology into children's hands, we position them as communicators and artists, rather than as powerless or naive consumers. When we add inquiry, we help them achieve the "skills of expression" they need to be literate in an ever-changing digital environment.

Integration: Making it Routine. Media literacy education is at its best when both inquiry and technology are seamlessly integrated into a child's day. This can be as simple as requiring children to articulate their plans for using a tablet before handing it over during choice time or providing easy access to tools like cameras so children can record at will things that they deem worthy of documentation.

Vivian Vasquez's description of children's "Tomato Trials" provides an excellent example of more complex integration (Vasquez & Felderman, 2013).

Building on kindergartners' interests in growing tomato plants, Vasquez starts the project by asking, "How could we find out about growing tomatoes?" Note that instead of simply telling children what to do, she offers them the chance to think about where to find credible information.

The children decide to do an online search and to ask people in their lives who garden. Online they encounter a device in which plants grow upside down. The children are intrigued by a commercial for the device and decide to test the ad's claims by growing their tomatoes in both the traditional way and with the special hanger.

They are also intrigued by a phrase from the ad—"back-breaking work"—and by the ad's implication that such work was "manly." To make sense of the unfamiliar phrase, they acted out the scene, discussed the gender stereotype, and ultimately decided that the stereotype was "unfair." Later they would act out alternatives to the ad, using new (and more accurate) information they had learned about growing tomatoes. As their plant experiment continues, the teacher helps the children use a word cloud to compare websites. The results help them determine the credibility of each site.

In this example, activities involving and not involving technology flow naturally into one another, and technology is used—with intention—to do tasks for which it is particularly well suited (like research and word cloud comparisons). Inquiry, critical thinking and language development are woven into everything. This is what high-quality media literacy education looks like in practice.

Conclusion

Some advocates suggest that because children encounter so much media outside of child care or school, early childhood educators should provide balance by avoiding use of screen technologies (Campaign for a Commercial-Free Childhood, Alliance for Childhood, & Teachers Resisting Unhealthy Children's Entertainment, 2012; American Academy of Pediatrics, American Public Health Association, National Resource Center for Health and Safety in Child Care and Early Education, 2011). Media literacy educators look at that same increase in the use of electronic screens and come to a different conclusion: It is precisely because our culture surrounds us with media that we need to model healthy and productive ways to integrate digital media technologies into our lives.

Developmentally appropriate practice would suggest that with technology, as with everything else, we need to let children know what they *can* do, not just what they aren't allowed to do. If we want children to understand that digital media technologies can be used for art making, learning, and communication, as well as entertainment, we need to demonstrate those possibilities. And if we want them to think critically about the values that media convey, we need to show them how to ask and find answers to relevant questions. By making technology integration about inquiry rather than inoculation and skill acquisition rather than acquiescence to a sales pitch, media literacy education provides a pedagogical path to those ends.

Teacher Takeaways

- Develop effective media literacy lessons and methods that help children develop the "habits of inquiry" and "skills of expression" they need to succeed in a digital world
- Understand that because our culture surrounds us with media is precisely why we need to model healthy and productive ways to integrate digital media technologies into our lives
- Model technology integration based on sound pedagogy rather than clock management
- Give children opportunities to make media to help them internalize the notion that all media are "constructed"—the concept from which all media analysis flows
- Teach critical thinking by actively involving children in decision making and reflection about the media they create and consume
- Help children learn to ask questions for themselves, by routinely modeling how to ask—and find answers to—relevant questions about the media you and the children use and create (not just about media that adults find objectionable)

Position Statement Alignment

> Early childhood educators who are informed, intentional, and reflective use technology and interactive media as additional tools for enriching the learning environment. They choose technology, technology-supported activities, and media that serve their teaching and learning goals and needs. They align their use of technology and media with curriculum goals, a child-centered and play-oriented approach, hands-on exploration, active meaning making, and relationship building. They ensure equitable access so that all children can participate. They use technology as a tool in child assessment, and they recognize the value of these tools for parent communication and family engagement. They model the use of technology and interactive media as professional resources to connect with colleagues and continue their own educational and professional development.
>
> NAEYC & Fred Rogers Center (2012), p. 10

References

American Academy of Pediatrics, American Public Health Association, & National Resource Center for Health and Safety in Child Care and Early Education (2011). *Caring for our children: National health and safety performance standards; Guidelines for early care and education programs* (3rd ed.). Elk Grove Village, IL: American Academy of Pediatrics; Washington, DC: American Public Health Association.

Campaign for a Commercial-Free Childhood, Alliance for Childhood, & Teachers. Resisting Unhealthy Children's Entertainment. (2012). *Facing the screen dilemma: Young children, technology and early education.* Boston, MA: Campaign for a Commercial-Free Childhood; New York, NY: Alliance for Childhood.

Galinsky, E. (2010). *Mind in the making: The seven essential life skills every child needs.* New York, NY: HarperCollins.

Hobbs, R., & Moore, D.C. (2013). *Discovering media literacy: Teaching digital media and popular culture in elementary school.* Thousand Oaks, CA: Corwin.

Jenkins, H., Clinton, K., Purushotma, R., Robison, A., & Weigel, M. (2006).*Confronting the challenges of participatory culture: Media education for the 21st century.* MacArthur Foundation White Paper. Retrieved from www.macfound.org/press/publications/white-paper-confronting-the-challenges-of-participatory-culture-media-education-for-the-21st-century-by-henry-jenkins/

Levin, D. (2013). *Beyond remote-controlled childhood: Teaching young children in the media age.* Washington, DC: NAEYC.

National Association for the Education of Young Children, & Fred Rogers Center for Early Learning and Children's Media at Saint Vincent College. (2012). *Technology and interactive media as tools in early childhood programs serving children from birth through age 8.* Washington, DC: NAEYC; Latrobe, PA: Fred Rogers Center for Early Learning and Children's Media at Saint Vincent College.

National Association for Media Literacy Education. (2007, November). *Core principles of media literacy education in the United States.* Retrieved June 2013, from http://namle.net/wp-content/uploads/2013/01/CorePrinciples.pdf

Prensky, M. (2006). *"Don't bother me mom—I'm learning."* St. Paul, MN: Paragon House.

Rogow, F. (2002). The ABCs of media literacy. *Telemedium, 1*(48), 3–5.

Rogow, F. (2011). Inquiring minds want to know: Media literacy education for young children. *Library Media Connection, 29*(4), 11–13.

Scheibe, C., & Rogow, F. (2012).*The teacher's guide to media literacy: Critical thinking in a multimedia world.* Thousand Oaks, CA: Corwin.

Vasquez, V., & Felderman, C. (2013).*Technology and critical literacy in early childhood.* New York, NY: Routledge.

Wiggins, G., & McTighe, J. (2005).*Understanding by design* (2nd ed.). Alexandria, VA: ASCD.

Resources

- Insighters Educational Consulting, www.insighterseducation.com
- Project Look Sharp, www.ithaca.edu/looksharp/
- *Mind in the Making*, www.mindinthemaking.org
- NAEYC/Fred Rogers Center Joint Position Statement, www.naeyc.org/content/technology-and-young-children
- National Association for Media Literacy Education, www.namle.net

Learn More . . .

- Scheibe, C., & Rogow F. (2012). *The teacher's guide to media literacy: Critical thinking in a multimedia world.* Thousand Oaks, CA: Corwin.
- Vasquez, V.M., & Felberman, C.B. (2013). *Technology and critical literacy in early childhood.* New York, NY: Routledge.

Chapter 8

Pioneering Literacy in the Digital Age

Lisa Guernsey and Michael H. Levine

Introduction

Early education has increasingly focused on language development and emergent literacy skills to prepare children to become strong readers by the third grade. Now, professionals are beginning to assess what role exists for digital tools and apps. In a multi-year project, New America and the Joan Ganz Cooney Center are exploring the early literacy landscape to determine how and if digital media and interactive technologies should be adopted—and to what extent programs have the resources and know-how to use them effectively. Previous studies have shown that many teachers are not yet prepared to use the new tools, and our 2012 scan of the app marketplace hinted at a mismatch: A plethora of new learning apps exists, but the most popular are primarily teaching basic skills such as how to identify the A, B, Cs. Parents and educators have been given little information on whether they work and how they should be incorporated into other literacy activities. Yet we also found several bright spots: Several programs are harnessing interactive media and new communications tools to assist parents and educators in promoting the skills and knowledge children need to read well. We call these programs "pioneers"— promising efforts that now need additional research and support to reach needed scale. We recommend that leaders in programs and communities should monitor digital innovation research and experimentation more closely, expand needed investments in program design and professional supports to effectively integrate technology, and take actions to inform parents and educators of the results.

Comienza en Casa: An on-the-ground example of iPads, Parents, and Early Literacy

One afternoon in rural Maine, a young woman steps up to the front door of a house trailer and knocks on the door. She works for a nonprofit organization called Mano en Mano/Hand in Hand, an early learning program funded by Maine Migrant Education. She has arrived for a home visit with a family from Mexico living in the area for most of the year, doing seasonal work such as fish processing, wreath making, and blueberry harvesting.

In her hands is an iPad—a tool incorporated into a new program called Comienza en Casa/It Starts at Home to help children develop early literacy, math and science skills, and promote their school readiness. Comienza en Casa uses carefully selected apps and tactile and hands-on early learning activities, and on this day, the home visitor has come to speak with the family about how various activities in the current unit have helped their children and to ask parents which learning goals should be a priority in the remaining two weeks of the unit. Families also attend an evening meeting once a month at the local elementary school with project staff and the local kindergarten teacher, which provides hands-on experiences using the iPads and trying out activities, before trying them at home.

One of the science units in the Comienza en Casa curriculum is "Life Sciences." It uses the e-book app Red Fox at Hickory Lane; an interactive app based on a Smithsonian picture book with an audio recording feature. Families can select and listen to the Spanish narration provided to participate together in the story experience and discussions about the fox. They might select an educational game, such as ABC Farm (available in English and Spanish), or the highly visual and interactive Seed Cycle app. They may decide to help their child tell a story using a creativity app such as Sago Mini Doodlecast or Puppet Pals Director's Pass, or they could use Book Creator to make a book about discoveries made while exploring living and nonliving things. Other activity choices include growing seeds, using the iPad to photograph and document growth, outdoor science explorations, and a group field trip to a local marine institute with a touch tank to learn about sea creatures, relevant in this coastal community. A one-page handout (in Spanish), How to Explore Plants with Your Children, is one of several family science resources offered during the season, available free online from the Peep and the Big Wide World website, including video clips in both English and Spanish.

"We wanted to be extremely intentional about the use of the iPad," said Bonnie Blagojevic, an Apple Distinguished Educator who co-designed the curriculum with her adult daughter, Ana Blagojevic, migrant education coordinator and advocate at Mano en Mano.

Blagojevic has seen children who are highly energized as soon as they see the tablet and start playing the games with their parents. One mother told the organizers that she appreciated the program's emphasis on "communication" and "spending more time with" her children, "teaching and learning with them." Her husband added: "She would say, come, come, come look at this, and she would show me something." Another parent of a young son said: "It was very valuable, very useful, as much for us as for the child. We learned a lot of things because we had never had one of these (an iPad)." One area sparked particular interest: making books. It was an eye-opener, the parent said, to see "the books that you can make and also the games, to learn counting and many other things. He really enjoyed the seed cycle app, planting and watching the seed grow."

The Literacy Challenge: How to Raise Strong Readers in a Digital Age

For many early childhood educators, the words *technology* and *reading* don't go together. Indeed, only recently after a 15-year hiatus did the field's most influential professional association, the National Association for the Education of Young Children (NAEYC) partner with the Fred Rogers Center to provide professional guidance to young child educators on the appropriate uses of technology (NAEYC & Fred Rogers Center, 2012). Literacy is one subject area that may require a special focus given that a recent national survey showed a drop in the amount of time children spend reading or being read to (whether online or off) between 2005 and 2011, while their time with TV or games increased (Common Sense Media, 2011). The follow-up study and report on screen media use, *Zero to Eight: Children's Media Use in America 2013* (Common Sense Media, 2013), found that overall screen time for children birth to 8 year old was down compared to 2011. Time spent on traditional screen media such as television, DVDs, and computers has decreased as access to mobile media devices has dramatically increased in 2 years, and time spent on mobile devices has increased for young children.

The rapid adoption of technology is roiling public debate over what young children should know and be able to do, but it has yet to forge a new pathway to reading success. Current education policies and practices have done little to address a national crisis in literacy that is sapping the potential of millions of young children. In 2012, the National Assessment of Educational Progress (NAEP), exam showed that only one-third of American fourth graders were reading at the proficient level (National Center for Education Statistics, 2012).

But the above story from rural Maine gives us hope. In 2012, New America and the Joan Ganz Cooney Center embarked on a project to scan the landscape for examples of literacy learning via technology. Comienza en Casa was one of several examples we encountered and labeled as "pioneers" for their innovative approaches to fostering early literacy skills in a digital age. The Comienza initiative embraces technology but relies not only on apps. Importantly, it embeds its tech-assisted approach within an already established migrant education program run by professionals who understand families. While it is still too soon to measure its long-term impact, the ingredients are there to make a positive difference in the children's early literacy and language development, not to mention the way families learn and grow together.

Our project is part of the national Campaign for Grade-Level Reading and started with our 2012 paper Pioneering Literacy in the Digital Wild West (Guernsey, Levine, Chiong, & Severns, 2012). We are basing our work on four principles:

1. To become proficient readers, children need to be raised in environments that support reading skills, background knowledge, and active discovery. Neither

skills (such as alphabet knowledge, word reading, and print awareness), nor knowledge (such as understanding concepts, oral language development, and vocabulary growth) are enough by themselves.

2. Technology can be a helpful ally in literacy development, but by itself is not the answer. What matters most is how parents, children, and educators use technology to strengthen their interactions with each other and improve children's familiarity with sounds, words, language, and knowledge.

3. Connected, engaged parents are crucial to children's success. Even parents without strong reading skills can make important contributions to their children's cognitive development and later reading success through conversation and joint engagement in learning via traditional and digital media.

4. To ignore technology is to miss opportunities for delivering new content and better teaching to the children who need it most, inadvertently allowing digital divides to grow wider.

The fourth principle is pushing us to help early childhood professionals become better versed in what new options may be available for themselves and the families they interact with. When used well, digital media can enable access to information and stories, while also connecting schools, teachers, students, and families within neighborhoods, around the nation and around the world. Blogging, social networking, podcasting, instant messaging, posting to newsgroups or boards, and the Internet itself have brought new ways to connect, collaborate, and share, transforming the way we live and work. Together, these advances have led to the emergence of what has been called a new "participatory culture" (Jenkins, Clinton, Purushotoma, Robinson, Weigel, 2009). This culture simultaneously requires a host of new literacy skills and affords a dramatic re-envisioning of learning environments for both children and teachers. Even young children are able to not only access but also produce content that can be shared and reacted to by a community beyond the classroom. New technologies also offer possibilities for augmenting traditional approaches to instruction, as well as providing more assistance to parents. They can help us develop mixed models that blend in-school and informal, out-of-school, learning.

In addition to Comienza en Casa, our initial scan, based in part on a "snowball sample" of examples drawn from interviews with early childhood leaders, led us to find several early childhood programs or initiatives that are using technology to reach parents and teachers: small but pioneering projects that help the adults in children's lives, especially those in disadvantaged families, learn how to promote literacy and use media to foster children's language development and eventual reading skills. Examples include using on-demand video to help illustrate best practices for parenting education, social media to provide new resources to parents and teachers, and daily texts and web-based messages to prompt storytelling and conversation. Our ongoing research for the Campaign for Grade-Level Reading and the Pritzker Children's Initiative is mapping and tracking creative ways to use technology.

These program innovations are emanating from across the professional landscape—from state libraries, public television, home-visiting programs, medical centers, school-based early reading programs such as Innovations for Learning and Success for All, and from science-based and professional development programs at organizations such as the TEC Center at Erikson Institute and the Ounce of Prevention Fund.

The App Marketplace: Tantalizing in Scope, Yet Promise Largely Unfulfilled

We also are exploring the marketplace—the products that one most associates with today's technology—the apps and interactive games that have become so plentiful. As of late 2013, the iTunes app store boasted more than 1,000,000 apps (W. Buckleitner, personal communication, December 8, 2013). In 2012, the Joan Ganz Cooney Center discovered that nearly 80% of the top-selling paid apps in the education category were aimed at children. Many of these apps claim they can help kids learn to read. We wondered: What features do they include that might back up such a claim?

In April 2012, we took a snapshot of the app marketplace on iTunes and in the Android store called Google Play. What we found was a digital Wild West, with tens of thousands of apps labeled educational and marketed to parents who receive little to no information about whether and how they work. Many of these apps claim to help teach reading, but as we found, the apps that parents are most likely to download are those that put a heavy emphasis on teaching letters, sounds, and phonics. Few address higher-level competencies that young children need in addition to basic skills to become strong readers. For example, among the iTunes App Store's most popular paid literacy apps, 45% targeted letters and sounds and half targeted phonics, but only 5% targeted vocabulary. None of the iTunes paid apps in the scan focused on comprehension, grammar and the ability to understand and tell stories, all critical to early reading competencies. (In 2014, we will take a second "snapshot" to determine if the marketplace is changing.)

This "market failure" comes as research shows that knowing the ABCs and other basic literacy skills, while important, are not enough to help children become strong readers. Children need background knowledge and vocabulary, too, and yet these abilities continue to be a tremendous weakness in children from low-income families' repertoires. The 2012 release of vocabulary scores from the NAEP is the latest evidence of this disconnect, with scores showing that students' vocabulary skills are tied to reading comprehension skills. On average, students from low-income families, as well as black and Hispanic students, received lower scores on the NAEP vocabulary test compared to white students and those from higher-income families. Until comprehension, knowledge and what many literacy experts describe as "deeper content expertise" are supported, American kids will continue to lag compared to children from nations in Asia and Europe whose reading competencies far outstrip our own. Currently, only a third of U.S. fourth graders and barely one in six children from low-income families are proficient readers by the fourth grade, contributing to wider achievement gaps and higher dropout rates.

Scaling Up: How to Go From Pioneering to Common Practice

The next phase is to document and explore the efficacy of several new strategies that policymakers and community leaders should consider to help parents and teachers "homestead" this digital Wild West. Schools and communities should conduct audits to determine whether and which families have access to technology and media and how they use it. Early childhood centers and schools should provide teachers with training on technology as a learning tool. Cities and neighborhoods should create physical places in partnerships with schools and libraries where parents and educators can come together to experiment with various media platforms (including print books and book-making projects) to foster literacy. And parent education campaigns should emphasize digital media's potential for learning and conversation between parents and children, not just for games or apps that children play alone.

Teachers have a huge role to play, but to enable them to fulfill their potential, we must start modernizing the early childhood teaching profession. In the 2011 report, *Take a Giant Step* (Barron et al., 2011), an advisory task force of teaching and learning experts led by the Joan Ganz Cooney Center and the Stanford School of Education, focused on changes required in teacher preparation programs, education schools, and inservice professional development. The taskforce found that to be effective, U.S. teachers need more robust professional preparation as well as more ongoing support than they currently receive, especially with respect to understanding children's learning and development, providing learning experiences with rich cognitive demands, and using new technologies to promote personalized learning and 21st-century skills. In the enhancing of teacher education, digital tools can play significant roles—for instance in online courses, connected learning communities, and in websites and other media offering video teaching examples, curriculum plans, and materials. Leadership at the school, district/community, state, and national level is essential for capitalizing on opportunities made possible by technology integration in the classroom.

Although some teachers are taking on the challenge of learning how to incorporate technology into the classroom on their own initiative, they are in the minority and typically have access to a strong social network of support, or work in pioneering programs and school districts. Yet, professional consensus is beginning to form, led by the 2012 joint position statement of the NAEYC and the Fred Rogers Center, that technology has an increasingly vital role in educational practices for teachers of young children. The box below (reprinted from *Take a Giant Step,* Barron et al., 2011) speaks to the growing consensus.

Excerpts from policy statements and position papers authored by educational organizations

Statements from the International Reading Association, 2009:

- Internet, multimedia and other information and communication technologies (ICTs) need to be considered and integrated in literacy education.
- Providing adequate education and staff development will ensure that each teacher is prepared to effectively integrate new literacies into the curriculum.
- Teacher education programs can play a critical role in preparing teachers to use new technologies for instruction.
- Creative initiatives to increase access, provide professional development, and enhance teacher education should be supported by professional literacy organizations.
- An intensive program of research on literacy and technology will enable us to better understand the rapid changes taking place in the nature of literacy and literacy instruction.
- We must pay particular attention to the critical literacies that new technologies demand.

Barron et al. (2011)

Position Statement Alignment

Digitally literate educators who are grounded in child development theory and developmentally appropriate practices, and who are technologically and media literate, have the knowledge, skills, and experience to select and use technology and digital media that are appropriate for the ages and developmental levels of the children in their care, and they know whether, how, and when to integrate technology into the program effectively.

Educators need positive examples of how to successfully adapt and integrate technology into the classroom to enhance children's learning.

Educators need guidelines for the informed, intentional, appropriate, and integrated selection, use, and evaluation of technology tools with young children.

In the digital age, educators need pre-service and professional development opportunities to test new technology tools, learn about appropriate use of technology, and gain the knowledge and skills to implement them effectively.

NAEYC & Fred Rogers Center (2012), p. 4

Table 8.1 identifies a handful of pioneering projects where creative uses of technology help support families and communities.

Table 8.1 Pioneering Projects: Supporting Families and Communities With Creative Uses of Technology

---

- **The Baby Elmo Program:** Using "Sesame Beginnings" videos as a launch pad for interaction with their children, incarcerated fathers are provided with models for positive engagement with their children during visits and after release from prison. The videos are from Sesame Workshop, which has hundreds of video clips, literacy games, and tools.

- **Comienza en Casa/It Starts at Home:** This program, which is part of the Maine Migrant Education Program, incorporates iPad use, traditional early learning activities and information to help parents improve school readiness and literacy skills for preschool and kindergarten children who speak little to no English.

- **The Early Learning Environment from Fred Rogers Center:** In an interactive online space, parents and educators can customize "playlists" of videos, games, and activities online and offline, designed by early childhood experts.

- **Mind in the Making Learning Communities:** Thirty-five organizations in 22 states have created communities of parents, educators, and health professionals who come together regularly to watch video clips from baby experiments and discuss ideas from *Mind in the Making,* a critically acclaimed book by Ellen Galinsky of the Families and Work Institute.

- **Pocket Literacy via Ounce of Prevention Fund:** The Ounce of Prevention Fund, a national nonprofit, has partnered with Parent University's Pocket Literacy Coach in sending daily texts to parent's mobile phones with ideas for literacy activities and reassurances to lessen the stresses of parenting. In 2013, 1,500 Head Start parents will participate in an evaluation of the service.

- **Storytimes Online:** The Idaho Commission for Libraries offers a DayByDayID. org website with daily messages to parents about literacy-building activities and daily featured e-books from Tumblebooks, a subscription service free to library users. Virginia and South Carolina, the origin of the idea, have built similar programs.

- **Wonderopolis:** Daily tweets, Facebook posts and links to videos about the "wonder of the day" designed to inspire conversation, vocabulary building and further exploration. From the National Center for Family Literacy, which has published more than 700 wonders so far.

Conclusion

We are at an opportune moment for harnessing digital media to support parents, educators, and children in building the next generation's reading skills. It's time for new roadmaps and new roles for educators and families, especially given the growing numbers of young children already swimming in digital media. Tech tools and social networking are becoming a bigger part of parents' and educators' daily lives, and pioneering programs are already thinking outside the box by using technology to promote literacy. But as we have discovered in our research, technology's potential to be a game changer across the country will not be reached unless technology is tapped to provide vital new supports for parents and educators. At its best, the technology *complements* the work of trained teachers and parents. It should not and cannot effectively replace it.

Teacher Takeaways

- Consider the use of e-books, videos, digital slide shows, "wonder of the day" online entries and more along with printed books to stimulate language development and conversation in the classroom.
- Be aware that popular apps for teaching reading may focus primarily on decoding skills (such as letter identification and phonics); research on literacy shows that learning to read involves a focus on vocabulary development, comprehension, and oral language skills in addition to decoding skills.
- Remember that the technology world is changing every day, but that the needs of students, who may be advanced digital navigators and still emerging readers, are not.
- Rely on your craft knowledge and research on effective literacy instruction to separate the fashion of the day from promising innovations of the sort described in this chapter.
- Integrate new tools with proven approaches that already work to become a strong early literacy educator.

References

Barron, B., Cayton-Hodges, G., Bofferding, L., Copple, C., Darling-Hammond, L., & Levine, M. (2011). *Take a giant step: A blueprint for teaching children in a digital age.* New York, NY: The Joan Ganz Cooney Center.

Common Sense Media. (2011). *Zero to eight: Children's media use in America 2011.* San Francisco, CA: Author.

Common Sense Media. (2013). *Zero to eight: Children's media use in America 2013.* San Francisco, CA: Author.

Guernsey, L., Levine, M., Chiong, C., & Severns, M. (2012). *Pioneering literacy in the digital Wild West: Empowering parents and educators.* Washington, DC: Campaign for Grade-Level Reading.

Jenkins, H., Clinton, K., Purushotma, R., Robinson, A. J., & Weigel, M. (2009). *Confronting the challenges of participatory culture: Media education for the 21st century.* Chicago, IL: The John D. and Catherine T. MacArthur Foundation. Retrieved from www.macfound.org/media/article_pdfs/JENKINS_WHITE_PAPER.PDF

National Association for the Education of Young Children & Fred Rogers Center for Early Learning and Children's Media at Saint Vincent College. (2012). *Technology and interactive media as tools in early childhood programs serving children from birth through age 8.* Washington, DC: NAEYC; Latrobe, PA: Fred Rogers Center for Early Learning and Children's Media at Saint Vincent College.

National Center for Education Statistics. (2012). *The nation's report card: Vocabulary results from the 2009 and 2011 NAEP reading assessments,* (NCES 2013–452). Washington, DC: Institute of Education Sciences, U.S. Department of Education.

Resources

Apps, Software, Online Resources, and Activity Sites

- *ABC Farm,* Peapod Labs, http://peapodlabs.com
- The Baby Elmo Program, http://elp.georgetown.edu/pdf/Barretal2011.pdf
- *Book Creator*, Red Jumper Studio, www.redjumper.net/bookcreator/
- DayByDayID.org, http://daybydayid.org/
- Early Learning Environment (Ele), Fred Rogers Center, http://ele.fredrogerscenter. org
- Google Play, https://play.google.com/store?hl=en
- Innovations for Learning, www.innovationsforlearning.org
- iTunes App Store, https://itunes.apple.com/us/genre/ios/id36
- *Mini-Doodlecast*, Sago Sago, www.sagosago.com/app/sago_mini_doodlecast
- Peep and the Big Wide World, www.peepandthebigwideworld.com
- Pocket Literacy Coach, https://pocketliteracy.com
- *PuppetPals HD*, Polished Play, LLC, www.polishedplay.com
- *Red Fox at Hickory Lane*, Oceanhouse Media, www.oceanhousemedia.com/products/ redfoxhickorylane/
- *Seed Cycle*, Seed Pod Productions, www.seedpodproductions.com
- *Storykit*, ICDL Foundation, http://en.childrenslibrary.org/about/foundation.shtml
- Storytimes Online, http://youthliterature.com
- Wonderopolis, http://wonderopolis.org/

Websites

- Campaign for Grade-Level Reading, http://gradelevelreading.net
- Comienza en Casa/It Starts at Home, www.manomaine.org/programs/mep/comien zaencasa
- Common Sense Media, www.commonsensemedia.org
- International Reading Association, www.reading.org
- Mano en Mano/Hand in Hand, www.manomaine.org/
- Mind in the Making, http://mindinthemaking.org
- NAEP, National Assessment of Educational Progress, http://nationsreportcard.gov
- NAEYC & Fred Rogers Center Joint Position Statement, www.naeyc.org/content/ technology-and-young-children
- National Center for Families Learning, http://familieslearning.org
- Success for All, www.successforall.org

Learn More ...

- Joan Ganz Cooney Center, www.joanganzcooneycenter.org
- *Learning at Home: Families' Educational Media Use in America,* www.joangan zcooneycenter.org/publication/learning-at-home/
- New America's Early Education Initiative and Learning Technologies Project, http:// education.newamerica.net
- Ounce of Prevention Fund, www.ounceofprevention.org/home/index.php
- *Pioneering Literacy in the Digital Wild West,* www.joanganzcooneycenter.org/ publication/pioneering-literacy/

- Shuler, C., Levine, M., & Rhee, J. (2012) *iLearn II: An analysis of the education category of Apple's app store*. New York, NY: Joan Ganz Cooney Center. www.joanganzcooneycenter.org/publication/ilearn-ii-an-analysis-of-the-education-category-on-apples-app-store/
- TEC Center at Erikson Institute, http://teccenter.erikson.edu
- *Zero to Eight: Children's Media Use in America 2013*, Common Sense Media, www.commonsensemedia.org/sites/default/files/research/zero-to-eight-2013.pdf

Chapter 9

Technology to Support Dual Language Learners

Karen N. Nemeth

Introduction

Early childhood educators are faced with an extraordinary rise in the linguistic diversity of the children they teach. At the same time, there is an extraordinary growth in the array of technology supports teachers can access to make sure they succeed in working with diverse groups of children, families, and colleagues. The goal of this chapter is to inform educators of young dual language learners (DLLs) about the technology options available to you and help you feel comfortable selecting and using them.

One in four preschool-aged children live with a parent who speaks a language other than English, and the number is closer to 30% for Head Start children (Schmit & Firgens, 2012). While Spanish is, by far, the most frequently appearing non-English language in early childhood classrooms (about 75% of DLLs), there are more than 150 other languages that teachers may encounter (Batalova & McHugh, 2010). Throughout the United States, we see early childhood classrooms with three or more languages, and each year may bring new and different languages. According to the Office of Head Start, any child who speaks a language other than English at home is considered a dual language learner or DLL ("Dual language learners," 2009). Whether or not they also speak English, children who are growing up with a home language other than English have learned and will continue to learn some concepts in that home language. While they are in the early childhood years, DLLs need teachers who understand the unique needs and assets they bring to school. This level of diversity brings five key challenges to early childhood educators:

1. How can I help each child feel welcome and safe?
2. How can I communicate with each child in her home language?
3. How can I connect with each child to help him learn English?
4. How can I communicate with the families?
5. How can I help DLL children and their families communicate with and be engaged in the community?

Technology has much to offer as teachers and administrators search for solutions to these challenges. Developmentally appropriate early childhood education programs also have a responsibility to ensure equitable access to technology resources (NAEYC & Fred Rogers Center, 2012). Understanding the needs of DLLs and their families is the first step toward making decisions about technology that will meet the needs of the students with whom you work.

Position Statement Alignment

> Because every child needs active practice in the four domains of language and literacy (speaking, listening, writing, and reading), technology resources should support active learning, conversation, exploration, and self-expression. Technology should be used as a tool to enhance language and literacy, but it should not be used to replace personal interactions. The role of language in developing self-esteem and social skills must also be considered in making technology plans for diverse classrooms.
>
> NAEYC & Fred Rogers Center (2012), p. 9

What Do DLLs Need?

Key recommendations have appeared in recent reviews of the research (Castro, García, & Markos, 2013, Espinosa, 2010, 2013; Goldenberg, Hicks, & Lit 2013). As leading researchers are reading the same body of research and coming to very similar conclusions, these recommendations are very compelling. Later in the chapter you will read about technology resources and strategies that can address all of these recommendations related to:

- Home language
- Family engagement
- Adaptations
- Professional development

Home Language. Early childhood educators must support each child's development in language and literacy in both home language and English in some way. How this happens will vary depending on the languages spoken by the teacher and the availability of resources. Support of the home language helps the child to build on prior knowledge developed in that language and, therefore, supports both home language and English development. Supporting the home language is also an important way to respect the unique assets each child brings to school.

Family Engagement. While family engagement is considered an important component of any school program, it takes on added significance for programs working with linguistically diverse populations. When teachers don't speak the language of the child, it is very important that they help parents fill the gap with good home language literacy practices at home. Connections with families help teachers bring authentic and relevant aspects of each child's culture into the school environment. Building relationships with families and helping them understand and participate in their children's school experiences is of utmost importance when working with young children who are DLLs.

Adaptations. One point that has come up repeatedly in the research reviews is that elements of high quality early childhood education are valuable for DLLs, but are not sufficient to help them achieve success. Adaptations that address the unique needs of language learners in the early years must be provided. In today's environment of increasing scrutiny related to meeting national and state standards, documenting outcomes with assessments and data, and maintaining funding by meeting these requirements, educators are concerned about how they can make sure that DLLs are learning and performing as they should. Increased recognition of the importance of authentic conversations and teacher-child interactions are making the ability to communicate with each student a primary concern (Dickinson & Porche, 2011). The adaptations needed for each DLL will be unique and all the more challenging because of the lack of language-specific resources available in most classrooms.

Professional development. With the rising numbers of DLLs in early childhood education, it is safe to say that most early childhood education teachers will have at least some children who are DLLs in their class at some point. Nationwide, there is still a significant shortage of qualified early childhood teachers who speak any of the many languages appearing in preschool and early elementary classes. Yet, general education and special education teachers need to learn about the developmental and educational needs of young dual language learners, and they need to learn how to work effectively with them. ESL and Bilingual Education teachers may know about supporting DLLs, but their teacher preparation programs rarely provide enough information about meeting the unique learning needs of children in the early years. Resources must be made available and accessible for early childhood educators as they prepare for their teaching careers and as continuous support while they are working in the field.

What Affordances Can Technology Provide?

Technology has many advantages to offer early childhood educators. After all, this whole book is devoted to sharing those advantages with readers. Here we will focus on particular advantages that technology can offer to early childhood educators and families to improve the early learning experiences of DLLs.

- *Internet connections* allow teachers and children instant access to a window to the world of different languages, countries, and cultures.
- *Digital devices offer flexibility* so that the learning experience can be individualized for each student and can include supports for each child's language.
- *Digital devices are critical for supporting different languages.* They can provide instant translations with audio pronunciations, access to people who can serve as interpreters, specialized programs that teach new languages, and materials or activities that allow users to switch languages as needed.

- *Technology-based activities* may offer tracking capabilities so the learning progress of each individual child can be tracked—as with websites like Smarty Ants or My Child—even when the teacher doesn't speak the same language as the child.
- *Here and now responsiveness*—also called temporal proximity—is an affordance of digital technologies that makes it possible to answer questions, clarify concepts and expand on vocabulary for DLLs right at the moment they arise. This is so important in helping all young learners, and particularly for young DLLs, to make instant connections between words and concepts and take advantage of teachable moments.
- *Cultural responsiveness and flexibility* can be at the teacher's fingertips with the use of technology at websites like Mama Lisa's World or apps like Lulu in Polynesia. Teachers and students can learn about each other's cultures and culturally appropriate content can be added to learning centers and lesson materials as needed.
- *Organization and searchability* are features that can make teachers' jobs much easier as their collections of materials grow with the new languages they must serve. Loading music, e-books, activities, and assessment records into digital files like iTunes makes it possible for the teacher to store what he or she needs in any language needed without overloading shelves and closets. Once stored, these items can be searched instantly with a few key words so the teacher can find just the right song or story to expand learning as it happens and to find it in the language needed at that moment for one child, a small group, or the whole class.
- *Portability* is something we all appreciate about smartphones and tablet devices. For early childhood educators in diverse programs, portability takes on added significance. If a young DLL starts crying and tries to tell the teacher what's wrong, does the teacher have to find and interrupt a bilingual staff person to help solve the problem? No, not if that teacher could be allowed to pull out her smartphone and use an instant translation app to find out what the problem is and what needs to be done. Out on the playground, children might gather around an unusual bug, but the children who are DLLs won't understand the teacher's explanation. Consider how this experience might be different if the teacher pulls out a tablet and finds a video that shows more about the insect.
- *Self-paced learning* can be an important advantage for children who are challenged with learning a new language while also trying to learn new content. It allows students to repeat an activity until they understand both the concept and the vocabulary involved. Many learning programs and apps provide instant feedback that can build the students' confidence and help them feel that they are staying on track. Some examples include Sharing app or the online games by Duckie Deck, or Left Right Pup by Mrs. Judd's Games. They also make it possible for a child who is a DLL to have learning time without the pressure and scrutiny of teacher and classmates who don't speak

the same language. While it would certainly be important to avoid creating a sense of isolation for a child, some opportunities for self-paced learning can provide a welcome break and an experience of competence.

- *Multi-touch capabilities* of tablets and tables give DLLs the chance to play and learn collaboratively with friends who may or may not speak their same language. All of the children can benefit from the social time and from learning each other's languages (McCann, 2012).
- *Digital cameras, recorders, interactive whiteboards, tablet devices* are among the options that allow teachers to create their own materials. This feature goes from being a luxury to a necessity when teachers find they need to create class books that can be produced in any language needed at the time, or games and activities that support the language learning needed by their students.

Technology Solutions for Creating a Language Ready Environment

Technology can play an important role in helping the teacher, the student, the family, and the classroom be ready for the school year to start in a welcoming way. Teachers can use technology to reach out to families before school starts and find out more about the home language, culture, interests, and assets they will bring to the school when their child gets started. Begin with a home language survey that has been translated into the family's native language (Nemeth, 2012b).

Find out which mode of communication families prefer. Some teachers are using text messages to stay in touch, while others find that email works better. Using technology resources like the My Child website or Tadpoles.com makes it possible to have linguistically and culturally appropriate music, books, materials, and displays ready for the child's first day even on short notice. Every child and family should walk into the classroom on the first day and see his or her native language represented and respected. When teachers have contact with families before the start of the school year, they may be able to recommend language learning apps such as the Pocoyo learning activities from the HITN Early Learning Collaborative, or the Rosetta Stone Kids Lingo Word Builder app that families can use at home or at the public library to work with their children on preparing to learn and play in their new school.

Technology Solutions for Expressive Language

For young children, practicing oral language is an essential component of their continuing language development and for early literacy development as well. Young DLLs need encouragement and opportunities to express their thoughts and knowledge in their home language and in English. Teachers struggle with this goal when they don't understand the child's home language well and are unsure about how well the child is doing with their expressive language progress.

- Use any device available to record the child's oral language and save for their portfolio. Parents or other staff can help translate their speech for the record (Nemeth, 2009).
- Digital storytelling apps like My Story by Hi Def and websites like VoiceThread.com allow children to create stories alone or collaboratively and recording their expressive language is integral to this process (Nemeth & Simon, 2013).
- Apps that use fun or game-like formats encourage children to play with their voices like SmackTalk app for iPad and iPhone and can be very encouraging to shy DLLs who can talk to the device sometimes, instead of performing for a teacher.
- Speech recognition software has been appearing in a growing number of apps like the Rosetta Stone Kids apps. This type of activity actually gives the young student feedback on whether or not their pronunciation is close enough to the target language. For older students, using voice to text dictation is another way to fine-tune their oral language so that the text more closely reflects what they try to say.

Technology Solutions for Receptive Language

Technology tools can help each individual child increase their receptive vocabulary of rich, interesting, and useful words in their home language and in English. Also in this category are resources that help teachers learn to communicate with DLLs in both their home language and English.

- E-books with audible stories in two languages such as the iPad and Android versions of bilingual stories by Ana Lomba help both students and teachers learn each other's languages (Simon & Nemeth, 2012).
- Using digital photographs of the real people, places, and things in the child's environment to create class books, manipulatives, puzzles, and games is the best way to ensure DLLs make the learning connections they need in English and their home language (Nemeth & Simon, 2013).
- Computer games and apps with verbal cues and simple, audible instructions like the Memory Train app by Piikea Street give DLLs opportunities to show what they know and can do in either of their languages.
- Translation apps such as iTranslate or Google Translate will help teacher and child communicate with each other and learn to recognize words in each other's language.
- Ask families to record favorite stories, rhymes, and fingerplays in their home language to bring authentic representations into the classroom for DLLs and their friends who speak different languages to share (Nemeth, 2009).
- Translation software can help teachers make classroom labels in multiple languages as needed (Nemeth, 2012b). Smart pen technology like the Anybook Reader pen or scanable QR codes can allow teachers to create

"talking labels" to support receptive language throughout the classroom (Simon & Nemeth, 2012).

Technology Solutions for Content Learning

Give careful consideration to the real role of language in the child's early learning and social interactions. Look for resources and activities that reflect developmentally appropriate practice. If you wouldn't use ditto sheets or flashcard memorization assignments in your classroom, then don't select apps or interactive whiteboard activities that work just like ditto sheets or flashcards (Nemeth, 2012a). Focus on using technology to help young DLLs learn the content and concepts they need to know in your grade or age group. Keep in mind that when a young child learns a concept securely in their home language, they will have a relatively easy time transferring that knowledge to English, so the most important focus is helping children learn—not just helping them learn English (Nemeth, 2009).

- There are a number of apps that have been developed to help young children practice and learn key concepts in engaging ways but with little or no language involved, such as Toca Boca Store app. They make it possible for a DLL to practice sorting or counting, for example, without being impeded by a language mismatch in the instructions.
- Fiction and nonfiction e-books can provide rich content learning for young DLLs in whatever language they need. Some are even available online for free. Just be sure to have a bilingual adult review the books you choose in different languages to make sure they don't contain any inappropriate content.
- Apps and games that involve cooking or baking, like Cupcake or Cookie Doodle, can be very useful because they allow realistic depictions of measuring, counting, predicting, and spatial reasoning to be practiced no matter what language the child may speak.
- Video examples from websites such as Youtube.com, teachertube.com, and nationalgeographic.com provide detailed visual learning supports. If the children become fascinated by equipment at a nearby construction site, showing them some videos about how that equipment works will build knowledge for all of the children, especially the ones who don't understand the teacher's verbal explanations (Nemeth, 2013).
- There are apps, app systems, and websites available that provide a tracking and reporting feature so teachers can assess each child's progress toward learning key concepts while using these technology resources such as My Child and Smarty Ants.

A word of caution is warranted here. There are hundreds of free apps available that claim they "teach" skills in math or literacy domains. An app that does not adapt to different children's ability and progress, or that simply presents unrelated words or skills for rote memorization will not likely result in much learning. Providing mindless busy work for DLLs is a sure way to prevent them from using their time for real content learning. Look for games and activities that grow with the child's ability, present appropriate challenges, and provide content that is based in meaningful contexts. Apps that give students opportunities to solve problems, plan structures, or facilitate interactions, for example, will be a more valuable use of the young DLL's time.

Technology Solutions for Embedding Authentic Culture

Helping young children stay in touch with their home countries shows that this aspect of their identity is respected and valued in class. Learning more about each child's previous and current culture will also make it possible for the teacher to create authentic and relevant cultural references in the classroom environment and in activities and lessons.

- Use communication platforms like Skype or Google Hangout to arrange conversations with family members or "pen pals" in other countries. This can be a great way to help a young child stay in touch with his or her heritage and to share insights about the culture and community of origin for each child.
- Rather than making music choices based on assumptions, ask each family to provide you with information or recordings of the music they feel represents their home culture.
- Print images from the Internet to enhance the cultural relevance of each area of the classroom. Some examples might include photos of buildings in other countries for the block area or artworks for the art area.
- Use customizable flashcard apps as portable picture communication tools so the child can point to a picture that will show you what she needs (Nemeth, 2013).

Technology Solutions for Family Engagement

Family engagement is not an event—it's a process. Technology tools give the early childhood educator many ways to stay in touch with families, to keep them informed about their child's learning and experiences in school, and to keep learning more about the family to continuously adapt learning environment and activities for each child.

- For many families, the main connection to the Internet happens via smartphone. Short messages may be easier for families to understand and use than lengthy newsletters and handouts. Be sure that the majority of your messages are positive and informative. If families hear negative comments about their child, constant reminders of rules and requirements, or complaints about their child's progress or behavior, they are not as likely to keep in touch with the teacher or the school. Each program needs to have its own policy about what can and cannot be sent digitally. Some programs encourage teachers to send photos of young DLLs engaging happily in the day's learning and play activities to families who may not understand if the teacher simply tries to tell them about the child's good day. Other programs forbid texting, or sharing photos, due to concerns about misuse, privacy, and confidentiality issues.

- Asking families to help by discussing certain topics with their child, by reading and singing to their child in their home language, or by volunteering in the classroom can be accomplished with the easy access of communications technology.
- To empower families and help them feel like important partners in their child's education, provide opportunities for them to have their say in school plans, policies, and activities via Facebook page, blog comments, or direct email.

Position Statement Alignment

Digital technologies can be used to support home languages by creating stories and activities when programs lack the funds to purchase them or when languages are hard to find. Technology can be used to explore the cultures and environments that each child has experienced, and it allows children to communicate with people in their different countries of origin. Technology may be needed to adapt existing materials; for example, by adding new languages to classroom labels, translating key words in books and games, or providing models for the writing area. With technology, adults and children can hear and practice accurate pronunciations so they can learn one another's languages. If teachers do not speak a child's language, they may use technology to record the child's speech for later translation and documentation of the child's progress.

NAEYC & Fred Rogers Center (2012), p. 9

Evaluating the Quality and Appropriateness of Technology Choices

Each school, and each teacher within the school, will be faced with many technology choices to make. Other chapters in this book will address concerns about digital media literacy and safe Internet practices. Answers that may seem simple in some contexts become more complex when considering culturally and linguistically diverse families. For example, it may be easy for a school to create a policy banning all sharing of digital photos by phone or Internet. Teachers may realize, however, that photos are the only effective way they have of communicating with newcomer parents who don't speak English. In that case, they may decide to print out pictures to hand to parents or mail home.

Teachers may find they depend more on technology solutions for DLLs once they get to know the options. It then becomes important to keep a balance such that it doesn't become too easy to just leave the DLLs alone with the computer or tablet for too much time. Other teachers may find they worry too much about keeping technology use to a minimum so that they may actually deprive DLLs of important learning experiences. This can only be determined on a case-by-case basis.

In a recent Early Childhood Technology Network blog post, "Designing a Rubric for Preschool Bilingual Apps" (Nemeth, 2012a), I shared some key points that can help early childhood educators select apps (and other technology resources) that will be appropriate for young DLLs. Here are some questions to consider:

- What languages are available?
- Are all the languages included or will they be an added expense via in-app purchases?
- Does the app provide home language and/or English support activities?
- Does the complexity of the language in the app match the needs of the students? Is it meant to provide isolated vocabulary words or sentences in conversational or conceptual contexts?
- What is the learning purpose of the app and does it match the learning objectives of your students?
- Does the app focus on low-value words like shapes, animals, or the alphabet? Or does it focus on sentences within stories, or songs?
- Can you see samples of the English and the other languages used in the app to decide if the translations are clear and culturally appropriate?
- Will the app offer rote memorization or will it stimulate interaction and conversation between students or between the student and the teacher?
- Are the images and characters culturally appropriate and respectful?
- Does the app provide features needed for your students such as sound recording, progress tracking, or offer choices and levels of play?

Individual teachers can use questions like these to make their own purchases, but putting these questions into the hands of a technology leader or an acquisition committee can be even more effective. The answers are not often simple.

Position Statement Alignment

> As linguistic and cultural diversity continue to increase, early childhood educators encounter a frequently changing array of languages. Appropriate, sensitive use of technology can provide the flexibility and responsiveness required to meet the needs of each new child and assure equitable access for children who are dual-language learners.
>
> NAEYC & Fred Rogers Center (2012), p. 9

While it is possible that children can learn a small bit of language from passive viewing or listening, this is often lost when not used productively (Espinosa, 2013). Active learning, ample opportunities to use the home language and

English in conversations and discussions, and appropriate challenges for each child are key quality indicators to seek.

Conclusion

In a nationwide survey of early childhood educators about their use of technology, only 60% of respondents said they use technology to teach young DLLs (Simon, Nemeth, & McManis, 2013). The options described in this chapter will hopefully pave the way to a significant change in views and practices for diverse early childhood programs. The more educators learn about the technology resources available and how to use them, the more they can elevate the quality of their programs for young DLLs and their ability to successfully individualize learning for every student.

In keeping with the NAEYC & Fred Rogers Center joint position statement (2012), "Technology should be used as a tool to enhance language and literacy, but it should not be used to replace personal interactions. The role of language in developing self-esteem and social skills must also be considered in making technology plans for diverse classrooms" (p. 9). Since DLLs make up 25% of the population of young children in the United States, and they are the fastest growing segment of the population, finding new and innovative ways to ensure their academic success is of critical importance to the overall success of our national education system. Careful, intentional, and creative uses of technology can make it possible to elevate the entire field by improving outcomes for this key quarter of the young children served in early childhood education. No matter how sophisticated it may be, technology is still just one of the tools at a teacher's disposal. It is how a teacher masters and uses these tools that really leads to the success of young DLLs.

Teacher Takeaways

1. Use technology to improve your ability to connect with and build relationships with young children who are DLLs and their families.
2. Use technology to make every day learning experiences more responsive, meaningful, and understandable for young DLLs.
3. Use technology to give young DLLs opportunities to demonstrate what they know and can do in English and in their home language.
4. Use technology to bring children together, to build cross-language communication, and to strengthen cultural connections.

References

Batalova, J., & McHugh, M. (2010). Top Languages Spoken by English Language Learners Nationally and by State. Washington, DC: Migration Policy Institute. Retrieved from www.migrationpolicy.org/research/top-languages-spoken-english-language-learners-nationally-and-state

Capps, R., Fix, M. E., Ost, J., Reardon-Anderson, J., & Passel, J. S. (2005). *The health and well-being of young children of immigrants.* Washington, DC: The Urban Institute. Retrieved from www.urban.org/UploadedPDF/311139_ChildrenImmigrants.pdf

Castro, D. C., Garcia, E. E., & Markos, A. M. (2013). Dual language learners: Research-informing policy. Chapel Hill: The University of North Carolina, Frank Porter Graham Child Development Institute, Center for Early Care and Education—Dual Language Learners. Retrieved from http://cecerdll.fpg.unc.edu/sites/cecerdll.fpg.unc.edu/files/imce/documents/%232961_ResearchInformPolicyPaper.pdf

Dickinson, D., & Porche, M. (2011). Teachers' language practices and academic outcomes of preschool children, *Science, 333*(6045), 964–967. Retrieved from DOI:10.1126/science.1204526

Dual language learners. (2009). Office of Head Start, National Center on Cultural and Linguistic Responsiveness. Retrieved from http://eclkc.ohs.acf.hhs.gov/hslc/tta-system/cultural-linguistic/center/Dual%20Language%20Learners/DLL_%20Resources/OHSDefinitionof.htm

Espinosa, L. M. (2010). Classroom teaching and instruction "best practices" for young English language learners. In E. García & E. Frede (Eds.), *Young English language learners: Current research and emerging directions for practice and policy.* New York, NY: Teachers College Press.

Espinosa, L. M. (2013). PreK–3rd: *Challenging common myths about dual language learners: An update to the seminal 2008 report.* Foundation for Child Development. Retrieved December 17, 2013, from http://fcd-us.org/sites/default/files/Challenging%20Common%20Myths%20Update.pdf

Goldenberg, C., Hicks, J., & Lit, I. (2013). Dual language learners: Effective instruction in early education, *American Educator, 37*(2), 26–29.

McCann, C. (2012, January 3). What influence do peers have on preschoolers' language skills? [Web log post]. Retrieved http://earlyed.newamerica.net/blogposts/2012/what_influence_do_peers_have_on_preschoolers_language_skills-61978

National Association for the Education of Young Children, & Fred Rogers Center for Early Learning and Children's Media at Saint Vincent College. (2012). *Technology and interactive media as tools in early childhood programs serving children from birth through age 8.* Washington, DC: NAEYC; Latrobe, PA: Fred Rogers Center for Early Learning and Children's Media at Saint Vincent College.

National Center on Cultural and Linguistic Responsiveness. (2009). *OHS definition of dual language learners.* Retrieved from http://eclkc.ohs.acf.hhs.gov/hslc/tta-system/cultural-linguistic/center/Dual%20Language%20Learners/DLL_%20Resources/OHSDefinitionof.htm

Nemeth, K. (2009). *Many languages, one classroom: Teaching dual and English language learners.* Beltsville, MD: Gryphon House.

Nemeth, K. (2012a, March 6). Designing a rubric for preschool bilingual apps [Web log post]. Retrieved from www.ecetech.net/blog/dll/designing-a-rubric-for-preschool-bilingual-apps-by-karen-nemeth/

Nemeth, K. (2012b). *Basics of supporting dual language learners: An introduction for educators of children from birth through age 8.* Washington, DC: NAEYC.

Nemeth, K. (2013, July 16). Technology for young dual language learners [Web log post]. Retrieved from www.fredrogerscenter.org/blog/technology-for-young-dual-language-learners/

Nemeth, K. & Simon, F. (2013). Using technology as a teaching tool for dual language learners in preschool through grade 3. *Young Children, 68*(1), 48–52.

Simon, F., & Nemeth, K. (2012). *Digital decisions: Choosing the right technology tools for early childhood education.* Beltsville, MD: Gryphon House.

Simon, F., Nemeth, K., & McManis, L. D. (2013). Technology in ECE classrooms: Results of a new survey and implications for the field. *Exchange,* 68–75.

Schmit, S., & Firgens, E. (2012). *Expanding teacher competencies to support young dual language learners.* CLASP: Policy solutions that work for low-income people retrieved from www.clasp.org/issues/child-care-and-early-education/in-focus/expanding-teacher-competencies-to-support-young-dual-language-learners

Resources

- Anybook Reader Pen, www.anybookreader.com
- Bilingual Story Apps, Ana Lomba, www.analomba.com
- *Cookie Doodle*, Shoe the Goose, www.shoethegoose.com/CookieDoodle.aspx
- *Cupcakes*!, Maverick Software LLC, www.mavericksoftwaregames.com/Cupcakes!.html
- Google Hangouts, www.google.com/+/learnmore/hangouts/
- iTranslate, www.itranslateapp.com
- iTunes, www.apple.com/itunes/
- *Kids Lingo*, Rosetta Stone, www.rosettastone.com/lp/kidsapp/
- *Left Right Pup*, Mrs. Judd's Games, www.mrsjuddsgames.com/games/
- *Lulu in Polynesia*, Zanzibook, www.zanzibook.com/en/
- Mama Lisa's World, www.mamalisa.com
- *Memory Train*, Piikea Street, www.piikeastreet.com/apps/memory-train/
- My Child, www.mychildnow.com
- My Story—Book Maker for Kids, http://mystoryapp.org
- National Geographic, www.nationalgeographic.com
- Pocoyo Learning Activities, HITN Early Learning Collaborative, http://earlylearningcollaborative.org
- *Sharing with Duckie Deck*, Duckie Deck, http://duckiedeck.com/sharing-with-duckiedeck
- Skype, www.skype.com/en/
- *SmackTalk*, marcussatellite, www.marcussatellite.com/SMACK_TALK/
- Smartyants, www.smartyants.com
- Tadpoles, www.tadpoles.com
- *Toca Store*, Toca Boca, http://tocaboca.com/game/toca-store/
- VoiceThread, www.voicethread.com
- YouTube, www.youtube.com

Learn More . . .

- Early Childhood Technology Network, www.ecetech.net
- Language Castle, LLC, http://languagecastle.com/Language_Castle/LANGUAGE_CASTLE_HOME.html

- NAEYC & Fred Rogers Center Joint Position Statement. (2012). Retrieved from www.naeyc.org/content/technology-and-young-children
- Nemeth, K. N. (2012). *Many languages, building connections: Supporting infants and toddlers who are dual language learners.* Beltsville, MD: Gryphon House.
- Simon, F. & Nemeth, K. (2012). *Digital decisions: Choosing the right technology tools for early childhood education.* Beltsville, MD: Gryphon House.
- Teacher Tube, www.teachertube.com

Chapter 10

Including All Young Children in the Technology-Supported Curriculum: A UDL Technology Integration Framework for 21st-Century Classrooms

Howard P. Parette and Craig Blum

Introduction

Today's early childhood teachers want *all* children to benefit from the exciting and engaging learning experiences that occur in their 21st-century inclusive class-room settings. For many teachers, learning experiences in their classrooms are supported in varying degrees by a range of instructional technologies used with diverse groups of young children. Other teachers may not yet be using technology in meaningful ways in their classrooms, but they are gaining interest in learning how to integrate today's technologies effectively. This interest may be influenced by a growing recognition among education professionals that young children are surrounded by technology in their home and community cultural settings (Parette, Blum, & Quesenberry, 2013; Peurling, 2012; Simon & Nemeth, 2012). Additionally, effective practices and standards have been developed that guide professionals in using technology, so it is now considered a developmentally appropriate practice for young children (National Association for the Education of Young Children [NAEYC] & Fred Rogers Center, 2012; Parette & Blum, 2013b).

Position Statement Alignment

For children with special needs, technology has proven to have many potential benefits. Technology can be a tool to augment sensory input or reduce distractions. It can provide support for cognitive processing or enhancing memory and recall. The variety of adaptive and assistive technologies ranges from low-tech toys with simple switches to expansive high-tech systems capable of managing complex environments. When used thoughtfully, these technologies can empower young children, increasing their independence and supporting their inclusion in classes with their peers. With adapted materials, young children with disabilities can be included in activities in which they once would have been unable to participate. By using assistive technology, educators can increase the likelihood that children will have the ability to learn, move, communicate, and create.

NAEYC & Fred Rogers Center (2012), p. 9

More importantly, acceptance of the role of technology in early childhood classrooms is reflected in the recent release of the technology position statement jointly published by the NAEYC & Fred Rogers Center (2012). This position statement provides guiding principles to help teachers understand that technology integration in today's classroom settings is indeed developmentally appropriate practice and can prevent teachers from "missing the boat" (Parette, Quesenberry, & Blum, 2010) by failing to intentionally integrate technology into planned classroom activities. But for many early childhood teachers, intentionality, or understanding how to effectively integrate technology into planned classroom activities for diverse groups of children may be elusive even though its importance is now at the forefront of the discipline (HITN Early Learning Collaborative & TEC Center at Erikson Institute, 2013).

Washington (2013) recently noted that a well-trained early childhood education workforce is critical for helping children reach their full potential. Lack of knowledge or training has been identified as a barrier to effective and efficient technology integration (Barron et al., 2011; Campbell & Scotellaro, 2009; Ertmer, Ottenbreit-Leftwich, Sadik, Sendurur, & Sendurur, 2012; NASBE Study Group on the Role of Technology in Schools and Communities, 2012; Schomburg, Chen, Johnson, & Wartella, 2007; Parette, Blum, & Quesenberry, 2013). Teacher attitudes have also been attributed to acceptance and use of technology to deliver early childhood curricula (Ertmer et al., 2012; Parette, Blum, Quesenberry, 2013; Parette & Stoner, 2008).

The HITN Early Learning Collaborative and TEC Center at Erikson Institute (2013) examined issues related to how content and experiences related to classroom technology integration may effectively be incorporated into both preservice and inservice personnel preparation venues. Case studies were presented to "thought leaders" in the field to stimulate conversation and to develop action steps to move the discipline forward. Paralleling this most recent thinking, Rosen and Jaruszewicz (2009) suggested that a central question for personnel preparation address identification of "the most developmentally appropriate instructional strategies for incorporating technology into children's educational experiences" (p. 163). This issue is compounded by the fact that there are so many technologies currently available that can be used in learning activities, making it is impossible for any teacher to have knowledge and skills about the full array of these technologies. Making decisions is even more problematic if teachers have no understanding of universal design for learning (UDL) principles that are important planning considerations for today's inclusive learning environments (Center for Applied Special Technology [CAST], 1999–2012; Lieber, Horn, Palmer, & Flemming, 2008; Rose & Meyer, 2002, 2006; Stockall, Dennis, & Miller, 2012).

Early childhood classrooms that use UDL principles in the design and delivery of curricula hold immense potential both for young children with disabilities (Buysse, 2009; Stachowiak & Hollingworth, 2013; Stockall et al., 2012) and typical peers (HITN Early Learning Collaborative & TEC Center at Erikson Institute, 2013; Morrison, 2012; Parette, Blum, & Luthin, 2013; Stachowiak &

Hollingworth, 2013). Thought leaders at the HITN Early Learning Collaborative and TEC Center at Erikson Institute noted the importance of these principles in guiding the early childhood discipline to more effectively integrate technology into classroom settings. But this recognition raises two particularly problematic questions for today's early childhood teachers who have not been trained either at the preservice or inservice levels to use UDL principles to make decisions about technology:

- What is UDL?
- What is its role in selecting and using technology in early childhood planned classroom activities?

The Role of UDL in Today's Early Childhood Classrooms

There are three principles integral to the use of the UDL framework when developing technology-supported learning activities:

1. Multiple means of representation
2. Action and expression
3. Engagement (Rose & Meyer, 2002, 2006).

Key Terms Defined

- *UDL, universal design for learning,* is a proactive process of designing and delivering curricula that provides multiple means of engagement, representation, and expression (CAST, 1999–2012).
- *Assistive technology:* The Individuals With Disabilities Education Improvement Act of 2004 (IDEA) describes assistive technology as "any item, piece of equipment, or product system, whether acquired commercially, modified, or customized, that is used to increase, maintain, or improve functional capabilities of individuals with disabilities."
- Assistive technology is a tool or strategy that allows a child to do a task they could *not* do without the tool at the expected performance level (Parette, Peterson-Karlan, Wojcik, & Bardi, 2007).

Multiple means of representation refer to how the teacher and young children are allowed to present information and content in classroom activities. Children differ in the ways they perceive and comprehend presented information; thus, there is no single means of representation that will be effective for all young children (Blum & Parette, in press). For example, children with physical disabilities, problem solving and organizational challenges, and language barriers all approach classroom learning tasks very differently. Multiple representations are used because they allow students to make connections within, as well as between, concepts.

Multiple means of action and expression refer to the teacher's consideration of varying opportunities provided to children to express what they have learned during a planned classroom activity and/or through participation in other early childhood classroom settings. Many young children will be able to communicate well orally, while others may draw pictures to represent their thinking. Some children who are unable to communicate verbally may prefer to use a picture communication board or electronic communication device to express themselves. Not only may young children vary in means of expression that are most effective or with which they are more comfortable, but they may be more comfortable expressing themselves in different settings (e.g., small group, large group, electronic environment; with a parent, different teachers, and/or different children) (Blum & Parette, in press).

Multiple means of engagement refer to consideration given to planned classroom activity design and delivery characteristics used to recruit children's interest in the activity; provide children with multiple options for sustaining their effort and persistence; and enhance children's self-regulatory behavior (Blum & Parette, in press). Of particular importance is the concept of flexibility, wherein an array of options for participation and choice are afforded young children (Parette & Blum, 2014). Some children prefer individual work, while others enjoy group and/or collaborative activities. Having multiple opportunities for "choice" regarding materials, supplies, characters, learning activities, learning content, and other elements of the curriculum afford diverse students with engagement opportunities.

The Promise of UDL and a New Model for Technology Integration

Guidance on using specific technologies to support learning has recently been presented to help guide the discipline (cf. Parette & Blum, 2013b; Puerling, 2012; Simon & Nemeth, 2012). Similarly, in Figure 10.1, we propose a model technology integration framework—EXPECT IT-PLAN IT-TEACH IT-SOLVE IT—that is couched in the use of UDL principles, is not based on use of specific technologies, and is developed specifically for use in early childhood classrooms (Parette & Blum, 2013a).

The initial three phases of the framework requires the early childhood teacher to:

1. EXPECT IT—Identify a learning standard and associated learning objective (or benchmark) for a planned classroom activity
2. PLAN IT—Consider various technologies, instructional strategies, and assessment methods that would be used in the planned classroom activity
3. TEACH IT—Teach the planned activity using the identified assessment methods

Participation of most children in planned activities will be supported using the first three phases of the technology integration framework, given that careful

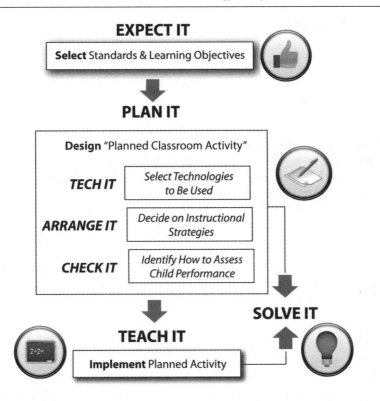

Figure 10.1 The EXPECT IT-PLAN IT-TEACH IT-SOLVE IT Technology Integration Framework

© *H.P. Parette & C. Blum, 2013. Used with permission.*

planning occurs with UDL principles in mind. However, even with such careful planning for diverse groups of young children, *some* children with disabilities will still be unable to participate in certain steps of the activity. Thus, a fourth component—SOLVE IT—helps the early childhood teacher identify specific problems demonstrated by children with disabilities in participating in the activity and arrive at solutions to help them be included (Peterson-Karlan, Parette, & Blum, 2013).

We feel that use of the first three phases of EXPECT IT-PLAN IT-TEACH IT will enable most teachers to make informed decisions using UDL principles and connect technology with which they are familiar to both instruction and assessment, even if they have a limited knowledge base! Understanding of SOLVE IT adds yet another dimension to the early childhood teacher's skill sets and ensures that all young children with disabilities are also included in planned classroom activities. Let's examine each of these elements of the technology integration framework and consider the connections to UDL.

Step 1: Expect It

This initial step in using the technology integration framework simply requires the early childhood teacher to select a learning standard and associated benchmark/learning objective that will be the focus of the technology-supported planned classroom activity:

> Ms. Hill wants to focus on helping her preschool students make progress toward a learning standard in her curriculum—"Recognizes at least 20 letter sounds." She selects "recognition of four beginning sounds—/p/, /c/, /b/, and /d/"—as a learning objective for her planned activity. Once this decision is made, Ms. Hill proceeds to plan the activity.

Step 2: Plan It

After a benchmark/learning objective is selected that will guide development of the planned, technology-supported classroom activity, thoughtful consideration is given in PLAN IT to each of three interrelated elements that support the targeted benchmark/learning objective—decisions made about:

1.   TECH IT—The technology
2.   ARRANGE IT—Instructional groupings and strategies
3.   CHECK IT—Assessment methods

A special connection is present between a technology decision made, the instructional strategy (or strategies) used with the technology, and the curriculum or support tier available in the classroom. Three levels of support tiers exist in many early childhood classrooms where instruction is delivered (Blum & Parette, 2013). These include whole class, small group (for remedial or more intense instruction needed for at risk students when learning doesn't occur in whole class settings), and 1:1 (for children with disabilities who cannot receive appropriate instruction in whole or small group settings) (Blum & Parette, 2013). Specific technologies lend themselves for use in one or across settings, and instructional strategies may vary depending on both the technology used and the content delivered. Decisions made regarding both will help identify assessment methods used in the planned activity. Each decision made in these interrelated elements is couched in UDL principles as illustrated in Figure 10.2. Exemplars of UDL characteristics that may be considered by teachers when making decisions during PLAN IT are presented in Figure 10.3.

While these are not exhaustive examples, it is important to note that flexibility is especially important in TECH IT, ARRANGE IT, and CHECK IT. The availability of multiple options for participation and opportunities for child choice should be available to the greatest extent possible. It does not mean that *most* characteristics presented in Figure 10.1 are present but that consideration is given to characteristics that afford flexibility and choice in the planned activity

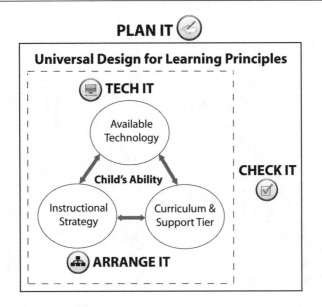

Figure 10.2 Planning Any Technology-Supported Classroom Activity Is Couched in UDL Principles and Is Connected to Assessment

© *H.P. Parette & C. Blum, 2013. Used with permission.*

being developed. We have also noted the importance of "flexible participation" strategies being embedded in all planning, particularly when children with disabilities are members of the classroom (Parette & Blum, in press). Flexible participation strategies include flexible curriculum and technology use, flexible use of peer or adult support, flexible skill sequences, and flexible rules as illustrated in Figure 10.4.

Ms. Hill decides that there will be four steps in her planned activity and that children will:

1. Transition to the SMART Board when the teacher signals
2. Interact with a Starfall ABCs activity
3. Draw pictures of things beginning with targeted sounds
4. Transition to Centers

Having decided to use the ABCs activity at starfall.com for her planned classroom activity, Ms. Hill recognizes that it lends itself to use in whole class, small group, and 1:1 instruction. However, she decides that she will use it with the entire class to "introduce" the four targeted sound concepts. Her SMART Board affords flexible means of representing content, particularly when the Starfall ABCs activity is launched given that sound,

UDL Principles and Characteristics

TECH IT (Selecting technologies that support the learning standard and benchmark/objective)

Multiple Means of Representation	*Multiple Means of Action and Expression*	*Multiple Means of Engagement*
The technology:	The technology:	The technology:
• Illustrates through multiple media.	• Has varying response and navigation features.	• Provides varying levels of challenge and individual choice.
• Visual and sound enchantment: e.g. sound adjustment, magnification, removing background images, changing the contrast.	• Uses multiple media for communication (e.g., app, on-line access, traditional curricular material).	• Provides opportunities for practice.
• Uses audio accompanied by signing, captioning, pictures, video, animation.	• Allows children to record voice, text, video, or draw.	• Enhances relevance, value, and authenticity (connects to prior knowledge).
• Decodes text with text-to-speech.	• Has built in prompting and scaffolding.	• Minimizes threats and distractions.
• Enables text transcription paired with text-to-speech/pictures.	• Enables transcription of text paired with text-to-speech.	• Varies demands (e.g., different levels of challenge) and resources to optimize challenge.
• Provides translation tools paired with English, for ESL learners.	• Is compatible with assistive technologies through USB port or other means permitting expression or action (e.g., an accessible keyboard might work with a computer).	• Fosters collaboration.
• Supports planning and strategy development.	• Allows name to be transcribed on tablet app (e.g., using pencil grip, typing name).	• Provides mastery-oriented feedback.
• Clarifies vocabulary and symbols.		• Facilitates/scaffolds coping skills.
• Highlights patterns or critical features.		• Develops self-assessment and reflection.
• Activates or supplies background knowledge.		• Highlights critical features.
• Clarifies syntax and structure.		• Provides signals and prompts.
		• Activates background knowledge.
		• Supports memory and transfer.
		• Has variable controls for mouse, touch, auditory or other input/control.
		• Enables assistive technology to be connected to tool use/features enabling access.
		• Enhances capacity for monitoring progress.

ARRANGE IT (making grouping decision and deciding on instructional strategies used with the technology)

Multiple Means of Representation	Multiple Means of Action and Expression	Multiple Means of Engagement
The grouping and instructional strategy (when paired with the technology):	*The grouping and instructional strategy (when paired with the technology):*	*The grouping and instructional strategy (when paired with the technology):*
• Provide multiple examples of content.	• Enable children to express themselves using: verbally; using drawing, signs, or pictures; constructing or performing.	• Allow flexible grouping (e.g., whole-class introductory discussions of big ideas content followed by small group or paired work).
• Highlights critical features of content.	• Allow flexible models of skilled performance and opportunities for demonstrating skills.	• Allow flexible participation in activities (i.e., flexible curriculum, skill sequences, rules, and peer/adult support).
• Provide verbal, visual, and tactile input with content.	• Provide opportunities for practice with support.	• Engage children with information through singing, music, movement, or dance.
• Include pictures (or real life objects) with labels in content.	• Provide ongoing, relevant feedback.	• Vary activities within instruction.
• Use various formats such as: online resources, videos, podcasts, PowerPoint presentations, manipulatives, and e-books.	• Use communication boards with a variety of pictures enabling children to express wants, needs, and preferences.	• Scaffold learning, supplies hands-on materials, and accesses children's background knowledge.
• Visual support background context when presenting content.		• Provide adjustable levels of challenge.
		• Pair a peer with strong social skills with another student to model appropriate communication.

(Continued)

CHECK IT (Deciding on assessment methods to document child outcomes)

Multiple Means of Representation	Multiple Means of Action and Expression	Multiple Means of Engagement
The assessment method (when used with the technology and instructional format):	*The assessment method (when used with the technology and instructional format) allows use of:*	*The assessment method (when used with the technology and instructional format) enables:*
• Uses a variety of formats: written products, visual products, audio products, performance products. • Provides text-to-speech for students having difficulty with reading.	• Demonstration, singing, matching, choosing/pointing, constructing, and/or manipulating. • Use of electronic portfolio or multimedia product. • Marks in book, oral responses, audio-recorded responses, demonstrations, experiments, and/or how-to sessions. • Recording of child's performance, movies, and/or digital portfolios. • Switch responses, and use of scribe, dictation, oral presentations, and/or interviews. • Diagrams, scrapbooks, and/or collages. • Blogs, e-journals, PowerPoint presentations, and/or slide shows. • Posters, pictures, cartoons, illustrations, models, diagrams, exhibits, and/or dioramas. • Software to create graphic organizers (e.g., *Kidspiration*), illustrations, and/or posters. • Role playing, skits, real-world problem-solving, music, drama, creative play, and/or dance.	• Students to choose assessment method that maximizes strengths and learning modalities. • Students to have choice regarding content of assessment to focus on their areas of interest. • Students to share their learning with others. • Performance feedback to be provided that is individualized, specific, and given in an accessible format. • Appropriate instructional level assessment for each student.

Figure 10.3 Exemplars of PLAN IT UDL Characteristics for Technology-Supported Classroom Activities

© H.P. Parette & C. Blum, 2013. Used with permission.

Flexibility Strategy	Description	Classroom Examples
Flexible Curriculum and Technology Use	Designing curricula that permit multiple means of representation, action and expression, and engagement to maximize activity participation.	**Representation:** Use visuals (pictures) or three-dimensional items (the actual item the word represents (e.g., a real pot when teaching 'pot') and auditory (i.e., words spoken) when teaching vocabulary. **Action and expression:** Use AT (e.g., a voice output device) to retell a story, either with or without teacher scaffolding. **Engagement:** Use visual and verbal cues (scaffolding) presented within the learning objective. Objectives should allow for multiple levels of relevant participation that are authentic to each child's ability.
Flexible Use of Assistance-Peer or Adult Support	Used to provide a 'scaffold' or in collaboration to maximize activity participation.	**Representation:** Permit peers to re-state instructions using a visual guide and verbal expression in collaboration with a partner. **Action and expression:** Allow peer assistance to child with disability to position wheelchair for Circle Time. **Engagement/action and expression:** Allow peers to collaborate together to choose a story to be read. One child expresses choice orally while another expresses it using a voice output device (AT).
Flexible Skill Sequence	Permitting order of skill sequence changes to maximize participation.	**Representation:** During a unit overview use a visual organizer on a SMART Board or iPad paired with the verbal presentation. Allow for concrete objects to be held by children to represent each skill sequence. **Action and expression:** Instead of re-telling a story and identifying main characters, re-tell the story by simplifying the sequence. **Engagement:** Permit each child to identify what is most important to learn and allow choices (individually and collaboratively when appropriate) about what to learn first.
Flexible Rules	Allows for broader and more universal rules that maximize activity participation.	**Representation:** Present rules visually and paired with an icon or picture. **Action and expression:** Define class rules as broad expectations (e.g., 'clean up after activities'), allowing for peer assistance or flexible completion of the task for a child with a disability. **Engagement:** Permit choice regarding the classroom task a child will complete; allow task sharing to foster collaboration.

Figure 10.4 Flexible Participation Strategies in Planned, Technology-Supported Preschool Activities

Source: Parette, H. P., & Blum. C. (in press). Using 'flexible participation' to include young children with disabilities in technology-supported, universally-designed preschool activities. Teaching Exceptional Children. Used with permission.

animation, and pictures will be presented. Built-in "signals" on each screen call attention to buttons that children must click. Children will volunteer to come to the SMART Board and make button selections on the Starfall activity screens. Starfall is flexible enough for her to use several instructional strategies, including guided discovery to pause as screens are shown and ask questions and show other objects beginning with the four sounds; provide models and reinforcement to students to access background knowledge; and scaffold children's responses. She uses her iPad to capture short videos of each child's interactions with the Starfall activity that she will archive in the children's digital portfolios.

After the Starfall activity, each student will be given four response cards having letters of the four beginning sounds that will be used as an assessment method. Ms. Hill will pronounce words having the four beginning sounds, and students will be expected to hold up a letter card and say the sound to identify the pronounced word's beginning sound. Ms. Hill can quickly scan the classroom and see if any students inaccurately identify a sound, allowing her to record errors made on a data-recording sheet. She can also provide immediate remediation to any student who makes an error, using modeling and reinforcement. Since she knows that several of her students are nonverbal, she will use flexible participation by having several four-message communication devices available that have the four sound letters presented along with prerecorded sound pronunciations. Nonverbal students can simply press a button on the communication device to provide an oral response. For any students who have physical disabilities, are nonverbal, and have difficulty pressing buttons on the communication device, Ms. Hills will use peer assistance as a flexible participation strategy. A peer selected by the student with a disability will point to each letter presented on the communication device and press a button when a nod is provided by the nonverbal student. If the student makes an inaccurate selection, the peer will provide a model for the proper button selection. Ms. Hill captures this interaction with her iPad so that she can share the student's participation with his parents via email. After this step, students will be asked to gather materials from the art bin and to draw four pictures of things represented by the sounds on their response cards. Students with disabilities who need help gathering art materials will be paired with typical peers, who can provide communication supports and physical assistance.

Ms. Hill will provide several of her students with an iPad having the app Educreations available and paired with a peer helper. This will allow students with difficulty holding a pencil to use their fingers to draw and record pictures on the screen. These students and/or peer helpers can record their voices while drawing is taking place, providing several means of representing content. Student's drawings are collected, to be photographed and archived in children's portfolios, and can be sent to families as email attachments. Educreations recordings can be saved and sent home to families as well.

In the foregoing example, many opportunities have been created by Ms. Hill for flexible use of Starfall in teaching the four beginning sounds combined with varying instructional strategies. She has also considered flexible assessment methods and flexible participation strategies. Now she can teach the planned, technology-supported activity and use her targeted assessment methods to document the success of the learning activity.

Step 3: Teach It

Having systematically developed her planned, technology-supported activity by considering UDL in TECH IT, ARRANGE IT, and CHECK IT, Ms. Hill now has a well-designed plan for delivering her instruction. Since UDL characteristics are present across all elements of the activity, and she has recognized the flexible participation needs of some of her students with disabilities in advance, she anticipates successful learning outcomes for her children. However, in the process of teaching—even though Ms. Hill felt that she had anticipated all potential problems that might arise—one student with disabilities was unable to successfully participate in certain aspects of the four steps of her activity.

> When Ms. Hill signals the class that it is time to transition to the SMART Board, she observes Cierra, a nonverbal student with physical disabilities who uses wheelchair, engaged in playing with a toy in the free play area. Cierra ignores the signal to transition, and a peer selected by Ms. Hill has to remind her that it is time to change activities and moves her wheelchair to the SMART Board area. After students have transitioned to the SMART Board and seated themselves on the floor, Ms. Hill notices that Cierra is inattentive as Starfall screen presentations, teacher demonstrations, and student questioning occur. As a result, she appears not to know what to do as Ms. Hill proceeds through this step of her planned, technology-supported activity. She also observed that Cierra had great difficulty holding up response cards and using her finger to draw on the *Educreations* screen. On reflecting on these observations at the conclusion of the activity, Ms. Hill engages in problem solving to find a solution to ensure Cierra's participation.

Step 4: Solve It

Technology-supported classroom activities typically adhere to a predictable structure and revolve around "procedures" used by the teacher to deliver instruction. All activities have a transition step into the activity (e.g., lining up, washing hands, gathering materials to be used, getting carpet square from storage shelf, seating oneself in the Morning Message area). This transition is then followed by a number of steps wherein specific content is taught using UDL principles that guide the use of technology, instructional strategies including flexible participation, and one or more assessment methods. Finally, the activity concludes with a transition step out of the activity (e.g., children return art materials or carpet squares to a storage bin, and then move to Literacy Center).

Each step in a planned activity is characterized by having certain things required of children to successfully participate. We categorize these demands as DO, SAY, and REMEMBER.

1. DO demands include anything *perceptual* (e.g., listening to/hearing the teacher, seeing/watching the SMART Board) or requiring *physical manipulation* or *mobility* (e.g., retrieving a carpet square from the shelf, drawing a picture, making a selection on an iPad screen, moving to SMART Board area, returning materials to a storage area).
2. SAY demands include any oral language demands required of children in the activity step (e.g., asking/answering questions, commenting on the work of others, telling a story, explaining one's thinking).
3. REMEMBER demands focus on recall of facts (e.g., days of the week, months of the year, word recognition); routines (e.g., Morning Message is followed by Centers which is then followed by snack time); and task sequences (e.g., gather your materials, draw a picture, put picture in bin).

Understanding demands placed on young children in steps of planned, technology-supported activities is critical in the problem solving process to ensure children with disabilities are included. We have found it helpful to use a Break It Down approach to problem solving. Presented in Figure 10.3 is a format that can help early childhood teachers organize their thinking and help them make decisions about additional flexible participation strategies or assistive technology (AT) that can be used to help these children participate in steps of planned activities. Some have noted that AT includes any tool that can help young children do things (demands in steps) that they could not do without the tool at some expected level of performance (Parette, Peterson-Karlan, Wojcik, & Bardi, 2007).

In the SOLVE IT process, the problem/s observed for a particular child must be stated in specific terms. Rather than identifying a problem broadly (e.g., The student could not participate in the activity step), a more targeted problem statement must be made (e.g., The student could not make SMART Board button clicks using his hand). Once the problem statement is identified, each of the steps of the planned activity is examined in terms of DO (including perceptual demands of seeing/hearing), SAY, and REMEMBER demands required for all children to perform the step successfully. Then, what is known about the student of concern and his or her ability and what was observed in the activity step is recorded. This helps the early childhood teacher understand the "discrepancy" that exists, that is, what is expected of the child and what the child can actually perform. Once this is known, additional flexible participation solutions and/or AT devices can be identified to support the student's participation by helping the student meet the demand/s that present difficulty. Let's see how Ms. Hill handles problem solving.

Ms. Hill first identifies the specific problems that she observed about Cierra while she was teaching her planned activity (see Figure 10.5): Cierra does not understand rules for participation in the Starfall activity and has problems holding up response cards and drawing using Educreations. She then lists the four steps for her planned, technology-supported activity and notes all DO, SAY, and REMEMBER demands that are present. While Cierra doesn't have perceptual (DO) challenges, Ms. Hill knows that this exercise makes her cognizant of the specific demands present in each of her steps, which will contribute to her use of UDL principles in planning in the future.

In all four of her steps, she has planned for use of flexible participation by having a peer provide physical assistance for Cierra to help her meet identified DO demands (i.e., gathering and returning materials; however, Ms. Hill had chosen the peer helper in the activity. She decided that to build in opportunities for *choice*, Cierra could be provided with an assistive technology (AT) solution—a Peer Helper Choice Board having pictures of peer friends. Using this AT tool, Cierra could point to a picture of a peer whom *she* wanted to help her in activity steps, *not* a peer assigned by the teacher! To help her with demands for communication, Ms. Hill decides that she can use a four-message communicator having preprogrammed sounds created by a peer helper. To support Cierra's DO challenges with drawing, she will be given choice regarding use of traditional drawing materials, including a pencil inserted into a tennis ball to make it easier to hold the pencil. If Cierra chooses to use *Educreations*, an iPad stylus inserted into a tennis ball will be offered. Finally, to provide support for Cierra's difficulty remembering rules for participation, Ms. Hill uses Boardmaker Plusto create two picture rules strips: (1) one for use during the Starfall activity ("Watch," "Listen," and "Choose"), and (2) one for use during the final transition step ("Listen," "Put away," and "Move quietly").

Conclusion

The EXPECT IT-PLAN IT-TEACH IT-SOLVE IT technology integration framework holds great potential for the early childhood field given that it connects UDL to elements of planning and teaching technology-supported classroom activities, as well as problem solving for young children with disabilities. Having UDL principles as an underpinning for all decisions made connects technology, classroom pedagogy, and assessment in powerful ways that ultimately results in a more engaging classroom environment that ensures flexible means of participation by all children. This approach is being successfully used at Illinois State University in a course titled Technology for Young Children With Disabilities. Classroom observations of students using the EXPECT IT-PLAN IT-TEACH IT-SOLVE IT framework over the past several years suggest that preservice students find it to be a useful approach for integrating technology. More recently, greater emphasis placed on UDL decision making as planned activities are being developed

Define the Problem: Cierra does not move in the classroom without assistance, doesn't understand rules for participation in Starfall activity and has difficulty holding up response cards and drawing using *Educreations*.

Activity Description: SMART Board large group guided discovery activity using starfall.com and response cards for letter recognition (/p/, /b/, /c/, /d/), followed by drawing activity to allow children to draw and comment on their drawings.

| Planned Activity Steps (including transitions) | Planned Activity Requirements | | | Child Performance (What we know [bold]/what was observed) | SOLVE IT: ASSISTIVE TECH IT: What's the Answer (AT Solutions/Flexible Participation*)? |
	DO	SAY	REMEMBER		
Transition to SMART Board area	See SMART Board Hear teacher directions Move to SMART Board & sit down		Recall location of SMART Board Remember rules for quiet transition	**Cierra relies on peer assistance with her wheelchair** She waited on someone to push her to the SMART Board area	• Peer Helper Choice Board
Participate in introductory Starfall activity	See *Starfall* screen/ teacher Hear *Starfall* audio, teacher questions, & peer responses Hold & show response cards	Pronounce beginning sounds	Recall sounds associated with letters Remember rules for participation	**Cierra has poor hand strength and difficulty holding objects; she is nonverbal and forgets participation rules** Cierra could not hold response cards and was unable to pronounce sounds. She made noises throughout the instructional session.	• *Cierra points to response card and Peer Helper holds it up • 4-Message Communicator • *Boardmaker Plus Rules Strip* (Watch, Listen, Choose)
Participate in drawing activity	Gather paper and pencil from bin Hold pencil & draw pictures See paper or *Educreations* screen and drawing materials	Pronounce beginning sounds Comment on drawing	Recall sounds represented by drawings Remember steps for drawing using Educreations	**Cierra cannot move to the art materials storage bin independently, cannot hold a pencil due to poor grip, cannot speak, and has difficulty remembering multi-step rules**	• *Peer Helper to get to storage bin, retrieve materials • Tennis ball pencil grip or iPad stylus with tennis ball grip • 4-Message Communicator with recorded sounds made by a selected peer

Transition to Centers	See storage and Center area Hear teacher signal Hold & return drawing materials Move to Center area	Recall location of storage area & Center Remember rules for quiet transitions		
	Hear teacher instructions and peer comments		Cierra sat in her wheelchair waiting for assistance; she made efforts to hold her pencil but could not grip it; she could not click the mouse to make a comment button selection and did not make a comment	
			Cierra cannot use her wheelchair independently; she has poor hand strength and difficulty holding objects; she forgets transition rules When directed to go to Center area Cierra did not move in her wheelchair; her *Educreations* drawing remained on her laptop tray; she began making loud noises when pushed by the teacher	• *Peer Helper to get to storage area, return art materials • *Boardmaker Plus* Rules Strip (Listen, Put away, Move quietly)

*Flexible participation

Figure 10.5 Completed Break It Down Table for Cierra

Source: Parette, H. P. (2013, July). TEACH IT-SOLVE IT: Including young children with disabilities in planned technology-supported classroom activities. Workshop presented at the Region 4 Education Service Cooperative Preschool Summer Institute, Houston, TX. Used with permission.

has heightened the understanding of teacher candidates regarding flexibility in decisions made about classroom technologies, grouping and teaching strategies, and assessment methods. And recognition of the importance of the framework is emerging (Family Center on Technology and Disability, 2013; Parette, 2013a, 2013b, 2014; Parette & Blum, 2013a).

Teacher Takeaways

- Consider the individual learning needs and preferences of all students when planning any technology-supported classroom activity.
- Build in flexibility both in strategies used to teach planned activities and the manner in which learning is assessed.
- Ensure that children have opportunities for choice both during teaching and assessment of learning outcomes.
- Consider developmentally appropriate practice, that is, intentional and meaningful use of technology to support young children's development.
- Use UDL principles when making classroom planning decisions and delivering technology-supported instruction in classroom activities for young children.

References

Barron, B., Cayton-Hodges, G., Bofferding, L., Copple, C., Darling-Hammond, L., & Levine, M. (2011). *Take a giant step: A blueprint for teaching children in a digital age.* New York, NY: The Joan Ganz Cooney Center at Sesame Workshop.

Blum, C., & Parette, H.P. (2013). Using instructional strategies in early childhood classrooms (ARRANGE IT). In H.P. Parette & C. Blum (Eds.), *Instructional technology in early childhood* (pp. 51–72). Baltimore, MD: Paul H. Brookes Publishing Co.

Blum, C., & Parette, H.P. (in press). Universal design for learning and technology in the early childhood classroom. In K.L. Heider & M.J. Jalongo (Eds.), *Promoting information and technology literacy.* New York, NY: Springer.

Buysse, V. (2009). Program quality and early childhood inclusion. Recommendations for professional development. *Topics in Early Childhood Special Education, 29*, 119–128. doi: 10.1177/0271121409332233

Campbell, A., & Scotellaro, G. (2009). Learning with technology for pre-service early childhood teachers. *Australian Journal of Early Childhood, 34*(2), 11–18.

Center for Applied Special Technology (CAST). (1999–2012). *Transforming education through universal design for learning.* Retrieved from www.cast.org/index.html

Ertmer, P.A., Ottenbreit-Leftwich, A.T., Sadik, O., Sendurur, E., & Sendurur, P. (2012). Teacher beliefs and technology integration practices: A critical relationship. *Computers and Education, 59*, 423–435. doi: 10.1016/j.compedu.2012.02.001

Family Center on Technology and Disability. (2013). Instructional technology in early childhood: A new way for a new day. *Technology Voices, 136*, 1–15. Retrieved from www.fctd.info/assets/newsletters/pdfs/307/FCTD-TechVoicesmar13.pdf?1372995063

HITN Early Learning Collaborative, & TEC Center at Erikson Institute. (2013, August). *HITN Early Learning Collaborative summer faculty symposium.* Symposium conducted for teacher educators at Erikson Institute, Chicago, IL.

IDEA. (2004). Building the Legacy of IDEA 2004, http://idea.ed.gov

Lieber, J., Horn, E., Palmer, S., & Fleming, K. (2008). Access to the general education curriculum for preschoolers with disabilities: Children's school success. *Exceptionality*, *16*(1), 18–32. doi: 10.1080/09362830701796776

Morrison, G. S. (2012). *Early childhood education today* (12th ed.). Boston, MA: Pearson.

NASBE Study Group on the Role of Technology in Schools and Communities. (2012). *Born in another time. Ensuring educational technology meets the needs of students today—and tomorrow.* Arlington, VA: National Association of State Boards of Education. Retrieved from www.nasbe.org/study-group/technology-study-group-2012/

National Association for the Education of Young Children, & Fred Rogers Center for Early Learning and Children's Media at Saint Vincent College. (2012). *Technology and interactive media as tools in early childhood programs serving children from birth through age 8.* Washington, DC: NAEYC; Latrobe, PA: Fred Rogers Center for Early Learning and Children's Media at Saint Vincent College.

Parette, H. P. (2013a, December 11). Framework for including young children with disabilities in planned UDL-supported classroom activities [Online webinar]. Retrieved from www.atia.org/i4a/member_directory/feResultsListing.cfm?directory_id=10&viewAll=1

Parette, H. P. (2013b, July). *TEACH IT-SOLVE IT: Including young children with disabilities in planned technology-supported classroom activities.* Workshop presented at the Region 4 Education Service Cooperative Preschool Summer Institute, Houston, TX.

Parette, H. P. (2014, January). *TEACH IT-SOLVE IT: Including young children with developmental disabilities in universally designed, technology-supported classroom activities.* Preconference workshop presented at the 15th International DADD Conference on Autism, Intellectual Disability, & Developmental Disabilities, Clearwater Beach, FL.

Parette, H. P., & Blum, C. (2013a, August). Contemporary issues for teacher preparation: Meeting the needs of young children in the age of digital media and technology. In E. Green (Chair), *HITN Early Learning Collaborative Summer Faculty Symposium.* Symposium conducted for teacher educators at Erikson Institute, Chicago, IL.

Parette, H. P., & Blum, C. (2013b). *Instructional technology in early childhood.* Baltimore, MD: Paul H. Brookes Publishing Co.

Parette, H. P., & Blum. C. (2014). Using flexible participation in technology-supported, universally designed preschool activities. *Teaching Exceptional Children, 46*(3), 60–67.

Parette, H. P., Blum, C., & Luthin, K. (2013). Pedagogy and use of apps for early literacy: Making connections in planned classroom activities. In J. Whittingham, S. Huffman, W. Rickman, & C. Wiedmaier (Eds.), *Technological tools for the literacy classroom* (pp. 180–195). Hershey, PA: IGI Global.

Parette, H. P., Blum, C., & Quesenberry, A. C. (2013). The role of technology for young children in the 21st century. In H. P. Parette & C. Blum, *Instructional technology in early childhood* (pp. 1–28). Baltimore, MD: Paul H. Brookes Publishing Co.

Parette, H. P., Peterson-Karlan, G. R., Wojcik, B. W., & Bardi, N. (2007). Monitor that progress! Interpreting data trends for AT decision-making. *Teaching Exceptional Children, 39*(7), 22–29.

Parette, H. P., Quesenberry, A. C., & Blum, C. (2010). Missing the boat with technology usage in early childhood settings: A 21st century view of developmentally appropriate practice. *Early Childhood Education Journal, 37*, 335–343. doi: 10.1007/s10643–009–0352-x

Parette, H. P., & Stoner, J. B. (2008). Benefits of assistive technology user groups for early childhood education professionals. *Early Childhood Education Journal, 35*, 313–319. doi: 10.1007/s10643–007–0211–6

Peterson-Karlan, G. R., Parette, H. P., & Blum, C. (2013). Technology problem-solving for children with disabilities. In H. P. Parette & C. Blum, *Instructional technology in early childhood* (pp. 95–122). Baltimore, MD: Paul H. Brookes Publishing Co.

Peurling, B. (2012). *Teaching in the digital age. Smart tools for age 3 to grade 3*. St. Paul, MN: Redleaf Press.

Rose, D. H., & Meyer, A. (2002). *Teaching every student in the digital age: Universal design for learning*. Alexandria, VA: ASCD.

Rose, D. H., & Meyer, A. (Eds.). (2006). *A practical reader in universal design for learning*. Cambridge, MA: Harvard Education Press.

Rosen, D. B., & Jaruszewicz, C. (2009). Developmentally appropriate technology use in early childhood teacher education. *Journal of Early Childhood Teacher Education, 30*, 162–171. doi: 10.1080/10901020902886511

Schomburg, R., Chen, M., Johnson, P., & Wartella. (Eds.). (2007). *Early learning leadership: Challenges and opportunities for applications of technology and media content*. Retrieved from www.fredrogerscenter.org/media/resources/June_2007_Briefing_Monograph-Final.pdf

Simon, F., & Nemeth, K. (2012). *Digital decisions. Choosing the right technology tools for early childhood education*. Lewisville, NC: Gryphon House.

Stachowiak, J. R., & Hollingworth, L. (2013). Technology toolbox for the K–12 literacy teacher. In J. Whittingham, S. Huffman, W. Rickman, & C. Wiedmaier (Eds.), *Technology tools for the literacy classroom* (pp. 159–179). Hershey, PA: IGI International.

Stockall, N. S., Dennis, L., & Miller, M. (2012). Right from the start: Universal design for preschool. *Teaching Exceptional Children, 45*(1), 10–17.

Washington, L. (2013). CD 2.0. Supporting people and advancing our field. *Young Children, 68*(4), 68–70.

Resources

- Boardmaker Plus, www.mayer-johnson.com/boardmaker-plus-v-6
- Boardmaker Share, https://br.boardmakershare.com/register
- Educreations, www.educreations.com
- SMART Board, http://smarttech.com/smartboard
- SMART Exchange, http://exchange.smarttech.com/
- Starfall, www.starfall.com

Learn More . . .

- CAST, Center for Applied Special Technology, www.cast.org
- Edutopia Assistive Technology: Resource Roundup, www.edutopia.org/assistive-technology-resources
- FCTD, Family Center on Technology and Disability, www.fctd.info
- HITN Early Learning Collaborative, http://earlylearningcollaborative.org
- IDEA, Individuals With Disabilities Education Improvement Act of 2004, http://idea.ed.gov

- NAEYC & Fred Rogers Center Joint Position Statement, www.naeyc.org/content/technology-and-young-children
- Parette, H. P., & Blum, C. (2013b). *Instructional technology in early childhood*. Baltimore, MD: Paul H. Brookes Publishing Co.
- SEAT, Special Education Assistive Technology Center at Illinois State University, http://education.illinoisstate.edu/seat/
- TEC Center at Erikson Institute, http://teccenter.erikson.edu

Stepping Into STEM With Young Children: Simple Robotics and Programming as Catalysts for Early Learning

Kate Highfield

Introduction

For many of us, when we think of robotics, we conjure concepts from television and movies (such as R2-D2 and C-3PO from Star Wars™), or think of intricate tools used in manufacturing, devices far too complex for use with young children. Programmable toys are much simpler tools, ideal for use with children. This chapter focuses on simple robotics and coding as tools for early learning in science, technology, engineering, and mathematics (STEM).

STEM in the Early Years

Early childhood educators have long recognized the importance of integrated approaches to learning, with a sound understanding that children's learning doesn't occur in neat, segregated curriculum boxes. This integrated approach is increasingly a priority for educators working with older children, with the STEM areas suggested as being of national importance for 21st-century learners. In recent years, engagement in STEM with young children is also increasing. In the United States, this has in part been prompted by President Obama's 2009 "White House Initiative: Educate to Innovate," while internationally, the promotion of 21st-century learning skills along with the development of new curriculum and learning frameworks have provided the impetus.

Work highlighting the benefits of STEM with young children is growing; researchers including Lindeman, Jabot, and Berkley (2013) and Bers, Seddighin, and Sullivan (2013) are highlighting particular benefits for young learners. This work adds to the body of work with older children and adults, espousing benefits of STEM and exploring factors of engagement and retention within STEM and STEM careers (Anderson & Kim, 2006; National Science Foundation, 2006, 2010; Wang, 2013). In the context of early childhood education, some educators prefer to use STEAM (STEM + Art), while others have proposed STREAM (STEM + Art + Reading and Writing). In this chapter, STEM, robotics, and coding are all integrated into and across the curriculum in a constructivist and whole-child approach to early learning and child development.

Position Statement Alignment

> Early childhood educators always should use their knowledge of child development and effective practices to carefully and intentionally select and use technology and media if and when it serves healthy development, learning, creativity, interactions with others, and relationships.
>
> National Association for the Education of Young Children
> [NAEYC] & Fred Rogers Center (2012), p. 5

Lilian Katz (2010) describes the differences between *academic* and *intellectual* curriculum goals, with intellectual goals focusing on "reasoning, hypothesizing, predicting, the quest for understanding and conjecturing, as well as the development and analysis of ideas" (p. 2). She suggests that project-based learning is an opportunity to develop STEM concepts, understandings, and dispositions. Here the project approach suggests three main stages of investigation: (1) topic selection; (2) firsthand investigation; and (3) concluding or debriefing of the project (Mendoza & Katz, 2013). Within this chapter, it is suggested that children's engagement with simple robotics and programming, using a project approach, is a way to explore both *academic* STEM goals such as counting and measuring, while integrating *intellectual* STEM goals such as reasoning, hypothesizing, and analyzing ideas.

Programming and Simple Robotics

There is a long history of research focusing on young children programming and coding, with tools such as "turtle" geometry or Logo (where learners program a turtle to move around the screen) present in classrooms for over three decades. Research suggests that children engaging with programming are given opportunity to explore spatial concepts, problem solving, measurement, and geometry and engage with metacognitive processes (Clements & Meredith, 1993; Yelland, 1994). Logo programming and the visual nature of this tool can be seen as a way to "externalize" ideas and make concepts "more accessible to reflection" (Papert, 1980, p. 145).

Given the increasing interest in programming and coding as a 21st-century literacy, there has been increasing focus on how to make these challenging concepts accessible to young learners, including the examination of alternate programming tools and commercial products such as Lego WeDo and Bee-bots. A growing body of research with robotics and young learners is developing with a particular focus on tangible tools for use in programming (Bers, 2010; Bers & Ettinger, 2012; Horn & Jacob, 2007; Horn, Solovey, Crouser, & Jacob, 2009; Horn, Solovey, & Jacob, 2008; Sullivan & Bers, 2012). These studies suggest that robotics can be engaging for young learners and promote collaboration and problem solving, with tangible interfaces and hybrid graphical-tangible tools enabling participation by younger learners.

Programmable toys, commercially available products, such as the Bee-bot (Figure 11.1) Roamer (Figure 11.2), and Pro-bot (Figure 11.3) can be classified as simple robotics as they have a basic interface that allows the user to program movement with pre-set distances and rotations (without the need for external or numeric inputs). The simplest toy (a Bee-bot) allows a user to program one forward step (moving a distance of the toy's length) by pressing the forward arrow and "go" or a rotation of 90 degrees by a side arrow and "go." The tool allows right and left rotations and forward and backward movement, storing up to 40 movements. The simple interface means that very young children can explore these toys through play, without the need to understand numerals or programming software. The Bee-bot, Roamer, and Pro-bot simple interface, can be linked to measurement concepts, unit iteration, and number concepts such as counting. The Pro-bot has additional programming options and can also be programed using numeric inputs to indicate rotation in degrees and movement in centimetres or via simple software.

Figure 11.1 A Bee-bot, TTS Group

Courtesy of TTS Group

Figure 11.2 Roamer, Valiant Technology

® *Roamer, © All rights reserved by Roamerrobot, Valiant Technology Ltd.*

Figure 11.3 A Pro-bot, TTS Group

Courtesy of TTS Group Ltd.

Studies focusing specifically on Bee-bots, suggest that these affordable programmable toys have potential to be motivational and engender engagement in mathematics (Janka, 2008; O'Meara, 2011; Stoeckelmayr, Tesar, & Hofmann, 2011). Further, studies suggest that simple robotics have the potential to promote mathematical thinking, measurement, and development of number concepts (Highfield, 2012) to develop semiotic systems and encourage investigation, reflective thinking, and problem solving (Goodwin & Highfield, 2013; Highfield 2012; Highfield & Mulligan, 2009; Highfield, Mulligan, & Hedberg, 2008). These tools offer opportunity for young children to investigate and reason, integrating scientific and engineering processes such as problem identification and development and evaluation of solutions.

Current Research—"The Robots Are at Kindy"

This project included 31 children, aged 3 to 7 years and their teachers as they participated in a 12-week program using simple robotics. The study examined the children's learning and play in two contexts: a prior-to-school setting and Grade One in an elementary school. Data collated included videotaped experiences, semi-structured interviews, and children's drawn representations. Children engaged in a project-based approach that promoted a cycle of programming the robotic toys and reflective problem solving. This chapter describes a series tasks completed by 3- and 4-year-olds.

Introduction and Topic Selection

Children participating in this project started by working with the teacher to explore a range of robotic toys, including Lego NXT™, Robopet by Wowee Toys, a "recycled robot" made by one of the children with boxes, Bee-bots, and Pro-bots (TTS Group). After a brief exploration of the devices, the children came up with a series of questions including "How do they move?" "What makes them go?" and "What can they do?" Importantly, the children also wanted to investigate "what they can't do, what things they can't go on, and stuff." The children and their teachers documented these questions as a large mind map and began to use these as the impetus to investigate.

Firsthand Investigations

The 3-year-olds were particularly interested in the Bee-bots, making decorative "hats" for them, personalizing the toys with feathers, color, and sequins. These children gave the toys names, built homes for them, and used the toys as actors in pretend play. When working with the teacher the 3-year-old children engaged in investigations to explore ideas of how the toys move, how long a Bee-bot "step" (see Figure 11.4) was, and designing programs of movement. This early investigation integrated mathematical concepts of movement then the use of informal units and counting to ascertain how far the toy could move, integrating mathematical concepts and investigative processes.

The 3-year-olds attached pens to the Bee-bots to "watch how they moved" and described their toy's programs using descriptive language such as "bumpy," "straight," and "like that" (indicating straight movement) and "that" (indicating a turn of a 90 degree angle). Here the children were investigating then using descriptive language and gesture to explain their observations. They also worked with the teacher and in play to teach (program) their Bee-bots to complete a simple dance the Hokey-Pokey. This multi-step programing and practice took several days and provided evidence of one child's problem solving and persistent disposition.

Figure 11.4 Informal Materials

Courtesy of Kate Highfield

The 4-year-olds who participated in this investigation were a group of boys, who particularly investigated how the toys moved, focusing on Pro-bots and Bee-bots. The boys compared the distance travelled by each toy, the different types of rotational movement, had robot races, and explored the shapes that the toys could make. The children investigated ramps and roads, experimenting with the types of surface that helped the toys move best (smooth wood, plastic, or cardboard). The investigation of roads and ramps led to explorations and experiences with construction using a range of materials.

In free play, the boys investigated the Pro-bot toy's movement up ramps in the playground and found that some ramps were too steep for the toy to move along (see Figure 11.5). The children hypothesized the reasons why the toy couldn't travel up the ramp: "perhaps it's (pointing to the ramp) covered in bark" (an appropriate observation given that the playground had a bark chip floor). They then cleaned the bark dust only to find that the toy still couldn't move up the steep ramp. Another child suggested that Pro-bot was tired, saying "perhaps his batteries are tired" (another plausible explanation), with still another child suggesting that the ramp was too steep: "it's too deep (gesturing to indicate the steepness of the ramp), it's too up." This comment showed that the child had a concept of angle of incline, but hadn't yet understood the vocabulary, substituting the word deep. The teacher and children measured the ramps and indeed found some differences. This concept of ramps was then explored as a component of the project, with children exploring a range of ramps as they played and investigated. In later constructions the children demonstrated their understanding of the toy's limited

Figure 11.5 Exploring Why a Pro-bot Robot Cannot Move Up

Courtesy of Kate Highfield

ability to travel up steep ramps by carefully testing the toy's movement up an incline before finalizing their designs (see Figure 11.5).

Within this setting the robotic toys acted as a catalyst for investigations integrating science processes, investigations, and programming; technology through the use of the robotics and through the design process; and a range of engineering processes such as problem identification and resolution and through construction of roads and structures. The project also facilitated engagement with a number of mathematical concepts and processes including:

- *Measurement concepts* such as iteration of a unit, comparison, informal measurement, partitioning, and estimation of linear and rotational measures;
- *Geometric concepts* such as space, position, directionality, angles, Euclidean geometry, and use of a grid to support structural concepts; and
- *Numeric concepts* such as estimation, reading numerals, object, and ordinal counting.

Within this set of investigations the teachers played a fundamental role—in enabling learning and in modeling the process of learning and investigation. As teachers facilitated learning they completed a broad range of tasks such as provisioning the environment with resources and tools; guiding behavior while sharing and working as a team; and exploring content (e.g., through modeling of counting and measuring). In modeling the process of learning and investigation the teachers stepped back from the position of expert and became co-players, participants, exploring the technology—experimenting with what worked and what didn't, demonstrating dispositions for learning, and modeling reflection and revision. The teachers also modeled the thinking process out loud for the children "in the beginning I thought . . . now I think . . ." using questioning to promote active knowledge construction.

Concluding and Debriefing the Project

In this project the children and teachers discussed learning throughout the process and documented their work as drawn images, photos, and documentation written by the teachers. At the conclusion of the work, the children also participated in a discussion with the researcher, explaining what they'd been doing and what they'd learned, here children indicated that they'd enjoyed their exploration with statements such as "we've been playing and finding how they work," "I have been learning some turns and to go up ramps and learning some more turns," and "I just love the robots, can we play with them always?" Similarly, most teachers indicated a positive response "we did more maths than I thought we'd do, and it was fun . . . just playing with it," and "sometimes it was hard to explain but then when the children understood it, when they really got it, it was worth all the work of getting the roads and learning how to use them (the robots)."

Cycle of Investigation

Throughout the children's investigation the children reflected, accessed prior knowledge and operated on their understandings, suggesting a level of meta-cognitive learning (Clements & Sarama, 2009). This process, facilitated by the teacher, was cyclic as the child identified the task or goal and then planned how the toy would move. The child then inputted a program, observed the program as it progressed and evaluated it. If the program went as planned and met the goal then the child ended the task. If the programmable toy did something unexpected or didn't work, the child then had to reflect on their plan and revise it, thus re-entering the cycle. Figure 11.6 shows an overview of this reflective model. While it is acknowledged that the teacher (or peers) have the potential to play a role in encouraging this cyclic process, the project also showed that children can engage in this cyclic process through play without assistance.

Tasks That Provide Opportunity for Learning

In addition to some of the ideas presented here there are a vast number of tasks that you could explore with simple robotics. The following may prompt STEM investigations in your setting:

- *Build a bridge*—Construct a bridge that your robot can move across. Try a variety of materials to investigate opportunities.
- *Shape maker*—What shapes can your robot make? Have children draw the instructions so a friend would know how to make the shapes to extend this task.
- *How many steps?*—How many steps is it to the door or the chair or the desk? Teachers can scaffold this based on the child's number concepts and encourage children to work in pairs or small groups to scaffold learning and documentation.
- *Build a robot village*—Use cardboard boxes and objects from the environment to construct a bridge. Take into account the types of turns your robot can move (e.g., the Bee-bot can only turn at 90 degrees) and consider the size of boxes for the toy to move into.
- *Write a robot instruction book*—Integrate literacy skills to create a book for other children to know how they work.
- *Dancing Bots*—Teach (program) the robots to dance and then perform a dance with your robot.
- *Use other technologies*—Connect with children in other centers using tools like virtual classrooms, Skype, or email. For example, sending instructions for children to trial with their robot in another center.
- *Make robot movies*—Use digital cameras (e.g., attaching a GoPro or using an iPad or tablet) and make movies of the robots movement.

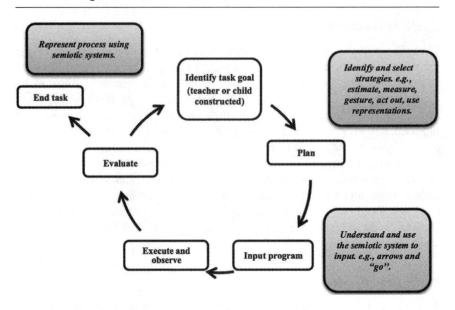

Figure 11.6 Model of Planning and Reflection

Courtesy of Kate Highfield

Position Statement Alignment

> Play is central to children's development and learning. Children's interactions with technology and media mirror their interactions with other play materials and include sensorimotor or practice play, make-believe play, and games with rules. Therefore, young children need opportunities to explore technology and interactive media in playful and creative ways.
>
> NAEYC & Fred Rogers Center (2012), p. 7

Conclusion

Simple robotics are affordable forms of technology and because most children see them as toys and play objects they have a natural desire to engage with them. The programmable nature of the toy and the children's playful response can act as a catalyst for learning in STEM and for the integration of STEM goals and concepts across the curriculum. They have potential to help children practice Katz's (2010) *academic* curriculum goals while developing skills in *intellectual* goals such as reasoning, predicting, developing ideas and analyzing options.

Teacher Takeaways

- *Teacher engagement:* As with all technologies, teacher engagement is key. Simple robotics aren't a form of digital babysitting, but a tool that teachers can co-engage with to prompt learning.

- *Language:* Teacher modeling of language is important and should expand the children's vocabulary to include STEM concepts (for example measure, distance, program, predict, experiment. . .). Teachers should consider their children's language and build on this, modeling and promoting words to extend the children's vocabulary.
- *Play:* It is unlikely that teachers will know how to use all the features of these toys (even after reading instructions!), so make sure that you also play, that you engage with the toys, playing and experimenting. Engaging with children as a participant and fellow learner helps generate the children's interest in the project and in their hands on tasks.
- *Multiple Representations:* Encouraging children to draw (for example, "predicting what they think the robot will do," "drawing what happened," or to document "the program so another player could also follow it") extends learning and makes concepts visible, so others can also discuss and participate. Various technologies (e.g., simple drawing apps, digital cameras and video) can also be used by the children to document what they've been doing— which can in turn act as a powerful memory aid and prompt for reflection.

References

Anderson, E., & Kim, D. (2006). *Increasing the success of minority students in science and technology.* Washington, DC: American Council on Education.

Bers, M., & Ettinger, A. (2012). Programming robots in kindergarten to express identity: An ethnographic analysis. In B. Barker, G. Nugent, N. Grandgenett, & V. Adamchuk (Eds.), *Robots in K–12 education: A new technology for learning* (pp. 168–184). DOI:10.4018/978–1–4666–0182–6.ch008

Bers, M.U. (2010). The TangibleK robotics program: Applied computational thinking for young children. *Early Childhood Research and Practice, 12*(2).

Bers, M.U., Seddighin, S., & Sullivan, A. (2013). Ready for robotics: Bringing together the T and E of STEM in early childhood teacher education. *Journal of Technology and Teacher Education, 21*(3), 355–377.

Clements, D.H., & Meredith, J.S. (1993). Research on Logo: Effects and efficacy. *Journal of Computing in Childhood Education, 4,* 263–290.

Clements, D., & Sarama, J. (2009). *Learning and teaching early math: The learning trajectories approach.* New York, NY: Routledge.

Goodwin, K., & Highfield, K. (2013). A framework for examining technologies and early mathematics learning. In L.D. English & J.T. Mulligan (Eds.), *Reconceptualising early mathematics learning* (pp. 205–226). New York, NY: Springer.

Highfield, K. (2010). Robotic toys as a catalyst for mathematical problem solving. *Australian Primary Mathematics Classroom, 15,* 22–27.

Highfield, K., & Mulligan, J.T. (2009). Young children's embodied action in problem-solving tasks using robotic toys. In M. Tzekaki, M. Kaldrimidou, & H. Sakonidis (Eds.), *Paper presented at the 33rd conference of the International Group for the Psychology of Mathematics Education* (Vol. 2, pp. 273–280). Thessaloniki, Greece: PME.

Highfield, K., Mulligan, J.T., & Hedberg, J. (2008). Early mathematics learning through exploration with programmable toys. In O. Figueras, J.L. Cortina, S. Alatorre, T. Rojano, & A. Sepulveda (Eds.), *Proceedings of the Joint Meeting of Psychology of*

Mathematics Education 32 and Psychology of Mathematics Education-North American Chapter (Vol. 3, pp. 169–176). México: Cinvestav-UMSNH.

Horn, M., & Jacob, R.J.K. (2007). Designing tangible programming languages for classroom use. Paper presented at First International Conference on Tangible and Embedded Interaction, Baton Rouge, Louisiana. Retrieved from http://hci.cs.tufts.edu/tern/horn-jacob-tei07.pdf

Horn, M., Solovey, E., Crouser, R., & Jacob, R. (2009). *Comparing the use of tangible and graphical programming languages for informal science education.* Paper presented at the 27th International Conference on Human Factors in Computing Systems, Boston, MA. Retrieved from http://web.mit.edu/erinsol/www/papers/chi09.horn.pdf

Horn, M.S., Solovey, E.T., & Jacob, R.J.K. (2008). Tangible programming and informal science learning: Making TUIs work for museums. Proceedings of Interaction Design and Children, (Chicago, IL, June 11–13, 2008). Proceedings of the 8th International Conference on Design. ACM, New York, NY. Retrieved from www.eecs.tufts.edu/~etreac01/papers/idc08.pdf

Janka, P. (2008). Using a programmable toy at preschool age: Why and how? Workshop Proceedings of SIMPAR 2008, International Conference on Simulation, Modelling and Programming for Autonomous Robots, Venice, Italy. November 3–4, pp.112–121. Retrieved from www.terecop.eu/downloads/simbar2008/%20pekarova.pdf

Katz, L.G. (2010). STEM in the early years. Early childhood research and practice. Collected Papers from the SEED (STEM in Early Education and Development) Conference. Retrieved from http://ecrp.uiuc.edu/beyond/seed/index.html

Lindeman, K.W., Jabot, M., & Berkley, M.T. (2013). The role of STEM (or STEAM) in the early childhood setting. *Advances in Early Education and Day Care*, *17*, 95–114.

Mendoza, I.A., & Katz, L.G. (2013). Nature education and the project approach. In D. Meier & S. Sisk-Hilton (Eds.), *Integrating nature across the early childhood curriculum* (pp. 153–171). New York, NY: Routledge.

National Association for the Education of Young Children, & Fred Rogers Center for Early Learning and Children's Media at Saint Vincent College. (2012). *Technology and interactive media as tools in early childhood programs serving children from birth through age 8.* Washington, DC: NAEYC; Latrobe, PA: Fred Rogers Center for Early Learning and Children's Media at Saint Vincent College.

National Science Foundation. (2006). *Science and engineering indicators 2006.* Arlington, VA: Author.

National Science Foundation. (2010). *Science and engineering indicators 2010.* Arlington, VA: Author.

O'Meara, M. (2011). *The use of programmable Bee-bot robots, as catalysts for the development of young children's mathematical problem-solving strategies, in a constructionist learning environment.* Unpublished Master of Education Thesis, St. Patrick's College, Dublin City University, Ireland.

Papert, S. (1980). *Mindstorms: Children, computers and powerful ideas.* Brighton, UK: Harvester Press.

Stoeckelmayr, K., Tesar, M., & Hofmann, A. (2011). Kindergarten children programming robots: A first attempt. Proceedings of 2nd International Conference on Robotics in Education (RiE 2011). Vienna, Austria. September, 2011, pp. 185–192. INNOC—Austrian Society for Innovative Computer Sciences. Retrieved from www.rie2011.org/conference/proceedings

Sullivan, A., & Bers, M.U. (2012). Gender differences in kindergarteners' robotics and programming achievement. *International Journal of Technology and Design Education*. DOI: 10.1007/s10798–012–9210-z.

Wang, X. (2013). Why students choose STEM majors: Motivation, high school learning, and postsecondary context of support. *American Educational Research Journal, 50*(5), 1081–1121. DOI: 10.3102/0002831213488622

Yelland, N.J. (1994). The strategies and interactions of young children in LOGO tasks. *Journal of Computer Assisted Learning, 10*, 33–49.

Resources

- Bee-bots, TTS Group, www.tts-group.co.uk/shops/tts/Products/PD1723538/Bee-Bot-Floor-Robot/
- GoPro, http://gopro.com
- Lego Mindstorms NXT, www.legoeducation.us/eng/search/Mindstorms
- Lego WeDo Robotics, www.legoeducation.us/eng/categories/products/elementary/lego-education-wedo
- Pro-bot, Terrapin, www.terrapinlogo.com/pro-bot.php
- Roamer, Valiant Technology, www.valiant-technology.com/uk/pages/roamertoohome.php?cat=8&8
- Robopet, WowWee Toys, www.wowwee.com/en/products/toys/robots/robotics/robo creatures/robopet
- Terrapin, www.terrapinlogo.com/bee-botmain.php

Learn More . . .

- Chaplin, H. (2012, January 31). Programming with Scratch Jr: When it comes to screen time and young kids, content and context are important. MacArthur Spotlight on Digital Media and Learning. Retrieved from http://spotlight.macfound.org/featured-stories/entry/programming-with-scratch-jr-when-it-comes-to-screen-time-and-young-kids/
- Guernsey, L. (2013, September 2). Very young programmers. *New York Times Science*. Retrieved from www.nytimes.com/2013/09/03/science/very-young-programmers.html?_r=0
- Gupta, V. (2013, November 12). Teaching programming to children using stories, music, and puppeteering [Joan Ganz Cooney Center blog]. Retrieved from www.joanganzcooneycenter.org/2013/11/12/teaching-programming-to-children-using-stories-music-and-puppeteering/
- Kazakoff, E., Sullivan, A., & Bers, M. (2013). The effect of a classroom-based intensive robotics and programming workshop on sequencing ability in early childhood. *Early Childhood Education Journal, 41*(4), 245–255. DOI:10.1007/s10643–012–0554–5
- ScratchJr., Computer Programming in Early Childhood, http://ase.tufts.edu/DevTech/ScratchJr/

Chapter 12

Innovate, Educate, and Empower: New Opportunities With New Technologies

Mark Bailey and Bonnie Blagojevic

Introduction

> Claire and Raven are huddled together, deeply engaged, as they problem-solve how to coordinate tasks; to sing and record a song they have learned about sunflowers at the same time as they create a story using an animated drawing tool on their iPad. Success! After thirty minutes they have completed their short production. They share their accomplishment with others in the classroom and with family members, playing their sunflower song as their drawing is recreated line-by-line. The qualities of the app and learning tool that allow the children to easily record and replay their creation, provide new learning opportunities and imaginative ways to share their understanding of sunflowers.
>
> Based on the stories shared in *Touch and Grow, Learning and Exploring Using Tablets* by Blagojevic, Brumer, Chevalier, O'Clair, and Thomes (2012)

Early childhood educators have always sought to provide children with the most effective tools available. In the past few years, the proliferation of digital tools has provided teachers with an amazing array of technologies designed to foster learning in new and innovative ways. The children in Clair and Raven's preschool classroom have examined real sunflowers and their parts and created sketches and paintings. They have counted sunflower seeds, tasted the seeds and planted them, read picture books and informational texts, and participated in a variety of learning activities across subject areas. Their teacher applied her understanding of child development and early learning standards and considered the interests and preferences of the children to determine the learning goals and plan the sunflower study. She used a range of educational tools and materials that engaged and supported the diversity of abilities, skills, interests, and learning preferences of the children in her class.

Alongside traditional early learning activities, the teacher used technology to provide the children in this rural New England community with new means of learning, as well as engaging and motivating ways to organize and share their ideas. Together, they conducted Internet searches to view sunflower photos and discover facts. They explored an e-book about van Gogh and took a virtual tour of

Figure 12.1 Collaborating With Tablet Computers

Courtesy of the Early Learning Community, Pacific University

a museum to view his sunflower paintings. The teacher is aware of their interests and provided the appropriate tools to support their work. The ability of children to create digital stories through pictures that represent their thinking; to record their songs or stories; to replay when they wish; and to share with a wider audience redefines the storymaking experience. The qualities of these educational tools offer another way to create, view, and share their ideas, and they can positively contribute to children's sense of themselves as authors.

Digital tools are playing an increasingly important role in the classroom learning of students of all ages. In order to design high-quality learning experiences for students like Claire and Raven, educators must be informed about the tools that are available and need to be insightful about the manner in which they select and integrate these new tools into their classrooms. Recent advancements in educational technologies have provided educators with the opportunity to reflect on the techniques with which classroom learning is supported and to reconceptualize the manner in which technological tools can support that process.

Educational technologies specifically designed to facilitate learning have a long and important history. The most effective of these tools are reflective of scientific innovation, based on learning theory, framed by pedagogy, and designed to be implemented with intentionality by skilled teachers. If we look at the work of Froebel and Montessori, we find educators who were at the forefront of their field. Based on their theories of the process of learning, they crafted tools that could facilitate this process and structured curriculum and pedagogy around these materials. Their innovations helped us rethink the use of manipulatives to support learning.

For the past few decades, early childhood educators have utilized advanced technologies in their classrooms with students. The advent of the computer, which could afford students unique opportunities to construct understanding, led Seymour Papert (1993) to refer to it as the "children's machine." Now we have access to a whole new generation of digital tools. With the introduction of laptop computers, which allowed for portability, followed by tablets and other mobile devices offering additional qualities such as a touch-screen interface, the children's machine has finally come of age. However, even Papert may not have predicted the techno-pedagogical transformations possible in digital classrooms.

Today, a plethora of ever-evolving devices and apps offer the possibility to revolutionize educational practice. However, as we imagine a boundless future for learning in a truly digital age, let us carefully consider the manner in which we might use technology in our classrooms. We encourage the recognition that technology can be used both in ways that offer highly engaging options for traditional early learning activities, as well as revolutionary ways in which new tools transform learning by offering educational opportunities previously inconceivable (Puentedura, 2006). Throughout this chapter, we re-envision ways in which technology can be utilized in the classroom, and we explore a sampling of innovative educational tools with an eye to the manner in which they empower young children to learn in new and pedagogically powerful ways.

The look and feel of these newer digital technologies differ significantly from traditional manipulatives. However, the purpose and distinguishing features of quality tools are still framed by pedagogical practice, underscored by an implicit theory of learning, and designed to be implemented with intentionality by thoughtful educators. While the tools may change, the importance of knowing how to use them in ways that support young children's learning remains constant; the need for high-quality classrooms and learning experiences is unchanging. So what do these classrooms look like, and how can we design them to support this vision of an engaged and empowered community of learners?

High-quality learning environments support children's freedom to learn through a nurturance of exploration and play. This learning should be facilitated through the use of strategically selected, developmentally appropriate materials of all types, including the opportunity to spend time interacting with nature. A high-quality early childhood learning environment seeks to provide young children with aesthetically embracing classrooms and natural areas in which to play and learn. Such a school should have books and blocks, crayons and music, paper and scissors, plants and areas for nature study, and when possible, outdoor spaces to explore with gardens and bugs. It can also benefit from the inclusion of a variety of strategically selected digital devices that provide a range of opportunities for learning.

It can be challenging for early childhood educators to learn how to select and use these digital devices, as there frequently is no system for professional development about technology provided in the workplace. After more than a decade of careful and thoughtful work, a joint position statement issued by the National Association for the Education of Young Children (NAEYC) and the Fred Rogers Center for Early Learning and Children's Media at Saint Vincent College, *Technology and Interactive Media as Tools in Early Childhood Programs Serving Children from Birth through Age 8,* has been published to provide guidance to the field (NAEYC & Fred Rogers Center, 2012). The position statement is a comprehensive synthesis of research on development, pedagogy, and technology. In the statement, we see interconnections between the work of countless developmental researchers and classroom practitioners. It offers a thoughtful perspective on effective and developmentally appropriate uses for technology.

The rapid pace of technological change and its proliferation into so many aspects of our lives impels educators, families, and other community members to look for strategies to apply these new tools in ways that support the healthy growth and development of young children. This is why it is so important that we become aware of the guidance provided in the position statement, and share these concepts with teacher candidates, family members, and others engaged in education throughout our community.

At the core of the statement is the notion that digital technologies are another form of manipulative that can empower children's learning; that child-initiated, child-directed, teacher-supported, intentional play with digital devices can serve as a powerful and positive learning experience. According to the position statement, effective uses of technology and media are active, hands-on, engaging, and empowering; give the child control; and can provide adaptive scaffolds to ease the accomplishment of tasks. Such devices can be used as one of many options to support children's learning.

Position Statement Alignment

> Effective uses of technology and media are active, hands-on, engaging, and empowering; give the child control; provide adaptive scaffolds to ease the accomplishment of tasks; and are used as one of many options to support children's learning. To align and integrate technology and media with other core experiences and opportunities, young children need tools that help them explore, create, problem solve, consider, think, listen and view critically, make decisions, observe, document, research, investigate ideas, demonstrate learning, take turns, and learn with and from one another.
>
> NAEYC & Fred Rogers Center (2012), pp. 6–7

The key is the use of technological tools in intentional and developmentally appropriate ways, with mindful attention to the quality of the content, to the child's experience, as well as to opportunities for collaborative engagement. These tools need to extend and support active, hands-on, creative, and authentic experiences. There is no doubt that, as noted in the position statement: "When used appropriately, technology and media can enhance children's cognitive and social abilities" (NAEYC & Fred Rogers Center, 2012, p. 7).

To begin the process of intentional technology use, teachers should take stock of the tools available to them. They should reflect on what tools they have and should be familiar with the capabilities and functions of the tools they want to utilize in their classrooms. This can be done in a multitude of ways including reading reviews, watching webinars or video tutorials, using social media tools, participating in online communities, and engaging in other types of professional development opportunities. Teachers should themselves play with these tools as a means of experiencing their capabilities. This is all part of the process of becoming a digital-age teacher proficient in the "skills and knowledge needed to teach, work and learn in an increasingly connected global and digital society" (The International Society for Technology in Education, 2008, 2012). The International Society for Technology in Education (ISTE) has developed a set of standards for teachers, the ISTE Standards-T, that helps to clarify the skills and behaviors expected of digital-age professionals. The standards encourage teachers to be informed about tools and their use by embracing the process of colearning with their students and colleagues around the world.

Position Statement Alignment

> The adult's role is critical in making certain that thoughtful planning, careful implementation, reflection, and evaluation all guide decision making about how to introduce and integrate any form of technology or media into the classroom experience. Selecting appropriate technology and media for the classroom is similar to choosing any other learning material. Teachers must constantly make reflective, responsive, and intentional judgments to promote positive outcomes for each child.
>
> NAEYC & Fred Rogers Center (2012), p. 6

The tools available in today's early childhood classrooms can transport students around the globe to visit the depths of the ocean or observe live pictures in the canopy of a distant rainforest. They can allow children to view minuscule objects in a manner impossible with the naked eye and explore the breadth of the world's knowledge with their fingertips. Students can connect with amazing resources and with each other, fostering inventive collaborations and unique creations of understanding. These are some of the things we are highlighting in this chapter: techniques to apply the power of new digital tools to transform the nature of learning for young children.

Digital Cameras

A range of digital devices that can capture photos and video are increasingly available for use by children and teachers. These tools have the ability to enhance as well as transform many learning activities. Cameras can provide opportunities for children to observe their world from a different perspective, to focus on and identify visual elements of their environment, and to document their learning activities in the classroom. The resulting images can serve as an inspiration for further learning.

Imagine it is cleanup time and a pair of collaborating children has just constructed the world's most amazing block castle. In it lives stories of magic and wonder, and now the children are expected to take it apart and put it away. Through the thoughtful use of a digital camera, not only can that castle be captured for all-time and committed to paper, but as an extension of their building activity, these two engineers can reveal the hidden secrets and rich stories of their construction by adding a narrative to a print-out of this picture during writer's workshop. Their structure and story can be posted near the block area as part of a collection, to be reviewed and discussed. Crisis not only averted, but redirected into creative collaborative storymaking (Mejia, 2013).

Young scientists can use digital cameras to document a variety of events. In our Oregon classroom, students photograph their sunflowers at regular intervals as they grow and then place the images on the wall as a means of observing and documenting growth: a visual representation of the concept of sequencing.

Figure 12.2 Extending a Block Construction Through Photography

Courtesy of the Early Learning Community, Pacific University

The hatching of butterflies and chicks in the spring can allow for careful study of the process of eclosion and a cross-species comparison of the emergence of these animals. Children use the digital camera to focus their attention, to look more closely, collect data, and support various aspects of the scientific process. The digital images that result provide visual support for revisiting an experience, examining details, and discussing and sharing this experience with others. This can lead to a deeper understanding of concepts and further growth in a variety of learning areas such as science, math, and literacy.

Digital camera scavenger hunts can further extend students' observational skills by encouraging them to look for and capture specific images. Shapes or letters formed in nature, different insects in the yard, or whatever concepts are being explored, can all be the focus of these forays into digital documentation. Photos can be displayed for the class as a closure activity and later posted on a classroom blog, with student descriptions that interpret and describe the activity. Documentation makes it available to family members and allows it to be shared with relatives near and far. Offering new and effective options to communicate with families about what is happening in the classroom and its significance, is important. It is one strategy for developing a mutual understanding of early learning goals and how they connect with children's classroom experiences. It also provides information that can promote conversations to extend learning at home.

Storyography (Collison, 2013) is a powerful pedagogical technique for story-making that begins with child-initiated and directed imaginative play and utilizes

Figure 12.3 Documenting an Exciting Butterfly Eclosion

Courtesy of the Early Learning Community, Pacific University

a digital camera. The approach allows a teacher to work closely with a child to document the narrative of his or her play and to turn this into a book. Here is the process.

> As children engage in play with manipulative materials, the teacher will inquire about the nature of the narrative on which they are working: dragon attacking a castle, horses playing in the forest, or whatever might be imagined. While the child is using the Legos or blocks or figures, the teacher will have the child narrate the actions and will use their words to transcribe the details of the story. As a next step the teacher reads the story back to the child and will ask about important elements that can be represented in a series of photographs as illustrations. The child will then pose each element of the story and take a series of photographs that the teacher will print. Combining the child's written words with the child's photographs, the teacher and child will create pages that will be spiral bound, creating a book that is their story. For many children this is their first "published" story, and the pride they have in this work is manifest in repeated readings and revisiting.

This simple use of digital cameras with preschoolers effectively inspires literacy emergent from play. It naturally builds on, extends, and integrates children's experiences. This approach can be strongly supportive of intentionality and creativity on the part of the child, and it allows the child to continue to revisit, retell, and refine the story with peers and family members long after it is written. It is a low-technology high-return approach to emergent literacy.

Depending on the children's and teacher's comfort and skills using technology, the use of digital tools and their impact on the learning experience may develop over time. Simpler activities, such as the one described above, may be the precursor to more sophisticated uses that transform the learning process, as both teachers and children become increasingly aware of the possibilities digital tools and media provide, and more fluent in their use.

We can consider technological tools and their use in early childhood classrooms in relation to well-known classification systems such as Bloom's Taxonomy (Bloom, 1956), with a hierarchy ranging from simply knowing or remembering, to at the highest level, creating (Anderson et al., 2000; Bailey, 2001; Churches, 2009). Puentedura's SAMR model (2006) is also taxonomic. It describes technology use as a substitute for traditional tools at the lowest level. At the highest level is the creation of unique new learning tasks using nascent technologies that allow students to accomplish pedagogical goals never before possible. In most contexts, the higher-level uses of tools can lead to significant improvements in student outcomes. These hierarchies are therefore designed to help teachers understand that there are differing qualities to the use of a technology depending on the context and learning activities. This insight should both empower teachers to recognize the range of possibilities, as well as encourage higher-level uses of tools where appropriate.

Figure 12.4 Teacher Scaffolding Photograph for a Narrated Story

Courtesy of the Early Learning Community, Pacific University

When Claire and Raven collaborated on their presentation, the teacher was supporting work at the highest taxonomic levels: creating in a way that would not be possible without technological support. Photographing block constructions and extending that work into storymaking as described above is another example of an innovative use of technology that allows students to create in powerful and innovative ways.

Another important classroom axiom is that the most effective educational tools and activities tend to be those that are open-ended and flexible for use by students in a variety of contexts. These are activities that energize learners to take the ideas or questions they have and empower them to explore or express in new ways; activities that expand a child's opportunity to do what interests them and that provide alternative ways to participate: activities that facilitate child-initiated, child-directed, and teacher-supported playful learning (Bredekamp & Copple, 1997). Pink (2011) speaks to this in terms of the intrinsic motivation provided by tasks and tools that provide autonomy, encourage mastery, and engage the individual in purposeful learning.

Digital Microscopes

Children are naturally curious about the hidden worlds around them. They wonder how and why, and want to view the unseen. One of the great joys of early learning occurs when children experience seeing the world from a new perspective. This makes digital microscopes a quintessential early childhood education technology. Good digital microscopes offer the power of Ms. Frizzle to transport learners to the level of fibers or textures, or to examine the scales on a butterfly's wing. Children can demonstrate an impressive ability to dwell in the role of the micro-explorer at the science table of wonders when a microscope is present.

Digital microscopes are also an eminently social tool that put children in control of what is explored. They allow children to make and share discoveries with others, either with the live images, or later through their photos. Intentionally providing learners with items that contain interesting textures and surfaces will allow them to connect their sense of touch with the image of the surface they are viewing. A transformative use of a microscope begins when a wireless microscope and

Figure 12.5 Digital Microscope Brings a Hidden World to Life

Courtesy of the Early Learning Community, Pacific University

tablet computer can be carried to objects of interest, rather than having to bring a specimen to the scope. A worm's hole and castings, drops of dew on a flower, spiders in their webs, bumble bees collecting pollen on an artichoke, all can now be explored in the wild.

The Proscope wireless microscope creates its own IP network allowing a teacher or student to display the microscope's images simultaneously on over 200 devices and to snap a photo to be sent to all those screens at once. We have found that setting them up at a learning station with specifically selected materials such as moss or shells or moldy pumpkins, and posing a carefully crafted provocation, can initiate dynamic investigative collaborations (Furgison, 2013).

The use of digital microscopes can foster authentic child-directed learning, promote exploration, and encourage higher-level thinking skills as students wonder or hypothesize. They are supportive of problem finding and problem solving. These microscopes are inherently motivating for children of all ages and are an excellent example of a digital tool that is really transcendent of any analog equivalent.

Tablet Computers

Tablet computers such as the iPad or Kindle have become a popular choice in many classrooms, just as they have in many homes (Common Sense Media, 2013). The tool offers child-centered portability and the intimacy of a touch screen. However, the tablet is only the platform; the quality of the learning is really dependent on the applications available to students, and these vary greatly with regard to educational quality and available features (Bailey & Appel, 2013; Buckleitner, 2013).

While the applications on this one tool can support a wide range of uses, this inherent flexibility can also be an issue. Our teachers in Oregon have found it works best to introduce the apps one or two at a time rather than all at once. Interested children are invited to join an iPad research committee at the end of each week. Those children spend time looking through all the apps on the iPad and are asked to think critically about which would help their peers learn new concepts. They are asked to choose a couple of apps and present their ideas to a teacher about which would be the best for their learning (and why). Teacher and children then decide on the apps that will be available for the whole class the following week.

When putting out a tablet for use, we have noticed that it is not uncommon for children to bounce from one app to another without thoughtfully dwelling on any of them. Teachers have helped students be more purposeful with their iPad use through the use of iPad plans (Bailey & Appel, 2013). During free choice learning time in the classroom, the kindergarten teachers have been successful in not making the iPad itself a choice, but asking children to choose one specific app from among those selected by the iPad research committee. Only this selection of apps is available on a given week. This has greatly reduced bouncing app syndrome.

An app we have used a great deal in our programs is StoryKit. It allows students to write or type their own stories, to add photographs and create illustrations, and then record audio to go with it. Stories can be posted on the Web for invited people to view. StoryKit also has the capability to share student-created stories via email and the app bookshelf. Kindergarten Teacher Aja Appel describes how she uses StoryKit in the classroom:

> In my classroom we use this app in several different ways. During Writers Workshop student authors sometimes choose to publish a story of which they are particularly proud. One means of publishing a story can be using StoryKit. To do this a student will use the camera feature of the app to snap a photograph of each page of his/her story. The author can then add an audio recording of him/herself reading each page of the story. This recording feature empowers students and enables even the most emergent writers to capture the rich details of their stories. For example, Aven spent 45 minutes illustrating and meticulously sounding out, looking up, asking peers, and writing out the words "school", "sister", and "me" which are the only words on his illustrated page. Without StoryKit, that would have been the end of his story. Fortunately, on this day Aven choose to use the StoryKit app to take a photo of his story and record the audio version.
>
> He recorded, "a long time ago my sister and me went to the ELC and it's the one we're in right now and when she came out a lot of times she would pick me up and we would talk together." I just love that ending. "And we would talk together." The depth and richness really comes through when Aven was able to record his story through both written words and an audio recording. It may take an emergent writer an entire class period to write a letter, a word, or a sentence. While it's critically important that students spend time learning to sound out words and practice the physical act of writing, without the support of the StoryKit app, the rich details of their stories would be lost.
>
> Bailey and Appel (2013)

Apps like StoryKit, Sago Mini Doodlecast (used in the sunflower study), Puppet Pals HD Director's Pass, and others that have an intuitive interface and are open-ended, can be used with young children in a variety of ways. While there are many creativity apps available, it is useful to note not only the features of each app, but also the specific formats for saving children's work. These factors should be considered when deciding what app to use and become important if you would like to save a child-created story for a digital portfolio of their work to be shared with families.

When teachers are very familiar with the features of an app, such as Puppet Pals HD, they are better able to offer activities that support different aspects of a curriculum. This app allows children to take and import a photo, which can be of a drawing they have created or something in their environment. They can then

Figure 12.6 Aven's Touching Story/Illustration

Courtesy of the Early Learning Community, Pacific University

use that image as a puppet character or background or use characters and back-grounds provided with the app to create an animated puppet show. They can eas-ily manipulate their characters, making them larger and smaller and moving them around the stage, while recording their own voice speaking the parts. Vocabu-lary and concepts introduced to the children, such as *big, small, over, under,* and *around* can be played out as the children move the characters and record their stories. Dialogue between characters is also supported as children develop the narrative of their presentation.

There are a variety of apps for tablets that support a range of children's plan-ning and problem-solving skills while being great fun. Newbie Chess is one of these. What makes this app effective for young children is the level of scaffolding it provides. All possible chess moves can be displayed for each turn. Once a move is made, it is possible to see its result and undo and try a different move. Kinder-gartners tend to engage in this game both in parallel play (each playing against their own tablets), or in collaborative play where they take turns making moves against the tablet and discussing what happened. The result has been a very social group cheering each other on, while developing a range of higher-level thinking skills. This collaborative problem solving with instantaneous feedback is a significant aspect of learning on any computing device. Not only does this apply to chess, but also to a variety of other problem-solving or instructional apps.

Foldify is another iPad application that supports higher-level thinking and that allows students to be creative in three dimensions. The program facilitates the design and printing of cubed creations, using painting tools, words, photos, and stamps. Classroom mathematicians then hone their small-motor skills by folding the printed paper into the six-sided structures or characters, which can then be incorporated into their dramatic play activities. Foldify is an unusual application that teaches mathematical concepts, while also being open-ended and creative. Students often use Foldify in a collaborative manner, working with partners or small groups to design new structures. The app requires students to design on the two-dimensional tablet, what will be folded into three dimensions after printing. This extends their skills of visualization as well as geometry and collaboration. The students are as fascinated with the process of creating the image, as they are of printing and bringing it to life through folding. They use the resulting creations for dramatic play as vehicles, superheroes, and structures. Great insight is provided into children's abilities and social skills as they problem-solve during design, folding, and dramatic play (Bailey & Appel, 2013).

While Google Earth is typically conceived of as an adult tool, it can also be empowering for young learners when used on a tablet or an interactive whiteboard. During a study of Komodo dragons that was initiated by a kindergarten class after a chance reference in a story, students read in library books that these creatures lived on Komodo Island in Indonesia. When students thirsted for more information about the island and its habitat, their thoughtful teacher was intentional in her reflection about what tools might support and extend the student's learning. She believed that Google Earth was the most appropriate choice. This software would visually zoom the students from their school, across the ocean, and down to land on the island. The app also allowed the students to view photos and video that others had taken from the island and posted to share. The class was able to view the national parks on the island, explore videos of the physical landmarks and of the island's dragon inhabitants (Bailey & Appel, 2013). This is one of those transformative tools that allows a redefinition of what is possible in the study of our world and creates unique learning opportunities for young students.

Cam has spent the past 15 minutes completely absorbed in the work he is doing on his iPad. Occupied by the interactive mathematics tool he is using, Cam appears oblivious to the swirls of activity around him even as cleanup begins, and ends. As children line up to head to lunch, Cam appears only distantly aware of the movement as he is deeply engaged counting to himself and constructing his next answer. Motivated to keep pushing himself to the next level of problem solving but recognizing the class is leaving, Cam slowly gets up to return the pad to its shelf, but standing in front of the shelf, he keeps calculating and answering.

Children enveloped in this immersive learning experience can at times be characterized by Csikszentmihalyi's notion of "flow" in which there is an optimal match between the challenge of the ideas or interface and the skills and interest that an individual brings to the task (Shernoff & Csikszentmihalyi, 2009). This can be observed at a basic level in a child enraptured by a book, or more complexly, by a complete immersion in constructing with Legos. There are numerous high-quality apps (Buckleitner, 2013) that can provide an immersive experience when matched with a specific learner. The challenge for teachers, as always, it to identify those that are higher quality and to make sure that children do not spend an inappropriate amount of time in solitary learning.

Luke is a kindergartner fascinated with the Titanic and other shipwrecks. Bringing a wealth of knowledge to his play, Luke has crafted amazing Lego replicas (including icebergs and the Carpathia), a four-foot wooden block facsimile at the dock, a giant outdoor block reconstruction and playdough version, and drawn the ship by hand. Most of these have been done in solitary play. Recently a virtual tour of the ship on CD (Chrisp, 2011) was added to the classroom computer.

Figure 12.7 Titanic Reimagined Through Blocks

Courtesy of the Early Learning Community, Pacific University

Figure 12.8 Sharing the Titanic Book and Interactive Program

Courtesy of the Early Learning Community, Pacific University

The ability for Luke to stand on deck or be in the wheelhouse or next to a lifeboat on the Titanic has given him a new first-person level of understanding of the ship. Furthermore, he has consistently had multiple peers at his side and engaged in explanations, demonstrations, and considerable social interaction around these explorations. His small motor skills have also improved as he has become more proficient at using the mouse to guide his movements through the ship. His subsequent personal constructions of the ship have been even more elaborative, informed as they are by his virtual experiences. This is a perfect example of what is coming to be referred to as transmedia play: student-directed thematically integrated play across a wide range of media. It is also an example of the utility of technology to empower children to experience new forms of learning.

> Nicholas is often busy in the block and dramatic play areas, but today decides to create a drawing on the computer using an open-ended art software program that allows him to draw, paint, and embellish his artwork in a variety of ways. To his teacher, he dictates his story about going to a birthday party during a strong storm. She types up his story in a text box, he selects from a variety of voice options, clicks "play", and is pleased to hear his story read

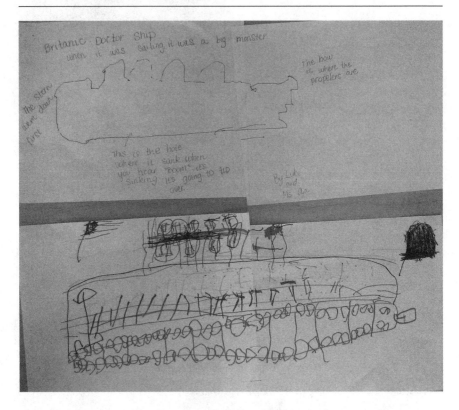

Figure 12.9 Before and After Drawings of the Titanic, 2 Months Apart

Courtesy of the Early Learning Community, Pacific University

aloud. After his teacher hands him his classroom name card, he uses the pencil tool to write the first letter of his name on the digital story. Not satisfied with the result, he uses the undo function, and tries again, happy with his second attempt. Despite frequent invitations involving paper, this is the first time that Nicholas has tried to write his name. His success appears to be meaningful, as he develops a new interest in writing his name in other situations including at the writing center. The affordances of this digital tool provided scaffolding enabling Nicholas to try something new.

Based on the stories shared in *Young Children and Computers: Storytelling and Learning in a Digital Age* by Blagojevic, Chevalier, MacIsaac, Hitchcock, and Frechette (2009)

Nicholas' teacher realizes that the children in her classroom have differing abilities, interests, and learning preferences. She brings a universal design for learning perspective to the planning process, offering a variety of ways to help children meet learning goals, including through the use of digital tools. Her understanding of child development, how all the tools in her classroom function, and why certain tools are effective in engaging specific children helps her to plan in ways that are considerate of the range of student needs in her classroom, assisting her in maximizing the learning experience for everyone.

The variety of activities possible using the range of available technologies, showcases the flexibility of these tools to support a diversity of learners. To help all children access the curriculum, universal design for learning concepts suggest there should be multiple means of representing content and information, opportunities for children to show what they know, and to be involved with activities that are engaging and motivating (CAST, 2013). For a child recently arrived from Mexico, unfamiliar with firefighters and what they do, being able to listen to the Spanish language version of an engaging informational app about firefighters provides knowledge that not only gives context when the firefighter comes to visit but also for subsequent firefighter play. The use of technology allows this child to more fully participate in the classroom community. In another example, "Caleb, who has cerebral palsy, lacks the motor skills to play with blocks, but he can stack digital blocks using an app on a tablet. While the goal remains to use real-world materials, the tablet offers Caleb valuable play experiences not possible before" (Blagojevic et al., 2012, p. 21).

How can we help *all* children benefit from enriching educational experiences using technology such as those described in this chapter? "Research and awareness of the value of technology tools and interactive media in early childhood education needs to be shared with policy makers who are interested in issues of access and equity for children, parents, families, and teachers." (NAEYC & Fred Rogers Center, 2012, p. 4). By learning about and modeling appropriate technology use, advocating for technology access and media balance, initiating conversations and developing collaborations between early childhood educators and community members, we can more effectively plan to use technology in healthy ways that can positively impact young children.

Conclusion

We encourage you to explore the wide range of uses and tools left undescribed in this chapter. Investigate the utility of iPods for hearing recorded stories and interact with a whole generation of literature brought to life with quality media enhancements or newly created by developers such as Moonbot Studios. Experiment with keyboards, interactive cubes, and microphones as a means of creating musical pieces or recording children's work. Review Web-based applications such as MapSkip or Storybird that allow informed interactive mapping or artful collaborative storymaking. Play with Littlebits, robotics, and many more emergent and imaginative tools still on the cusp of invention. Finally, look for what is on the horizon. Imagine how three-dimensional printing will contribute to a change in children's thinking about designing and creating in the classroom.

Re-envision the process of emergent literacy when a child can speak, and their words will accurately appear on a screen. Speech to text will provide yet another transformation in children's ability to convey their ideas and emotions.

These are exciting times to be an early childhood educator. As quality digital tools continue to be developed, they can support new opportunities to inspire young learners. As you consider the options for effective classroom technology use, be thoughtful in your planning. Design the use of tools that will support active, hands-on work, and use tools and plan activities that are engaging, empowering, and collaborative. Plan in advance for scaffolds to support authentic and appropriate learning and make sure that technology is only one of the many options you consider to support learning. As much as we might be advocates for innovative tools and pedagogies, please remember that children need to color and draw, to run and jump, to play with blocks and balls, and lie on their backs and watch the clouds. They need to be allowed to embrace their childhood, and they need teachers to be supportive of a wide range of appropriate developmental experiences. Make sure that your use of technology supports rather than supplants these essential activities. So play and learn along with your students using the full range of classroom materials that are available and have fun in the process.

Teacher Takeaways

1. Explore and play with technological tools to better understand how they can be used to support and extend students' learning.
2. Identify learning objectives and consider which tools, including technology, can provide young children with a range of developmentally appropriate, hands-on activities to achieve these objectives.
3. Provide provocations to facilitate technology use in ways that are engaging, empowering, collaborative, and that support student explorations ranging from playful to in-depth.
4. Join a community of practice, consult current research, and use social networking or other professional development opportunities to inform appropriate use of technology with young children.
5. Support important conversations in your community about topics such as media balance, use of technology to support not supplant other valuable early learning activities, and equal access to educational opportunities (including technology) for all children.

References

Anderson, L. W., Krathwohl, D. R., Airasian, P. W., Cruikshank, K. A., Mayer, R. E., Pintrich, . . . Wittrock, M. C. (2000). *A taxonomy for learning, teaching, and assessing: A revision of Bloom's taxonomy of educational objectives*. New York, NY: Pearson/ Allyn & Bacon.

Bailey, M. (2001, February 23). *Bloom, the brain and technology: Teaching and learning in the electronic classroom.* Paper presented at for the Oregon Association for Teacher Education Annual Conference, Eugene, OR.

Bailey, M., & Appel, A. (2013, February 10). *Effective, appropriate and intentional use of technology tools in early childhood classrooms.* Invited Webinar, Erikson Institute, Chicago, IL.

Blagojevic, B., Chevalier, S., MacIsaac, A., Hitchcock, L., & Frechette, B. (2009). Young children and computers: Storytelling and learning in a digital age. *Teaching Young Children, 3*(5), 1–5. Retrieved from www.naeyc.org/files/tyc/file/TYC_V3N4_Blago jevicexpanded.pdf

Blagojevic, B., Brumer, H., Chevalier, S., O'Clair, A., & Thomes, K. (2012). *Touch and grow: Learning and exploring using tablets.* Retrieved from www.naeyc.org/tyc/article/touch_and_grow

Bloom B.S. (1956). *Taxonomy of educational objectives, Handbook I: The cognitive domain.* New York, NY: David McKay Co Inc.

Bredekamp, S., & Copple, C. (Eds.). (1997). *Developmentally appropriate practice in early childhood programs* [Rev. ed.]. Washington, DC: National Association for the Education of Young Children.

Buckleitner, W. (2013). *Children's Technology Review: About the ratings.* Retrieved from http://childrenstech.com/about/ratings

CAST. (2013). *About UDL.* Retrieved from www.cast.org/udl/index.html

Chrisp, P. (2011). *Explore Titanic: Breathtaking new pictures, recreated with digital technology* [Har/Cdr edition]. Hauppauge, NY: Barron's Educational Series.

Churches, A. (2009) *Blooms digital taxonomy.* Retrieved from http://edorigami.wikispaces.com

Collison, L. (2013). *Storyography.* Published as part of Best Practices Website. Retrieved from http://fg.ed.pacificu.edu/cldc/cameras.html

Common Sense Media. (2013). *Zero to eight: Children's media use in America 2013.* Retrieved from www.commonsensemedia.org/research

Furgison, K. (2013). *Digital microscopes: Pumpkin investigations.* Published as part of Best Practices Website. Retrieved from http://fg.ed.pacificu.edu/cldc/microscopes.html

International Society for Technology in Education. (2008, 2012). ISTE standards for teachers. Eugene, OR: Author. Retrieved from www.iste.org/standards/standards-for-teachers

Mejia, R. (2013). *Digital cameras.* Published as part of Best Practices Website. Retrieved from http://fg.ed.pacificu.edu/cldc/cameras.html

National Association for the Education of Young Children, & Fred Rogers Center for Early Learning and Children's Media at Saint Vincent College. (2012). *Technology and interactive media as tools in early childhood programs serving children from birth through age 8.* Washington, DC: NAEYC; Latrobe, PA: Fred Rogers Center for Early Learning and Children's Media at Saint Vincent College.

Papert, S. (1993). *The children's machine: Rethinking school in the age of the computer.* New York, NY: Basic Books.

Pink, D.H. (2011). *Drive: The surprising truth about what motivates us.* New York, NY: Riverhead Books.

Puentedura, R. (2006). *Transformation, technology, and education.* Retrieved from http://hippasus.com/resources/tte/

Shernoff, D.J., & Csikszentmihalyi, M. (2009). Flow in schools: Cultivating engaged learners and optimal learning environments. In R.C. Gilman, E.S. Heubner, & M.J. Furlong (Eds.), *Handbook of positive psychology in schools* (pp. 131–145). New York, NY: Routledge.

Resources

- Foldify, www.foldifyapp.com
- *Google Earth*, Google www.google.com/earth/
- iPad, www.apple.com/ipad/
- Kindle, https://kindle.amazon.com
- Littlebits, http://littlebits.cc
- MapSkip, www.mapskip.com
- Moonbot Studios, http://moonbotstudios.com/#start
- *Ms. Frizzle,* The Magic School, Scholastic www.scholastic.com/magicschoolbus/
- *Newbie Chess*, Luminary Apps, http://luminaryapps.com/products/newbiechess/
- Proscope Microscope, www.bodelin.com/proscope
- *Puppet Pals HD Director's Pass*, Polished Play, www.polishedplay.com
- *Sago Mini Doodlecast,* Sago Sago, www.sagosago.com/app/sago_mini_doodlecast
- Storybird, http://storybird.com
- *StoryKit*, International Children's Digital Library, http://en.childrenslibrary.org

Learn More . . .

- Comienza en Casa/It Starts at Home, www.manomaine.org/programs/mep/comienzaencasa
- ISTE, International Society for Technology in Education, www.iste.org
- National Library of Virtual Manipulatives, Utah State University, http://nlvm.usu.edu/en/nav/vlibrary.html
- Pacific University Child Learning & Development Center Best Practices Page, http://fg.ed.pacificu.edu/cldc/bestpractices.html

Technology Tools for Teachers and Teaching: Innovative Practices and Emerging Technologies

Brian Puerling and Angela Fowler

Introduction

Basic technologies, such as rulers and scales, have been used in classrooms for many years. As technology across the globe quickly evolves and advances, people discover new and more efficient ways to manage calendars, communicate with others, and create content. In classrooms, teachers are using technology to do just the same. They are exploring the technology landscape for resources to help them streamline their documentation, gather information more efficiently, and more effectively communicate with the families in their classrooms. Additionally, teachers are on the lookout for new and innovative ways to provide meaningful experiences for children. Today, in a business meeting, a document camera can offer a quick way to spontaneously project and display a document or 3D prototype for a new product. In the classroom, it can offer teachers and students the opportunity to spontaneously project a drawing or piece of artwork created by a student, or a teacher can project various kinds of soil to compare texture.

Brian says . . . Teachers are increasingly seeing technology as another tool for their classrooms. As they explore strategies and reflect on their students' responses, they see the value in these experiences. A book is an amazing tool to invite children to become immersed in a story. When I was teaching preschool, I remember the expressions of anticipation when I would finish reading a chapter in the Magic Treehouse series. An iPad, projected on a screen can be a tool to extend enthusiastic read-alouds. Children can reach out and connect with authors via video-conferencing tools. iPads also invite opportunities to engage with and enjoy children's literature in another way. When children are familiar with a particular story, they can experience the same story through enhanced e-books (Chiong, Ree, Takeuchi, & Erickson, 2012), and they can see the characters they know and love come to life.

Cultivating Teachers as Learners

Angela says . . . In supporting teachers' understanding and innovative use of technology, we must look at two common challenges. As an early childhood instructor at Columbia College in Chicago, I see preservice teachers who are so familiar with technology that they tend to overuse it in developmentally inappropriate or less meaningful ways, and I also work with more experienced and less technologically savvy teachers who tend to ignore it all together. We know neither of these two extremes reflects best practice. The challenge is how to support these teachers where they are in their understanding and how to help them realize technology is a teaching tool that can support excellent teaching practice if used appropriately.

Brian says . . . As Director of Education Technology at Catherine Cook School in Chicago, I support teachers in all sorts of ways. Just like children, each adult learns in a different way. Given this, the support I give each teacher varies. In terms of planning, I meet with teachers individually, in grade-level teams, and as a staff. Teachers have varying comfort levels with technology, so leading up to a planned activity, teachers may need different types of experiences. Some teachers may need to observe my interactions with the children and the technologies, they may need me to observe them interacting with their students and the technologies, or they may need to sit back and observe an introduction with the entire class. When it comes to the actual planned experience, I may lead the entire lesson as the teacher observes, I may observe and chime in as a support voice as needed, or perhaps I pull small groups (see Figure 13.1). The frequency of support also varies depending on what the teacher would like to achieve. One teacher may like support every now and then when he or she recognizes the need

Figure 13.1 Brian Puerling Demonstrates Technology to a Class

Courtesy of Catherine Cook School

for an extra mind for ideas or an extra pair of hands. Other teachers may want to maintain a more consistent level of support, coming in for a given period of time on certain days. These various methods of support provide teachers with personalized and comfortable entry points into technology integration that is respectful of their experience, interest, and goals.

Angela says . . . In order to support best practice and innovative use of technology with young children, we must begin to shift teacher's beliefs about technology. Technology has become an everyday part of our lives, but many teachers still don't see technology as an "integrated" part of their classrooms. Many teachers fear technology integration or only know how to use technology as a game console or e-book. Learning how to integrate technology in developmentally appropriate ways requires a different mindset altogether. In order to facilitate this shift, we must support teachers in understanding that technology integration can be an opportunity for learning not only for students, but for themselves as well. Anytime we see ourselves as learners, we are more willing to explore, more willing to not know, and more willing to take chances (Hawkins, 2002). It is in this exploration and risk taking that developmentally appropriate technology integration will begin to happen.

In the past decade, technology has grown so fast that any teacher would be hard pressed to keep up with it. However, exploring and embracing this growth could also be the answer to making sense of the ever-changing landscape of early childhood education. Emerging technologies can be a teacher's biggest ally rather than their enemy. An excellent example of this is in the area of assessment. In early childhood, there has been a huge shift in the assessment of young children due to the need to compile hard data about student performance. Because teachers need to provide these data, they have shifted away from more authentic forms of assessment such as observation, anecdotal notes, and work samples to more data-driven systems of checklists and testing. Innovative technologies however, have the potential to change the way we think about hard data and how we collect and compile it. There are many new apps on the market for iPads and other devices that are supporting more authentic documentation and assessment.

At Columbia College, early childhood educators in collaboration with an educational resource company recently worked on an app, Childfolio, that has the capability to connect all forms of authentically collected assessment such as photographs, video clips, audio clips, anecdotal notes, and work samples. These individual collections of assessment can then be organized, tagged for keywords and standards, and saved in a searchable portfolio system. These portfolios are then automatically turned into a database and easily transformed into professional data-driven reports. These reports illustrate each student's developmental level, standards mastered, content areas addressed, and more. This is only one example of an application that was designed to help teachers more effectively and appropriately assess young children. There are many more applications like these being developed, and we are just beginning to see the impact of these emerging technologies on innovative teaching practices.

Position Statement Alignment

> When the integration of technology and interactive media in early childhood programs is built upon solid developmental foundations, and early childhood professionals are aware of both the challenges and the opportunities, educators are positioned to improve program quality by intentionally leveraging the potential of technology and media for the benefit of every child.
>
> National Association for the Education of Young Children
> [NAEYC] & Fred Rogers Center (2012), p. 1

Cultivating Communication Through Technology

Brian says . . . Communication technologies are another area where the sky could be the limit depending on the policies and capabilities of your school. This shouldn't mean we leave behind the personal phone call or carefully handwritten notes, but technology opens up new opportunities for communicating with families, other teachers, administration, and the worldwide early childhood community, and these opportunities need to be embraced. Schools are constantly trying to find ways to engage parents, and for better or worse, most parents are more "plugged in" than ever. The days of parents stopping by school just to chat, volunteering, and participating in every school event unfortunately is dwindling. There are many reasons for this including the need for stronger home/school partnerships. However, for parent engagement to be effective and meaningful, parents need to feel like they are part of the school (Epstein, 2005). They need to feel connected. It is this very idea of connection where we need to think more innovatively. Yes, parents are "plugged in," and we are not likely to unplug them. Most adults live in a world where being plugged in is paramount to their working lives and to managing personal and professional responsibilities. So instead of trying to compete with technology, we should be embracing it when appropriate. There are so many amazing and easy technological ways to keep parents informed about what is happening in the classroom that you might just find parents becoming so engaged they come back to the classroom.

Most schools these days have a website and many classrooms have webpages, but what do those websites communicate about your school or classroom? Think about your own Web searches. Let's say you are looking for a new dentist: Where is the first place you look? You search the Internet, and though your decision will not be solely based on the website of your chosen dentist, you will certainly take away a first impression from their website. What kind of first impression do you want to communicate to your parents, and the community? It is understandable that many schools, and especially teachers, once had very basic websites. They were cumbersome to create, and perhaps there wasn't someone on staff to build and manage the site, or there wasn't money in the budget to pay someone to create and maintain it. This has drastically changed over the past few years. There are a multitude of tools available online for easy website development and maintenance for very little expense or even for free. So, schools and teachers can easily update their websites and think about the message they are sending parents and the community.

It is important to note the differences between websites and blogs; the intentions of both resources are different (Puerling, 2013). Many settings and organizations are discovering that having both a website and a blog is effective in sharing various pieces of information.

Tools for Communicating

The Internet also holds a wealth of opportunities for communicating with families and the community beyond a website. In fact, there are different avenues for communication developed every day. Though we will point out a few in this chapter, by the time this book goes to print, there will be even more exciting opportunities for communication. When thinking about communicating with families and the community, you need to think about the ways that you communicate with your own family and community. These are the same ways that your student's families will be communicating. Facebook is still one of the most popular ways families connect and communicate, and though there are privacy concerns, it is still an avenue to pursue. Many teachers have classroom Facebook pages, but be sure to check your school's policies and procedures for participation in social media. Classroom blogs are another way to communicate. Though they are not as direct a connection as Facebook, they do allow a little more customization by the blogger. Just as there are a multitude of website development tools out there, there are also a multitude of blog hosting websites. A simple online search will give teachers lots of options that fit their level of technological understanding. Twitter and Snapchat are other ways teachers are staying in touch with families. These social media platforms allow teachers to quickly update followers about what is going on in the classroom on the fly, so to speak. This is particularly true of Snapchat, which gives quick updates via photos, video, and drawings that disappear after a few seconds. Snapchat also has the added feature of allowing teachers to control the list of people who are invited to see their Snapchat.

Website	Blog
Mission and Vision	Examples of curriculum experiences
Approaches to Curriculum	Reflections of school events
Faculty and Staff Information	Description of new programs
History of Program	Celebrations
	Updates for current families
	Guest bloggers

Tools for Sharing Photos

Angela says . . . Photo sharing, online photo printing, and book publishing sites are other ways to communicate what is going on in the classroom. Teachers have been using these kinds of tools for many years, and they just keep getting better. Photo sharing sites allow you to take pictures and share them with parents. Photo printing sites and book publishing sites go a step further and have the capability to turn your photos into published hard and soft back books. The online interfaces for these sites are easy to use and let you add text and other details. Most of these sites also publish your book with an official ISBN number. They also allow others with the login information to purchase books. Some can even help you raise money. Blurb for example, is essentially a self-publishing site and allows teachers to set their own price for published books. There are many sites to choose from, including Blurb, Snapfish, Walgreens, and Shutterfly, so teachers need to search and see which one is right for them. They are all easily searched, using tags like photo sharing, online photo printing, or online book publishing.

Innovative technologies for the classroom can come from unintentional places as well. Many of us have enjoyed Pinterest for years collecting all our great food ideas, decorating inspirations, and favorite travel destinations. But, at a recent educators conference that limited view of Pinterest was shifted forever. A professor of early childhood education shared how she used Pinterest in her course on Developmentally Appropriate Environments. She searched images and saved them to her boards and used the boards as assignments for students to evaluate environments. This shift in thinking immediately opened up a multitude of possibilities, especially for the use of Pinterest in the classroom. Teachers can easily share information about topics of study in the classroom for parents and children at home. They can post boards about suggested activities at home. They can ask parents themselves to create boards to share with other parents based on topics of interest. The possibilities are endless.

Tools for Sharing Video

Brian says . . . Webcams are another tool we can use in creative and innovative ways. Many teachers cringe when they think about webcams in the classroom. They don't want an eye on them all the time. Webcam's however, can be an excellent live connection to the classroom for parents and children and have much better uses than a blurry view of the whole classroom. Webcams instead should be used for focused observations. Have you ever studied monarch butterflies in the classroom only to have them emerge out of their chrysalis over the weekend? By using a webcam focused on the monarchs, you can allow children and parents access to the butterflies at all times. Webcams are great tools for keeping track of classroom pets, hatching chicks, and even watching your garden grow. Webcams are easy to set up and maintain. Most computers will already have the required software and an external webcam is inexpensive and easy to find.

Webcams are also a tool to expand the classroom walls (Puerling, 2012). They provide children with the opportunity to connect with individuals who may not be able to visit the classroom. Teachers can invite guest readers into the classroom virtually. These guest readers may be distant family members or previous classroom guests. In inquiry-based experiences such as the project approach, children use all sorts of resources to conduct research (Harris-Helm & Katz, 2010) including other people. In these experiences, children can use videoconference software such as Skype, FaceTime, and Google+ to virtually interview authors, artists, musicians, scientists, and other people of interest.

Tools for Connecting Home and Classroom

QR codes, those squares bar codes you see everywhere, are ways to help parents get a view into what is happening in the classroom (see Figure 13.2). At the Catherine Cook School, teachers have discovered that QR codes add a new layer of access to their bulletin boards. For example, kindergarten teacher Amanda Burns video records her students dramatizing stories they have written. After recording these stories, she posts a printed narrative of the child's story with a QR code linked to the recorded video. Posted in the hallway and in the classroom, visitors to the school and the students can access these experiences instantly.

Though most of the tools we have been talking about have been available for many years and may simply require a shift in your thinking for use in the classroom, there are new communication technologies emerging every day. One area of emerging technology is the ePortfolio for use with young children. There have

Figure 13.2 A QR Code

Courtesy of Brian Puerling

been basic forms of digital portfolios around for a while. Many institutions of higher education have used learning management systems that include ePortfolios for years. Tablet technologies, however, have made ePortfolios possible in the early childhood classrooms by changing the way we can collect, organize, and manage the work of children. It also changes the way we can communicate this information to parents, colleagues, administrators, and even governing bodies. There are basic applications available to help organize ePortfolios or anecdotal notes on children's development in any given area. Paperdesk and Confer are applications that provide a streamlined, yet flexible, way to gather and organize electronic documents, photographs, and notes. There are other applications that help teachers capture moments that can later be shared with parents. Doodlecast Pro is an application teachers can use to overlay audio on an image. For example, a child could reflect on a photograph of a field trip by recording his or her voice with the photograph, creating a shareable video.

Angela says . . . There are also more comprehensive assessment application like the one we spoke of earlier created at Columbia College. This app, Childfolio, allows teachers to document and organize learning in multiple ways. It then allows teachers to manage the documentation in ways that best suits their school or program. For example, a teacher may have certain documentation she has turned into data collections that provide required information to their governing body such as the state board of education or Head Start. However, she may also have documentation collections that are meant to help parents understand their child's development. Some ePortfolios allow for this kind of management and could potentially improve the way we assess young children, as well as communicate with parents and others. Though the information shared in the ePortfolios can be completely secured using password protections and encryption, online access to this kind of information is still a concern with many schools. As more and more information becomes Web-based, we hope teachers and schools will develop a better understanding of technology and feel more comfortable in its use.

Position Statement Alignment

> Technology and media should not replace activities such as creative play, real-life exploration, physical activity, outdoor experiences, conversation, and social interactions that are important for children's development. Technology and media should be used to support learning, not an isolated activity, and to expand young children's access to new content.
>
> NAEYC & Fred Rogers Center (2012), p. 5

Tools for Creativity

Brian says . . . Early childhood educators are learning what an amazing tool multi-touch mobile devices can be for young children. As Director of Education

Technology at Catherine Cook School in Chicago, I am always on the lookout for new ways for students to explore, develop, and share their creativity. Teachers thoughtfully plan units of study across the grades, students enroll in enrichment classes, they can participate in after school clubs, electives, and field trips, all of which provide children with opportunities to use their unique abilities, interests, and strengths to express themselves and share their learning. As I assess the multitude of tools available to teachers and students, I continue to be astounded by the opportunities technology offers students to explore their creativity. I have seen preschoolers record their remixes of nursery rhymes using an application, DJ MIX KIDS, and kindergartners learning about story elements by creating their own cartoons using Toontastic. In math, they are creating their own basic programs using our Bee-bot. In art, they are exploring symmetry and geometric shapes through the creation of stopmotion videos.

When I speak to educators and parents, I acknowledge how technology offers new ways for children to share their learning (see Figure 13.3). In the past, when children have drawn or illustrated something, it is put in their backpack and then put up on the refrigerator at home, viewed only by the immediate family. In the application Drawing Pad, children can email their illustrations off to family members near and far. Educreations, for example, an iPad application and Web-based resource, provides students with the opportunity to overlay audio recordings over photographs and/or electronic formats of illustrations. This combination creates a video that is Web-based and can be shared with anyone. Technology offers children opportunities to share their learning in so many ways.

Figure 13.3 One iPad and Many Engaged Children

Courtesy of Brian Puerling

Tools for Inquiry and Problem-Solving

Angela says . . . In September of 2013, I went with a group of colleagues from Columbia College to hear Greg Bamford, of Leading is Learning, speak about an intriguing approach to student problem solving. The design thinking approach, a popular problem solving approach in the business field at innovative companies such as IDEO, can also be applied to the classroom context. There are several variations of this model but the pillars of this approach include individuals doing needs assessments for given audiences, identifying problems through research, observations, interviews, and reflection.

There are several examples of this approach carried out in the middle school and high school context, for example, a high school student observed that individuals at a bus stop often do not engage in conversation. They spend a given amount of time in close quarters but often avoid conversation. This student wanted to develop a bus stop experience that invited engagement and conversation, so after careful observation and interviews, she developed a large etch-a-sketch for individuals to use while waiting for the bus. The etch-a-sketch required two people to operate, so conversation was more likely.

In early childhood classrooms, children are learning to solve problems on all sorts of levels. They are exploring how to fit all their winter gear in their cubby, they are figuring out how to share the limited number of blocks, and they are sorting out who will be first in line. They are also capable of solving larger, classroom community-based problems such as how many children in the dramatic play center is too many children, and how to keep other children from walking in the bathroom when someone else is using it. Young children, when given the opportunity, can think critically and develop thoughtful solutions to problems they encounter. Young children are also developing empathy for others. Children develop empathy when they interact with others in all sorts of ways. The basics are developed in the dramatic play center when they "try on" the roles of others such as a police officer, a post office employee, or a librarian. Empathy is also developed on a higher level when they discuss social conflicts that arise in the classroom.

Young children can use these important skills to solve problems for others in their community. For example, children in a kindergarten classroom notice that a door entering the school swings closed rather quickly, making it difficult and at times unsafe to enter through. Five and six-year-old children are not outside the cognitive capacity to arrive at authentic solutions such as a doorstop, a door holder, or interviewing the building engineer about replacing the hinge. Once they have identified solutions, they can observe how individuals interact with their solution to determine if in fact it is the best solution. Perhaps they use one of their triangular prism blocks as a doorstop, but they observe that the door keeps closing regardless of the doorstop. They may continue their conversation and 3D print their own custom-made doorstop to fit the door or perhaps they may invite in or videoconference with an individual from Home Depot to explore other options.

Position Statement Alignment

> True integration occurs when the use of technology and media becomes routine and transparent—when the focus of a child or educator is on the activity or exploration itself and not on the technology or media being used. Technology integration has been successful when the use of technology and media supports the goals of educators and programs for children, provides children with digital tools for learning and communicating, and helps to improve child outcomes.
>
> NAEYC & Fred Rogers Center (2012), p. 8

Tools Integrated Into Classrooms

On a recent trip to Reggio Emilia Italy with colleagues, I was once again reminded of what it means to explore the hundred languages of learning. Many early educators in the United States would be surprised to learn this also includes technology. The schools of Reggio Emilia are considering some of the most child-centered and developmentally appropriate early education programs in the world. They demonstrate a respect for children and learning rarely matched in educational systems, and they are highly regarded by well-known early educators worldwide (Edwards, Gandini, & Forman, 2012).

Walking into a Reggio classroom, you will see technology being used in many creative ways from low to high tech. Young children may be exploring images of space projected on the walls of the classroom through a projector while simultaneously adding their own images to the wall by drawing on a low-tech overhead projector. In another classroom, a group of children is around a desktop computer; they are working on a slideshow of photographs they have taken on a digital camera. One child is doing most of the editing work on the computer while the other children are excitedly chiming in with suggestions. We later learn the student who has been doing the editing had autism, and this was an area where he excelled. In yet another classroom, children are building intricate structures out of Lego blocks. As we watched the children completely involved in their exploration, we realized they were building, but had a small pen camera that they were inserting inside the structures. The pen camera was connected to a projector, which projected the image on a wall for the children to see. Even though we couldn't understand what they were saying in Italian, we could see the children were excited and more engaged in the activity. It was obvious this added another dimension to their explorations and learning.

It is in this rich integrated way we should be using technology to extend creative thinking in every early childhood classroom. Technology should not be replacing play or hands-on creative activities, but rather used to enrich the early learning experience. At Boulder Journey School in Boulder, Co, they have embraced technology in just this way. In a community project, preschoolers were asked to contribute their ideas of how to improve the city park. The preschoolers first visited the park, explored, drew pictures, and took photographs using digital cameras. The teachers used a photo editing application to turn these pictures into partially transparent images allowing the children to re-imagine what they wanted in the park and draw directly over the images. Once they had explored their ideas extensively, the teachers enlarged some of the same images and printed them using a large format printer placing them on a wall. They then invited children to once again re-imagine their ideas in the larger format by drawing or cutting out objects that they applied to the larger park image. All these ideas were pulled together and then presented to the city council.

Teachers could have taken this study even further with technology encouraging children to recreate park structures using wire, clay, and drawing. Then by taking digital images of these objects, they could have used photo-editing tools to create digital cutouts of the images. Then in a drawing application with a park image as the background used these digital cutouts to recreate the park in another re-envisioned way.

This is similar to the way schools in Reggio Emilia created bike study images by photographing images of interesting recycled materials and creating digital cutouts from these images. Children then used the digital cutouts combining them digitally to create different kinds of bikes. The images of these bikes adorn the train station viaduct in Reggio Emilia Italy. Taking this a step further, teachers could seek out libraries or schools that have 3D printers and work with someone to re-create students drawn images for the park in a 3D format.

Brian says . . . This technology is becoming more reachable every day with many schools actually owning their own 3D printers. 3D printers are offering individuals all sorts of new opportunities to create objects big and small. In 2013, the Urbee-2, a second prototype of a 3D printed car was created. Also in 2013, efforts at the University of Southern California are underway to create giant 3D printers capable of 3D printing a 2,500 square foot house in just 20 hours.

In schools 3D printers, such as the Cubify Cube and the Makerbot Replicator 2, are being used to create materials for all sorts of purposes. At Catherine Cook School, we are implementing an Innovation Center that will be comprised of an IDEA (Innovation, Design, Engineering, Arts) Lab and an AV Studio. In our IDEA Lab, staffed by our Director of Innovation, JD Pirtle, students will engage with a variety of emerging technologies such as 3D printers, laser cutters, and custom electronics. These technologies invite students to explore, express, and share their creativity in ways they could not have with previous tools. As a school, we continue our conversations regarding curriculum, and see these technologies complimenting our commitment to providing students with the necessary experiences to develop 21st-century skills: creativity, critical thinking, collaboration, and character.

A 3D printer may come with a price tag too high for many schools to consider it as a tool for their students and teachers. However, programs to help offset the costs are emerging. In mid-November of 2013, MakerBot teamed up with DonorsChoose.org in an attempt to get a 3D printer in every public school in America. Their initiative invites corporations to donate up approximately 95% funding, exponentially increasing the chances of full funding. These types of initiatives are evidence that these technologies can and will be used by populations in all socio-economic statuses. Authors of *Invent to Learn: Making, Tinkering, and Classroom Engineering on the Classroom*, Sylvia Libow-Martinez and Gary Stager, made a powerful point in their book, "Even if you do not have access to expensive (but increasingly affordable) hardware, every classroom can become a makerspace where kids and teachers learn together through an assortment of high- and low-tech materials" (Libow-Martinez & Stager, 2013, p. 3).

Tools for Sound and Music

Sound and music is another area of creativity that has only begun to be explored using technology. Yes, we want children to play instruments and explore music in hands-on ways, but this doesn't prevent children from expanding their experiences through technology. There are many musical apps available for children, but one of the more creative sound apps children can use is Mad Pad (an app that was not developed for children, but has proven to be excellent with preschoolers). Children can use the sounds provided in the app, record sounds, or use their voice to create unique songs and sound stories. The app is very easy for children to use and has broad creative possibilities. There are newer technologies being developed for young children, which allow them to program robots to do simple tasks. In the context of music, there is a robot, named Bo, developed by Play-i that can be programed to play a xylophone. There are all sorts of ways to invite children to explore music and creativity in the same experience.

Tools for Storytelling

Angela says . . . Creative storytelling and animation can be enhanced and enriched through technology tools. There are many apps that allow children to draw and dictate stories. One benefit of these kinds of storytelling apps is children can develop stories without the limitation of writing. This is very supportive of children's natural literacy development and creative thinking process. It also allows young children to work on their story knowledge in a more autonomous way.

Tom and David Kelley, authors of *Creative Confidence: Unleashing the Creative Potential Within Us All,* discuss the power in embracing your creative confidence (Kelley & Kelley, 2013). They challenge us and our students to trust the ideas we develop and ourselves. When we trust the ideas developed by ourselves and those around us, we are able to create and problem solve much more effectively.

Conclusion

We have shared our own stories and ideas to illustrate how technology can be a tool that enriches teaching and supports innovative best practices with children. In sharing this information with you, we became more aware ourselves that the concept of emergent technologies is very subjective. While exploring touch-screen devices might be an emergent technology for some, it may be an everyday part of some teachers' lives. Others may have such advanced technological skills that emergent to them is cutting edge technologies such as 3D printers or programming robots. Still others may be looking back for innovative emergent uses of older lower-tech devices such as overhead projectors. So the question of what is emergent technology actually becomes a question of "emergent for who."

We return to the idea of teacher as learner. As technology learners of the 21st-century teachers must constantly be willing to embrace what is "our" emerging technology and decide what technologies we are comfortable with, while always pushing ourselves to learn more. This is how we will discover best practices for teachers and teaching with technology.

Teacher Takeaways

1. Approach technology as a learner, it will always be new and improved and as a teachers we know being a learner is the most exciting way to approach what is new.
2. Look to low-tech options for exploration in your classroom if you are the most technological person in your school. Sometimes simple really is best. You would be surprised how young children can find the most amazing ways to explore and be innovative using these simple technologies, such as old digital cameras, overhead projectors, and light tables.
3. See technology as another support system. Technologies can support better communication with parents as well as more appropriate assessment. So though it may be difficult to embrace at first, you might just find it very supportive of your developmentally appropriate practice with young children and 21st-century skills.

References

Chiong, C., Ree, J., Takeuchi, L., & Erickson, I. (2012). *Print books vs. e-books: Comparing parent-child co-reading on print, basic, and enhanced e-book platforms*. New York, NY: Joan Ganz Cooney Center.

Edwards, C., Gandini, L., & Forman, G. (2011). *The hundred languages of children: The Reggio Emilia experience in transformation*. Santa Barbara, CA: ABC-CLIO.

Epstein, J. L. (2005). A case study of the partnership schools comprehensive school reform (CSR) model. *Elementary School Journal, 106*(2), 151–170.

Harris-Helm, J., & Katz, L. (2010). *Young investigators: The project approach in the early years* (2nd ed.). New York, NY: Teachers College Press.

Hawkins, D. (2002). *The informed vision: Essays on learning and human nature*. New York, NY: Algora Publishing.

Kelley, T., & Kelley, D. (2013). *Creative confidence: Unleashing the creative potential within us all*. New York, NY: Crown Publishing Group.

Libow-Martinez, S., & Stager, S. (2013). *Invent to learn: Making, tinkering, and engineering in the classroom.* Torrance, CA: Constructing Modern Knowledge Press.

National Association for the Education of Young Children, & Fred Rogers Center for Early Learning and Children's Media at Saint Vincent College. (2012). *Technology and interactive media as tools in early childhood programs serving children from birth through age 8.* Washington, DC: NAEYC; Latrobe, PA: Fred Rogers Center for Early Learning and Children's Media at Saint Vincent College.

Puerling, B. (2012). *Teaching in the digital age: Smart tools for age 3 to grade 3.* St. Paul, MN: Redleaf Press.

Puerling, B. (2013). Teaching in the digital age: Using social media. *Swings and Roundabouts. 5*(3), 12–13. Wellington, New Zealand.

Resources

- *Bee-bot*, Terrapin, www.terrapinlogo.com/bee-botmain.php
- Blurb, www.blurb.com
- *Confer*, David Lowe, www.conferapp.com
- *Cubify Cube*, 3D Systems, http://cubify.com/en/Products
- *DJ MIX KIDS*, Technolio Inc., https://itunes.apple.com/us/app/dj-mix-kids-pro-sound-exploration/id478653656?mt=8
- *Doodlecast Pro*, Zinc Roe, http://doodlecastpro.com
- *Drawing Pad,* Darren Murtha Design, http://drawingpadapp.com
- *Educreations*, Educreations, Inc., www.educreations.com
- Facebook, www.facebook.com
- *FaceTime,* Apple, www.apple.com/ios/facetime/
- *Google+ Hangouts,* Google, www.google.com/+/learnmore/hangouts/
- *MadPad HD*, Smule, www.smule.com
- *Magic Treehouse*, Random House Children's Books, www.magictreehouse.com
- *Markerbot*, Makerbot Industries, www.makerbot.com
- *Paperdesk*, WebSpinner, LLC, https://itunes.apple.com/us/app/paperdesk/id367563434?mt=8
- Pinterest, www.pinterest.com
- *Play-i*, Play-i Inc., www.play-i.com
- Shutterfly, www.shutterfly.com
- Skype, www.skype.com/en/
- Snapchat, www.snapchat.com
- Snapfish, www.snapfish.com/
- *Toontastic*, Launchpad Toys, http://launchpadtoys.com/toontastic/
- Twitter, https://twitter.com
- Urbee-2, KOR EcoLogic, INC, http://korecologic.com/about/urbee_2/

Learn More . . .

- Boulder Journey School, www.boulderjourneyschool.com
- Catherine Cook School, www.catherinecookschool.org
- Columbia College Chicago, www.colum.edu
- Puerling, B. Early Years: Teaching in the digital age. *Early Horizons*. Retrieved from www.asg.com.au/Assets/Files/ASG_EaryHorizons_2_2013_AU_Revised_WEB.pdf

- Puerling, B. (2012). *Teaching in the digital age: Smart tools for age 3 to grade 3.* St. Paul, MN: Redleaf Press. www.redleafpress.org/Teaching-in-the-Digital-Age-P691.aspx
- Puerling, B. (2013, May 7). How teachers are using digital media with kindergartners [Fred Rogers Center blog]. Retrieved from www.fredrogerscenter.org/blog/how-teachers-are-using-digital-media-with-kindergarteners/
- Puerling, B. (2013, August 27). Tips for supervising students on the digital playground [Fred Rogers Center blog]. Retrieved from www.fredrogerscenter.org/blog/tips-for-supervising-students-on-the-digital-playground/

Part III

Technology Beyond the Classroom

EDITOR'S INTRODUCTION

Whereas Part II focuses on technology in the classroom, Part III looks beyond the classroom with chapters on technology as a tool to strengthen the home-school connection and communities. We also look beyond formal education to learn about the role of children's librarians in supporting early learning in the digital age and conclude with a focus on becoming a connected educator and connected learner as a 21st-century teacher.

We begin with Chapter 14 by **Tamara Kaldor**, who identifies technology tools and strategies that can improve communication, build relationships, and strengthen the home-classroom and home-school connection. She offers stories and practical advice for teachers and describes a wide range of technology tools and how each can be used effectively. This chapter is loaded with resources to explore and ideas to try. As Kaldor says, "So now you have some great tech tools to use. The power of any communication is to make it purposeful. These tools and your creativity will be the powerful bridge to connecting with families."

In Chapter 15, **Luisa M. Cotto** reminds us that "technology puts resources for teachers, families and children at their fingertips." She introduces us to tools and strategies to build and strengthen the sense of ownership and community within the classroom, for the program or school, to the neighborhood and beyond. She shares stories and images that illustrate best practice and offers tips for using mobile devices, digital photography, email, videoconferencing, software and apps, and social media.

Cen Campbell and **Carisa Kluver** team up in Chapter 16, as they so often do, to explore the emerging role of children's librarians at the intersection of digital media and early learning, and as media mentors for young children, parents, and educators. They describe the digital context for informal learning—for example, in the library, at a children's museum, at a zoo or nature center, and in out-of-school time programs—and they suggest that the strategies libraries have used to support community early learning efforts are the place to begin. Their ACE model (Access, Content, and Engagement) provides a framework for thinking about the role of technology and digital media in the library and for responding to the needs of children, parents, and educators in the digital age.

Chapter 17, by **Amanda Armstrong**, looks at what it means to be a connected educator and connected learner, and the implications for teaching and learning in the 21st-century. Early childhood educators in the digital age need to take advantage of the technology tools at hand to connect to information, ideas, resources, and other educators. Armstrong offers examples, strategies, and specific resources to help educators dive in and begin to get connected or to connect in new and broader ways. She defines a professional learning network (PLN) and a community of practice (COP) and describes ways to connect with parents and families, as well as strategies for developing young connectors.

Chapter 14

Technology as a Tool to Strengthen the Home-School Connection

Tamara Kaldor

Introduction

"Sharing is caring!" repeats Annie to her teacher in the preschool classroom where I am working today. She says this as she passes a tablet device to a peer next to her, so she can add her own picture and voice recording to the "About Us" book they are making for their upcoming class party. The party will feature a family potluck. Parents will attend the party and see their children's faces light up as they hear their own voice recordings and see their pictures displayed on the classroom smartboard. In the world of technology, young children and education, Annie's statement could not be truer. The ability to share information using technology tools is one of the greatest breakthroughs for bridging the communication gap between the classroom and home.

As a developmental therapist, I spend much of my day communicating with parents, teachers, and other therapists to share information about my sessions. I build teams that move children forward using everything from text messaging and email to sending digital work samples from a session that may include comics, videos, art, and e-books we make. As you know, most young children have a difficult time recalling and explaining many of the events of their day. I work with a population of children that often doesn't have the verbal abilities to answer the question, "What did you do at school today?" Technology for this population is a game changer for communication. For the first time young children can *show* their parents what they did at school today. They can *show* their peers at circle time what they did with their family over the weekend or what they ate for dinner. These digital visual supports create opportunities for conversation and allow all of the members of the classroom or family to have a voice in the classroom at circle time and at home around the dinner table. As our classroom communities become more inclusive and multilingual, we need to provide additional opportunities for children and parents to communicate and to share their thoughts, feelings, and goals.

Technology as the Tool, Not the Reward

In a kindergarten classroom in Chicago where children speak up to twenty different languages, parents were asked to come to the classroom and record a fairy tale from their country in their native language. Parents shared important cultural lessons and explained why their fairy tale had meaning to them. The teacher set up listening stations for the children and then had children write their own fairy tales. The teacher had children compare and contrast fairy tale themes and characters. The teacher reported that the children's fairy tales were each unique and reflected many cultural influences. She also reported that parents were highly engaged in the writing process at home with their children (Flynn, 2013). The classroom community came together to understand, relate, and share. Technology was the vehicle that allowed this to happen.

Technology needs to stop being thought of as the reward system or just a gaming device and needs to start being tools we can use to relate and communicate. For educators and support teams, technology can alter the way parents and children from diverse linguistic, cultural, and economic backgrounds are able to communicate and share their knowledge with teachers and their children. For educators, this is your opportunity to teach parents how to use technology to learn and engage with their children.

I may be one of the only child development specialists you will ever hear asking parents and children to bring their own digital devices (BYOD) to back-to-school night and encouraging families to put a tech device in the middle of the dining room table one night a week. Yes, I am gasping and questioning right along with you. But I believe that when we learn together and share information about what we are learning, the results are that we all grow together and build more meaningful relationships, especially between families and classrooms. New tools that support "digital sharing" are creating opportunities for exciting and ongoing conversations. I hope you and the families you work with will become partners in exploring how to create meaningful and engaging relationships using the new tools you each have in your tech toolbox.

Position Statement Alignment

With technology becoming more prevalent as a means of sharing information and communicating with one another, early childhood educators have an opportunity to build stronger relationships with parents and enhance family engagement. Early childhood educators always have had a responsibility to support parents and families by sharing knowledge about child development and learning.

Technology tools offer new opportunities for educators to build relationships, maintain ongoing communication, and exchange information and share online resources with parents and families. Likewise, parents and families can use technology to ask questions, seek advice, share information about their child, and feel more engaged in the program and their child's experiences there.

National Association for the Education of Young Children [NAEYC] & Fred Rogers Center (2012), p. 7

Sharing and Communicating to Build Relationships and Community

Sharing is the name of the game for creating meaningful communication, experiences, and participation for children, parents, and educators. Bridging the digital divide is the challenge. The digital divide that exists is not just about economics, but also about exposure, learning, and embracing technology as a communication tool. Children will often be leading parents and educators in digital lessons. *Sharing* and *learning together* is what will bring excitement and enthusiasm into your classroom and the home environments.

A Warning: Using Technology to Report on Behavior or Developmental Concerns

I will not spend much time on applications and communication tools that help professionals share information about a child's behavior with a parent. There are many apps and programs that are designed to do this. However, I consistently hear from parents who receive electronic notifications, including brief emails, that tell them their child has had a bad day with little or no explanation as to why. This leads to anxious and confused parents who don't know how to talk with their child and teacher about what may or may not have occurred. I encourage professionals to think carefully about the language used to describe a child's behavior or development in the classroom before hitting the "send" button. Parents have different reactions and expectations that are cultural and emotional to children's behavior and development. When in doubt listen to your gut. I highly recommend you pick up the phone and ask parents to come in and meet with you face to face. You will all need to work together as a team to support a child's social and emotional development. Technology can assist you, but it can't read the important social cues that a parent's body language and facial expressions express when they hear concerns about their child's development. Being a strong communication partner and setting examples for high-quality parent-teacher communication is an important role you play in the school-home connection process.

All of the various tech tools and methods that educators and parents can use to share information with one another can seem overwhelming. In this chapter, we will explore how to create meaningful communication and build relationships with your families through technology. I will provide you with tools to help you think about how you can bring parents into the classroom and challenge you to go home virtually with your families.

When Sharing Feels Overwhelming

You may have been feeling excited and a little overwhelmed, as you've made your way through this book. Along the way you've picked up many new wonderful tools and research to support your work with young children, parents, and families. It is okay to feel overwhelmed by all of the options because the parents you work with probably do, too. Become partners with your families and be honest with them about your ideas, concerns, and questions. Create a classroom community that encourages everyone to experiment, explore, and inquire together. Create an ongoing dialogue and don't be afraid to ask your students and parents for help when you feel overwhelmed or stuck. When you open yourself up to ask for help you may feel vulnerable, but showing students and parents that you are an engaged learner and partner with them will be vital as your build your classroom community.

10 Basic Tech Tools for Your Communication Toolbox With Parents

1. Telephone
2. Email
3. Classroom blog
4. Twitter for your classroom
5. Texting
6. Digital newsletter (emailed newsletter)
7. Classroom video via YouTube or Vine
8. Video conferencing/Skype/FaceTime
9. Photo sharing via email, text, or twitter
10. Class website

Where to Start in Setting Up a New Communication Toolbox

My first piece of advice to any professional setting up a digital system for communicating with parents is to make as many adjustments to your settings as necessary to get your notifications, bells, whistles, and distractions turned off. Not sure how to do this on your devices? There are many YouTube videos you can easily find if you search for the name of your device and "notification settings." We now all have the ability to communicate 24/7, and that means busy parents may reply to your communication efforts during your sleep, class prep, family, and other inopportune times. The key to successful communication will be determining when and how you want to communicate! The other key to using technology with success is to lower your anxiety. Listen to your gut and determine how much time you feel comfortable learning, playing with, and using different modes of communication. It may mean that you only pick one new communication tool to master this school year.

Tips for Setting Boundaries on Communication

We don't communicate well when we are unable to focus, are feeling anxious, or are not in a positive frame of mind. I let my families know up front that I may send them work samples, videoclips, or a social story from my iPad or phone during a session with their child, but they will not be getting written communication, text messages, or calls from me during my time with their child. My focus is on the work I am doing and further communication occurs at pickup time or when I am not with clients. I also let clients know that I have a family, but respond to most emails and calls with 24 to 48 hours. These are the boundaries that allow me to be productive and effective in my work with children and families. What are yours? Let parents and your professional team know what to expect!

A note to administrators looking to help staff improve communication with parents. I recently worked with an early childhood program where the director was incredibly frustrated because she could not get her own staff to respond to her emails. She was fearful about introducing technology to her staff. We held a lunchtime training with a technology set-up guru where all of the staff, including custodial, brought their smartphones and laptops. We taught everyone how to set up email accounts on their devices. We also discussed how to appropriately correspond using email to parents and professionals. This proved to be a wonderful use of their digital training dollars and bridged a large digital divide amongst the professional team at the center. The center's director reports that her staff is now more effectively communicating internally with one another and with parents.

Teacher Takeaways for Communicating With Parents, Guardians, and Family Members

- Always start on a positive note!
- Add a tip for carrying over classroom lessons or themes at home.
- Communicate regularly throughout the year to prevent surprises when report cards arrive home or you have other concerns to share.
- Use a translator from your school to communicate with parents whose first language is not English, especially via email. Keep language very simple and messages short. If you are unable to find a translator to help you with communication then consider using iTranslate or Google Translate. Communication needs to be clear with parents, and due to many cultural differences and translation problems, often digital messages go awry (Nemeth, personal communication).
- Survey parents to find out what technology they have access to and use.
- Set boundaries for communication and provide a copy in writing for families.
- Set up an auto response to email and a voicemail message when you are away that states when you will be away, when you will be available, and how long it typically takes for you to respond to messages.
- Don't assume staff and families know how to use the tech basics such as email.
- Seek training and tech support to learn how to use basic communication tools.
- Model appropriate practices for children, parents, and families.

Important Questions to Ask When Selecting Communication Tools

- How can I make my communication purposeful?
- What do I want the parents to know?
- How can I send a communication to parents that will encourage a response and prompt a conversation?
- What technology do most of the families have access to on a regular basis? Basic cell phones with text messaging? Smartphones with email access? Home or work site computers? Tablets with WiFi access? Other?
- How often do I want to communicate with families? Daily? Weekly? Monthly?
- What is my school or center's policy on social media, photographing students, and sharing information digitally with parents?
- Talk with your fellow teachers and administrators about procedures and policies before hitting your first "send", "post," or "tweet" button!

Tips for Finding Digital Tools for Communicating With Families

Not sure how to correctly use a tool or set up the privacy or notification settings of a tech tool?

- Search on *YouTube* (www.youtube.com) for how-to videos

Want to know more about how to correctly use a tech tool as an educator?

- Go to *Google* (www.google.com) and search using the tech tool name + Educator

Looking for digital communication programs?

- *Kaymbu* (www.kaymbu.com) is specifically designed for early childhood teachers and classrooms. It allows teachers to safely and securely build student portfolios with video, pictures, and work samples that can be easily shared with parents via email and updates a secure website portal. For schools without their own iPads or technology support personnel to keep tech updated, Kaymbu offers a subscription program that includes iPads, support, and the student portfolio program.
- *Edmodo* (www.edmodo.com) allows teachers to safely and securely share information with students and parents about grading, behavior, and more.
- *Class Dojo* (www.classdojo.com) is an app that allows teachers to work with students on classroom behavior and character building through positive reinforcement. Teachers can share information with parents. Parents become more involved and can see if homework was checked in, understand their child's classroom participation, and communicate with the teacher.

Need a program that allows you to schedule emails?

- *Boomerang* for *Gmail* (www.boomeranggmail.com)
- *SendLater* for *Microsoft Outlook* (www.sendlateremail.com)

Do you want more information about using popular communications tools for strengthening the home-school connection?

- Try *Twitter* (www.twitter.com)
- Learn the *Twitter Basics* (www.engagingeducators.com/blog/2011/04/25/your-edtech-toolkit-twitter-basics/)
- Visit the *EdTech* (www.edtechmagazine.com/k12/article/2013/03/printable-list-best-education-hashtags-infographic) and *TeachThought* websites (www.teachthought.com/social-media/the-20-most-useful-hashtags-in-education/) to learn about popular education hashtags (#) on Twitter you can use to connect with other educators and to help parents search for information from.
- Use *HootSuite* (hootsuite.com) to manage and schedule social media.
- Try out *Remind 101* (www.remind101.com) and *Kikiutext* (https://kiku-text.com) programs designed for educators to safely send text messages to parents and students. Always check group text programs to make sure that teachers' and parents' phone numbers stay protected. Most require that you provide parents a code to activate the service securely.
- Explore *YouTube* (www.youtube.com), *Vine* (www.vine.com), and *Animoto* (www.animoto.com) as tools for sharing videos and using photos and pictures to create a video compilation. *Always check security and privacy settings before posting videos on any website.*

Are you interested in building a classroom website or publishing a blog?

- Try *Wordpress* (www.wordpress.com) for a free website creation tool or *Weebly for Educators* (www.education.weebly.com), a free website creation tool for educators.
- Visit *Scholastic.com* (www.scholastic.com/teachers/top-teaching/2013/06/create-impressive-class-website-under-hour) to create a class website in under an hour.

Great! I have all of these tools . . . How am I going to really use them?

Examples of Strengthening the Home-School Connection Through Technology

Before the School Bell Rings! The days and weeks before the first day of school, teachers are often feeling the same butterflies as parents and children. What to expect this coming year? What will my classroom be like? One way to settle butterflies and start the year off on a positive note is by giving your families a digital preview of the classroom and you!

Make a quick video or e-book to introduce yourself, the classroom, school, and staff that families will interact with throughout the year. Then, send an email with a link or post it on your classroom blog or website. Children will often ask their parents if they can view or read these e-introductions over and over again. They are an excellent way to set expectations for the classroom schedule and routines. You might also post a copy of the classroom schedule by creating a visual schedule that parents can show their children at home and you can use throughout your classroom. There are several apps that are easy to use to do this, enabling you to spend less time getting stuck to Velcro! Apps that have added the ability to email or print from within an app are a teacher's best new tool.

You can make these e-intros and visual schedules simply by shooting some video or taking photos with a smartphone or tablet. Consider following the routines a student should follow when coming to your classroom and your classroom schedule. You may want to include information such as where children will hang their coats, eat lunch, sit at circle time, keep supplies, go for recess, the library, gym, and after school programs. Keep your language simple and clear. Figure 14.1 shows a sample page from my classroom e-book, *This is My New*

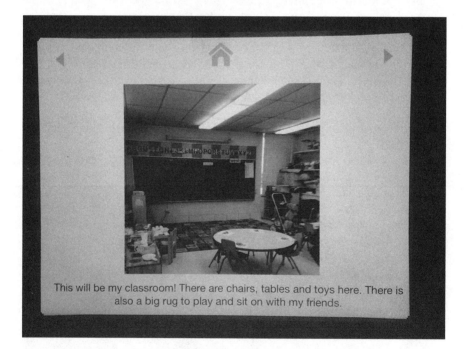

This will be my classroom! There are chairs, tables and toys here. There is also a big rug to play and sit on with my friends.

Figure 14.1 Sample Page From Classroom E-book *This is My New Classroom and School.*

Courtesy of Tamara Kaldor

Classroom and School, that I use to introduce the child and parents to important places and spaces in the classroom.

In your email to parents introducing the e-book or video, you might consider giving parents some simple tips for easing the transition back to school. Children and parents love knowing what to expect, and this digital solution is a great tool to use. For children with developmental differences and children who are having their first school experience, these books will act as social stories and help many children who are feeling anxious about their classroom experience. Figure 14.2 shows a sample page from my e-book on separation, *Saying Goodbye to Mommy and Daddy, Saying Hello to My Teacher*. The e-book helps children prepare for their classroom experience.

Include social-emotional learning in your e-book to support children who are struggling with the transition to school. Consider making a book about how first-time students may be feeling with pictures that show different emotions. Provide solutions for what children and parents can do to make the school transition and separation smoother. These will also help many children who experience separation anxiety when attending early childhood programs. You can make a book to help children and parents prepare to say goodbye at the start of the school day. Place printed copies of e-books you make throughout your classroom, as children will love reading them during the first weeks of school.

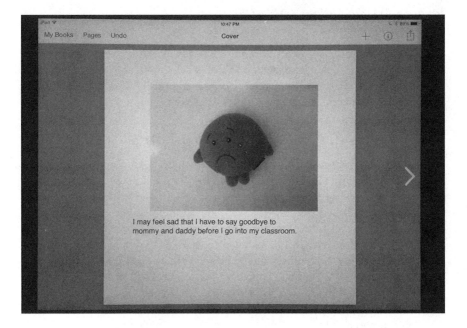

Figure 14.2 Sample Page From an E-book on Separation, *Saying Goodbye to Mommy and Daddy, Saying Hello to My Teacher.*

Courtesy of Tamara Kaldor

You can keep reusing your e-books every year, which will save you time! Administrators might consider adding an e-intro to their school website to connect parents to the school community.

Ideas in Action: Technology That Keeps Children and Parents Connected

Message from Me, a project of the Carnegie Mellon University Create Lab (www. cmucreatelab.org) uses camera technology to let children take pictures about daily activities, a digital audio device to record and attach voice recordings, and a system for sending those files to a family members' cell phone or email address. Message from Me stimulates communication between children and family members and helps to strengthen home-school connections. Children develop skill in communication and self-confidence using technology as they make choices about what they want to share about their day. The data logs from Message from Me allow teachers to document children's use of the kiosks, the development of communication skills, and a maintain records of anecdotal information for assessment purposes (learn more about Message from Me at www.cmucreatelab. org/projects/Message_from_Me).

Ideas in Action: A Website That Supports Parents and Families

The Fred Rogers Center Early Learning Environment (ELE) helps families support their children's early language and literacy development.

Mike Robb, Director of Education and Research at the Fred Rogers Center, offers advice for parents of young children in the digital age.

Advice for Parents of Young Children in the Digital Age

1. *Keep it interactive.* The way a digital tool is used is as important as the tool itself; adult-child interaction should be emphasized. Rather than putting on a television show or handing over your smartphone and walking away, create a dialogue. Sit and discuss what you are seeing, ask questions, encourage imaginative ways to explore similar subjects in the outside world.
2. *Match use with age.* Children's needs change as they develop. Any media use with infants and toddlers should be an interactive experience with adults, such as reading an e-book together; older preschool children may enjoy exploring a touch screen or using video to record and view their play.
3. *Have fun, stay engaged.* Children's media and technology are best when they support active, hands-on, creative, and authentic engagement with the people and world around them. Look for games, websites, and apps that encourage outdoor activity, healthy eating, critical thinking, and other real-world skills.

4. *Promote digital literacy.* By modeling appropriate use of digital media, adults can help children learn to use the wealth of tools at their disposal in smart, healthy ways that complement their growth and give them greater access to the opportunities of the digital age.

from *Advice for Parents of Young Children in the Digital Age*
from the Fred Rogers Center (2012)

For more information and resources, visit the Fred Rogers Center Early Learning Environment™—or *Ele* (pronounced El-Lee), a free online resource at www.yourele.org.

Making E-books for Social-Emotional Learning at School and Home

For early childhood educators, creating e-books that children can read at home and have in the classroom is wonderful way to connect with parents. Children love to see their pictures, hear their voice recordings, and read their words. Listed below are some of my favorite applications for creating e-books. I encourage you to make them for your classroom community and with the children in your classroom!

Apps and computer programs that act as slideshow creators are simple and quick to use for making books! The only limiting factor is your own creativity. Think about taking pictures of children, classroom artwork, field trips, children's emotional faces, and your day in the classroom.

Consider adding a page at the beginning with tips for parents on literacy and questions to ask their children while reading the book. One of my favorite e-books I made with a class included simple pictures of the children expressing different emotions and their own voice recordings saying how they felt. Kids loved having them at home to read with their families. You can print them out, email them, post them on your classroom website, and make them available on your classroom's digital devices. If you have access to a smartboard, you might consider projecting books the class makes and reading them together for important social-emotional lessons.

Make Your Own E-book Resources

- Book Creator (app), www.redjumper.net/bookcreator/
- Choiceworks (app) to make visual schedules. Contains other great tools such as social stories, waiting and feelings boards, www.beevisual.com
- Haiku Deck (app and website), www.haikudeck.com
- Keynote (app for iPhone, iPad or Mac desktop), www.apple.com/mac/keynote/
- PowerPoint (computer program), http://office.microsoft.com/en-us/powerpoint/
- Scribblepress (website and app), www.scribblepress.com

Bring-Your-Own-Device (BYOD) Night Is the New Back-to-School Night!

I am in a parochial school on the south side of Chicago and parents are finding seats, pulling out smartphones, tablets, and laptops. Several fathers are showing each other their favorite apps for following sports after dropping their children off in the gym. A mother at the table where I am sitting says to me, "I just have my old phone. I'm not sure I should be here." I ask her if it works and if it receives text messages. She nods and I reassure her that she did indeed bring her own device. The room is packed and buzzing with chatter. The school staff has placed the school's tablets and laptops on every table for parents to play with. We start the evening program by having myself and the school staff show and explain the school's digital policies, programs, and applications they are using with students. We get parents playing with several applications and programs that their children are using! Parents then rotate through several classrooms learning how to use the school's new digital communication tools. We have several "how to use____" classrooms set up for parents so they can learn how to follow the school and their child's classroom on Twitter; log in to their school's web portal; and set up email accounts on their smartphones and receive text messages from their child's teacher. Middle and high school students have been recruited to be teacher's assistants in each room, so parents can get some 1:1 help, if needed. We finish the BYOD event by having students give their parents a digital lesson, share e-projects they have made, and sign a digital contract with their parent. It is hard to clear the room at the end of the night!

Training and ongoing support for the learning needs of families will be imperative to keeping them engaged using technology for communication. The administration will need to maintain a budget and time to invest in supporting the school staff, parents, and children's ongoing technology learning programs.

We Provide the Following Handouts

- Digital contracts for parents to sign
- Copies of digital contracts they can use with their children at home
- Checklists with instructions on how to register for the school web portal, instructions and codes for receiving text messages from their child's teacher, the twitter handle names for the classroom, and the school twitter handle name

What Teachers Are Doing in Each Classroom

- Explaining and showing how and why they use technology in their classroom
- Encouraging parents to play with the classroom technology
- Providing tips to parents on using technology with their children for more than games and rewards

- Parents receive a text message in the middle of the program
- Teacher posts a picture of parents playing with tech and of kids in gym on Twitter and ask parents to respond

Why do you and your families need digital contracts? A digital contract is a written contract that parents sign with teachers and their children. The contract lays out the rules for communication and the use of technology. It acts as a reinforcer and a great conversation starter. It supports parents' efforts to have their children use technology appropriately and safely.

I encourage you to create a digital contract that you give to families to sign at back to school night or BYOD night that discusses how you will communicate, when you will require face-to-face meetings, when and where you are not available to communicate. I also encourage you to have families create a contract or hand out a sample for parents to use at home with their children. Parents look to teachers and professionals for guidance as they raise their digital natives.

Resources for Digital Contracts

- Family Safety Institute's Parent and Child Contracts, www.fosi.org/resources/257-fosi-safety-contract.html
- A Platform for Good has online safety cards and contract cards for families to use and give a child with a digital device gift. They have a contract card for each type device a parent might give a child available at www.aplatformforgood.org/pages/holiday-safety-cards-2013.
- Psychology Today guide to designing a family technology contract, www.psychologytoday.com/blog/parenting-in-digital-age/201301/designing-family-contracts-technology-use

Texting to Support Parents and Improve Child Development

As a teacher, it may seem against your grain to want to send a short text message to parents. The grammar of text messages alone makes many of us in education shudder! However, in the digital age of too many emails and junk email, text messaging can be a powerful tool to quickly and effectively get parents to stop in the moment to receive valuable child development tips and suggestions for educational activities to use with their children at home. According to a PBS Ready to Learn Cell Phone Study (2006) of *Learning Letters With Elmo,* a text message and video streaming program for parents, 95% of parents who received educational text messages to use with their child reported, "a cell phone used in this way can be an effective learning tool." Providing parents with regular, brief child development tips and activity ideas directly to their cellphones improves the home-school connection, offers a way to communicate with parents in a new way, and can give parents more confidence in their knowledge and ability to support their children's healthy growth and development.

Tips for Sending Meaningful Text Messages to Parents

- Use as more than just a homework reminder.
- Suggest a play theme or game that supports a classroom play theme, book, or academic lesson. Getting parents to engage in play with their young children is critical and important.
- Tell parents about books that are read in class and suggest topics for dinner conversation.
- Suggest an activity where parents help their child hunt for letters or numbers in the natural environment, at home, in nature, or at the grocery store, etc.
- Share photos of class projects with a question for parents to investigate with their child at home.

Conclusion

So now you have some great tech tools to use. The power of any communication is to make it purposeful. These tools and your creativity will be the powerful bridge to connecting with families. Families are living further away from their support systems and looking toward their children's teachers for more help navigating their child's development. This also means that families are under more stress and need to be part of supportive community programs. Ask yourself how you can use your tech toolbox to bring families in to the classroom and build a new community. I encourage you to find the tools that you feel comfortable using; ask students and parents for help; and challenge yourself to step outside your comfort zone.

Teacher Takeaways

- Be purposeful, positive, and supportive in your communication with parents!
- Survey parents so you can "meet them where they are" with technology.
- Determine if the purpose of the communication is to educate parents, elicit a response from parents, or share classroom experiences with parents.
- Pick tools that feel meaningful to you as the educator and that your families can have access to.
- Ask other teachers about tools they use and find reliable sources of technology recommendations to avoid becoming overwhelmed by too many tools.
- Be creative in your communication!
- Set appropriate boundaries for your own time and energy.
- Ask for help from colleagues, parents, and students. Don't be afraid to be vulnerable.

Administrator Takeaways

- Provide staff the opportunity to play and learn through small learning networks. Bring coffee and snacks in for monthly or weekly "staff tech show-and-tell" sessions. They don't need to be long. Even 10–20 minutes a week or month is fantastic!

- Invite parents to learn and play with BYOD nights and ask them to share their tech expertise with parents and teachers. For schools with limited budgets, parents can be a wonderful resource for training and support.
- Develop a budget for technology support, upgrades, and learning for staff, children, and parents.
- Create school wide digital contracts and policies to support teachers' efforts to communicate with parents and share their work with other learning networks.
- Create a classroom and school community where it is safe and fun to explore, question, and experiment with technology for you, the parents, and the children.
- Survey staff frequently to find out their successes, frustrations, and challenges in using technology to connect with families. Create problem-solving opportunities during supervision.

References

Flynn, C. (2013, October). Connecting technology with teaching. Symposium conducted at the Technology for The Early Years conference, TEC Center, Erikson Institute, Chicago, IL.

Fred Rogers Center. (2012). *Advice for Parents of Young Children in the Digital.* Retrieved from www.fredrogerscenter.org/media/resources/Elearticle_041712.pdf

National Association for the Education of Young Children, & Fred Rogers Center for Early Learning and Children's Media at Saint Vincent College. (2012). *Technology and interactive media as tools in early childhood programs serving children from birth through age 8.* Washington, DC: NAEYC; Latrobe, PA: Fred Rogers Center for Early Learning and Children's Media at Saint Vincent College.

PBS Ready to Learn. (2006). *Ready to learn cell phone study: Learning letters with Elmo project.* Alexandria, VA: Author. Retrieved from www-tc.pbskids.org/read/files/PBS_CPS_Report.pdf

Resources

- Animoto, www.animoto.com
- Book Creator, www.redjumper.net/bookcreator/
- Boomerang for Gmail, www.boomeranggmail.com
- Choiceworks, www.beevisual.com
- Class Dojo, www.clasdojo.com
- Edmodo, www.edmodo.com/
- Ele, Early Learning Environment, Fred Rogers Center, http://ele.fredrogers center.org
- Google, http://google.com
- Google Translate, http://translate.google.com

- Haiku Deck, www.haikudeck.com
- HootSuite, https://hootsuite.com
- iTranslate, www.itranslateapp.com
- Kaymbu, www.kaymbu.com
- Keynote, www.apple.com/mac/keynote/
- Kikiutext, https://kikutext.com
- Message from Me, www.cmucreatelab.org/projects/Message_from_Me
- PLAY is Work, www.chicagoplaypro.com
- PowerPoint, http://office.microsoft.com/en-us/powerpoint/
- Raising Digital Natives, http://raisingdigitalnatives.com
- Remind 101, www.remind101.com
- Scholastic, www.scholastic.com/home/
- Scribblepress, www.scribblepress.com
- SendLater for Microsoft Outlook, www.sendlateremail.com
- Twitter, www.twitter.com
- Vine, https://vine.co
- Weebly for Education, http://education.weebly.com
- Wordpress, www.wordpress.com
- YouTube, www.youtube.com

Learn More . . .

- Comienza en Casa/It Starts at Home, www.manomaine.org/programs/mep/comienzaencasa
- *Families matter: Designing media for a digital age,* The Joan Ganz Cooney Center, www.joanganzcooneycenter.org/upload_kits/jgcc_familiesmatter.pdf
- Harvard Family Research Project, www.hfrp.org
- healthychildren.org, www.healthychildren.org/
- *Learning At Home: Families' Educational Media Use in America*, Joan Ganz Cooney Center, www.joanganzcooneycenter.org/publication/learning-at-home/
- *Media, technology, and reading in Hispanic families: A national survey*, Center on Media and Human Development at Northwestern University and National Center for Families Learning, http://familieslearning.org/PDF/HispanicFamMediaSurvey_Dec13.pdf
- *The New Coviewing: Designing for Learning through Joint Media Engagement*, The Joan Ganz Cooney Center, www.joanganzcooneycenter.org/upload_kits/jgc_coviewing_desktop.pdf
- *The Parent App: Understanding Families in the Digital Age.* L.S. Clark, 2013. New York, NY: Oxford University Press.
- *Parenting in the Age of Digital Technology, A National Survey*, Center on Media and Human Development. Northwestern University, http://web5.soc.northwestern.edu/cmhd/wp-content/uploads/2013/05/Parenting-Report_FINAL.pdf
- PLAY Pro, www.chicagoplaypro.com
- Smart Apps for Special Needs, www.smartappsforspecialneeds.com
- *Strengthening Family Engagement Through Teacher Preparation and Professional Development,* Harvard Family Research Project, www.hfrp.org/publications-resources/browse-our-publications/strengthening-family-engagement-through-teacher-preparation-and-professional-development

- *Zero to Eight: Children's Media Use in America 2013*, Common Sense Media, www.commonsensemedia.org/sites/default/files/research/zero-to-eight-2013.pdf
- *Zero to Three,* Special Issue—*Media and Technology in the Lives of Infants and Toddlers*, National Center for Infants, Toddlers, and Families, www.zerotothree.org/

Chapter 15

Technology as a Tool to Strengthen the Community

Luisa M. Cotto

Introduction—Defining Community

Rapid advances in technology have changed the way we view our world today. Traditionally, when thinking about the concept of community, we tend to think about our immediate neighborhood or the people around us, but the Internet has made it possible for communities to have fewer or no geographical limitations (Wenger, 2006). In 2001, Project LinCS 2 Durham (Linking Communities and Scientists) was approached to define the concept of community among different populations in order to create collaborative models and measures that apply to most communities. After 113 interviews, LinCS was able to identify five core elements of a community: location, sharing a common interest, joint action, social ties, and diversity. Location was included in 77% of the definitions, while sharing the same interest was included in 58% of the responses. Ninety-three percent of the definitions included either shared location or sharing a common interest (MacQueen, et al., 2001).

All communities have two common threads—they cannot exist without a social component and they need members who share a particular interest. Each community, offline and online, is bound by a particular concern or curiosity that drives conversation and engagement. Community members meet to discuss and ask or answer questions regarding a particular topic, take action, or learn from one another (Henri & Pudelko, 2003). In some instances, community members are not geographically bound to each other, but rather share an interest in the topics they discuss.

Community members can also share similar characteristics, including language, ethnicity, age, and profession that contribute to the community. When a group is diverse in terms of knowledge and experiences, it can contribute positively to the learning process (Vygotsky, 1978). An important aspect of these communities is that their members do not act exclusively as experts or learners, but each individual in a community engages in meaning-making by sharing information that contributes to the content and learning experience (Bruner, 1985).

Before social media channels existed, emails, discussion boards, chats, and instant messaging systems were the online spaces people used for sharing ideas about a particular topic. People were able to create their own discussion boards by topics, and chat rooms were available by gender, age, nationality, and interests. These early communities and digital tools, which are still in use, were mainly used within organizations or homes (Wellman, 2002). With the arrival of new and more affordable technologies such as cellphones, tablets, and social media networks, people stay connected to each other at all times strengthening community ties through more frequent contact, both online and offline.

Even though advances in technology have expanded our notion of communities, we should begin the community building process by creating a culture of collaboration and communication within our immediate circles, which includes our classrooms, families, and neighborhoods, before expanding them outward. This will ensure that new connections beyond your geographical locations are meaningful and relevant.

Position Statement Alignment

Technology tools offer new opportunities for educators to build relationships, maintain ongoing communication, exchange information and share online resources with parents and families. Likewise, parents and families can use technology to ask questions, seek advice, share information about their child, and feel more engaged in the program and their child's experiences there.

National Association for the Education of Young Children [NAEYC] & Fred Rogers Center (2012), p. 7

Creating a Community Within Your Classroom Walls

The physical classroom has all the attributes of a community. It's comprised of a group of people in the same area, sharing some set of common characteristics, be it age, interests, language, etc. Yet those traits alone don't make a community. Keys to building community within a classroom include cultivating a culture of collaboration and engaging in effective, culturally sensitive communication. Children need to feel secure and see their classroom as their "school family," and the collaboration between teachers, children, and their families must be transparent in their everyday interactions, as illustrated in Figure 15.1.

Taking into account children's backgrounds is another important aspect to building a strong community within a classroom. The U.S. census of 2010 showed how more than 60 million of United Sates residents, 5 years old and older, speak a language other than English at home. Therefore it is up to educators to provide opportunities for young children that are culturally sensitive and that are developmentally appropriate (NAEYC & Fred Rogers Center, 2012). Every classroom, like any other community, has its own values and rules. Children in our classrooms come from different backgrounds, and by building a community within the classroom walls, teachers create an atmosphere that provides common threads and helps children and families connect to each other (see Figure 15.2).

Nearly 13 million children under the age of 5 in the United States are in some type of childcare arrangement every week (Laughlin, 2013). As children's first

Figure 15.1 Sharing an iPad

Courtesy of United Way Center for Excellence in Early Education

teachers, families play a fundamental and essential role in children's development. This is the first and most crucial relationship children have, and it sets pre-
cedence for future relationships (Halgunseth & Peterson, 2009). It is important
that teachers ask families in their classrooms what is the best way to communicate with them. As a teacher, I learned that not every family will come to your
classroom to volunteer, not everyone has a computer, and some just simply do not
have the time as they work several jobs. Accommodating parents' and families'
needs is a crucial task in building positive and strong relationships. In order to
engage your community, you cannot rely on one communication channel, but a
variety of them. This ensures equitable access to the resources and information
you provide to families.

Mobile Devices to Engage Children and Families

One of the fastest growing technologies is the cellphone. Ninety-one percent of
the United States adult population owns a cellphone, while 56% of them are
smartphone owners (Smith, 2013). Even though some families do not have access
to broadband connectivity at home, they are accessing the Internet through a variety of mobile devices and shrinking the digital divide (File, 2013).

Figure 15.2 Using Photos to Welcome Families and Build Community

Courtesy of United Way Center for Excellence in Early Education

Even though cell phone and smartphone technology might not be seen as an educational tool, when used properly, it can become a powerful learning tool (NAEYC & Fred Rogers Center, 2012). Qualcomm Wireless provided smartphones to low-income students in North Carolina, allowing them to conduct research and connect with classmates and teachers through their wireless devices. This means that learning did not stop in the classroom but continued after school. These students improved their standardized test scores by 30%. Teachers used the phones to facilitate collaboration through blogs, instant messaging, and email. Students were able to use the smartphones to take pictures or videos that captured their problem-solving strategies, allowing them to have further discussion with their peers (Project Tomorrow, 2011).

Smartphones have many potential uses in early childhood settings; they can connect families, be a source of information, and a tool for observation and documentation. I have met many teachers who own a smartphone, and they are willing to use it in the classrooms, but their early childhood centers prohibit the use of cellphones in the classroom. It is understandable that the use of the cellphone needs to be limited as teachers are responsible for children, but teachers should be allowed to use cellphones appropriately for research, documentation, or any learning and engaging activity. Each school has to develop their own technology protocols, so everyone is clear about how to properly use technology tools in the classroom and how to avoid their use for personal matters.

The following tools or apps are examples of how a mobile device may be used to engage children and families:

- *Remind101:* Provides a safe way for teachers to send text messages to students and engage families. With this tool, you can create up to 10 groups to send messages to. A great way to engage the community with this tool is by updating the community with public policy updates on early childhood or new research.
- *QR Codes:* If you send families a book to read with their children, you can add a QR code with a video version of you reading it, so families know how to be interactive with the book. This can also be helpful for children who are not yet reading. You can also create materials for the community with QR codes that lead to videos on best practices or how to advocate for early childhood.
- *Flickr:* Allows you to upload pictures and share them. The great thing about Flickr is that you can give permission to families to add comments and notes to pictures.

Building a Sense of Ownership Through Photography

Teachers have long used photographs to build a sense of ownership in their classroom by placing student pictures in cubbies, creating a classroom poster with each child's face on it, or a word wall with the children's name and pictures. When children see their pictures around the classroom, they feel a sense of belonging within their classroom community. This simple technology tool can enhance relationships from infancy through preschool, as illustrated in Figure 15.3.

In an infant classroom, one teacher placed pictures of the children on the floor (at their eye level). After a couple of days, teachers started to notice that children were crawling to the area and interacting with their own pictures. In their own marvelous ways, infants were developing a sense of belonging. In the same classroom, teachers shared pictures with families through a journal. Families were encouraged to take the journal home and write notes for their children. Teachers added pictures and notes every day as well. This two-way communication tool makes families feel secure that their child is being cared for and gives families and teachers insight about the activities the child can do at school and at home.

In a toddler class, teachers created a "watch me grow" chart in which they took pictures of each child every month and displayed them for families and children to see (see Figure 15.4). Not only did this activity engage families in a meaningful way, but it showed them what skills they were developing during those months.

In a preschool class, a teacher noticed that children were interested in learning about Japanese culture, so she went online and found pictures and videos of aspects of Japanese culture including dress, food, and transportation. The teacher

Figure 15.3 Using a Camera to Document Classroom Life

Courtesy of United Way Center for Excellence in Early Education

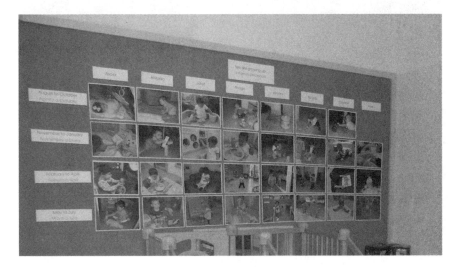

Figure 15.4 "Watch Me Grow" Chart

Courtesy of United Way Center for Excellence in Early Education

found a website called panorimo.com, in which people share pictures through a geosocial network. Geosocial networking allows users to provide their geographical location and, therefore, be found by people near them or that are looking for that specific location. The teacher used this website as a resource to learn more about Japanese culture through words, images, and graphics. In this case, photos were attached to a specific geographical location. Children in this preschool classroom were not only able to explore the Japanese culture, but they were able to explore their own cultures and those of their peers.

Another simple, but effective, way to create a sense of belonging and culture within your classroom is through documentation (see Figure 15.5). Taking pictures of children engaged in learning activities and displaying them in the classroom is an effective way to make learning visible. Documentation provides a vehicle in which teachers and students can create and transmit culture, values, and knowledge (Cox Suarez, 2006).

There is no particular recipe to create a community within your classroom and beyond. Each child, parent, and teacher brings different languages, cultures, values, and knowledge to the classroom; this difference must be valued and taken in consideration when planning the use of technology tools (NAEYC & Fred Rogers Center, 2012). Each year, as new children and families arrive, the process

Figure 15.5 Documentation in a Preschool Classroom

Courtesy of United Way Center for Excellence in Early Education

starts all over again, from getting to know the children and families to developing new ways to work together.

Strengthening Communities Through Email

In her article, Patricia Reaney (2012) identifies email as the most familiar online communication channel and people's top online activity. This asynchronous communication tool can play a great role in building strong communities both within and outside the classroom. Emails provide the capability to share children's learning through stories, pictures, videos; share resources to enhance learning; or extend conversations with families, practitioners, and the community at large.

A preschool teacher, who took pictures of the different learning activities during the day, used an email to share that day's learning experiences with the children's family. Through email, the teacher described how children were interested in the smell of the different herbs in the garden and how they made connections between the different smells and the one of the soap. She added a link to the soap recipe in the email, as the children were interested in learning how to make soap. The teacher encouraged parents to try to make soap at home, using the recipe, and take pictures that can then be shared back with the classroom. She also included a summary of some of the conversations children had and what they were able to learn. Since she teaches in a community where 66% of families speak Spanish, she worked with her Spanish-speaking co-teacher to translate the content of the email. In the email, she also copies other school teachers, teaching the same grade.

This teacher used the email to create a community among families and teachers at her school. In a short email, she was able to share relevant information, and be inclusive.

1. *She included each family in the email:* This allows each family to learn about their children and other children in the classroom. Allowing families to have conversations by simply clicking "reply all."
2. *She took into consideration the diversity of the families:* She knows the community she serves, so she translated the content of the email, so every family could benefit from it. You can use online translators such as Google and Bing translator if you don't have the luxury of having a person to do it for you. (Please note that these translation programs are not accurate at all times, but it will show how culturally sensitive you are. Also, don't hesitate to ask bilingual parents to translate items for your classroom communication or environment.)
3. *She used the email as an engagement tool:* The teacher explained the children's interest in learning about the soap, and she included a link with the soap recipe for families to do at home. This is a real opportunity to strengthen the home-school connection. Don't just inform families about your classroom happenings, but add an interactive activity they can do with their children at

home. By doing this, you get families interested in the topic being discussed in the classroom and will provide opportunities to further engage families.

4. *She shared her experience:* By copying other teachers at her school, she was able to inform other teachers about what is happening in her classroom. This act of sharing encourages other teachers to share ideas or even volunteer as a subject matter expert on the soap project. As early childhood practitioners, it is important to share and be open to suggestions.

Home visits and school meetings are very important; they give insights about the strengths and challenges children and their families have, and provide an opportunity to create strong relationships between teachers and families. These meetings and home visits, due to time constraints, often happen sporadically. Email communications have the power of enhancing face-to-face communications as they provide an ongoing communication channel for teachers and families. When teachers use technology tools like email on a regular basis, they increase the potential of having greater overall contact with children's families (Quan-Haase, Wellman, Witte, & Hampton, 2002).

Emails can also help to spark conversations with families. Some early childhood education centers host *family roundtables*. These meetings give families the opportunity to suggest a topic of interest such as behavioral management, developmental milestones, and early literacy, and have open discussions about the issue. These roundtables can be complemented by further discussions via email or by sharing relevant resources such as videos, handouts, or articles.

Using Videoconference Tools to Connect With a Broad Audience

Videoconference and Voice-Over-Internet-Protocol (VOIP) systems such as Skype and Google+ Hangouts allow people to have real-time communication from two or more different locations. These synchronous technology tools enable people to connect with others outside their geographical location and expand classroom walls. Synchronous technology tools provide real-world experiences by giving access to experts, authors, artists, musicians, and peers around the world, enabling learners to solve problems and develop understanding of other cultures. Unlike emails, videoconferences, and video chats are very similar to face-to-face communication as these tools allow you to see the person through a webcam in real time.

In an inquiry-based learning school, teachers work on several projects with children. In one of the preschool classrooms, the teachers and children were exploring the concept of airports. Everything started when a child came back from vacation and shared with others during "show and tell" the experience of clearing security at the airport and boarding the plane. Other children started sharing their experiences, and as the children played with blocks, the teacher noticed that they were building an airplane. As the classroom explored the topic more deeply, the teachers and students decided to ask experts to come visit. They invited a Transportation Security Administration (TSA) agent and a pilot to come to the classroom. After researching more, the students wanted to go and visit the airport and control tower, but for security reasons, the airport was not allowing fieldtrips. Teachers decided to make some calls to see if they could Skype with someone at the control tower. After many calls, teachers were able to Skype with a customer service employee. The classroom also used videos, pictures, and books to build background knowledge. The whole classroom was turned into an airport. With the help of some parents, children built an airplane and luggage out of cardboard boxes. They created plane tickets, signs, and brochures among other early literacy materials. The Skype conversation, the videos, and the online research were only a piece of the whole learning experience (see Figure 15.6). The teachers did not focus on the use of the technology itself, but how these technology tools would enhance children's learning experiences. Technology should never replace any learning experience, but enhance it (NAEYC & Fred Rogers Center, 2012).

Figure 15.6 A Video Chat With an Expert

Courtesy of United Way Center for Excellence in Early Education

Videoconference tools can also help to connect families that live abroad or do not live in the home with the child. Teachers can invite families to share their culture, read a book, or tell stories; they can also be invited as topic experts for a project. Also, as teachers, we know that it is sometimes challenging to have 100% attendance at family meetings. Google provides teachers with the ability to create a classroom page and also a Google Hangout account, which can be used to have conversations with families online. One of the features of Google Hangouts is that you can connect up to 10 people in the same conversation, allowing families that could not attend a school meeting the opportunity to join the meeting virtually. Another feature of Google Hangouts is that you can share your screen and documents. Google recently released a new product called Hangouts On Air. This tool allows you to stream a live meeting or a classroom activity, record it, and share it through YouTube. This tool can be used to share videos with families, other teachers, professional development, for assessment of learning or to simply share best practices.

Technology Tools That Are Strengthening Community

The Museum of Modern Art (MoMA) in New York started using Google Hangout to connect art educators with art enthusiasts to discuss topics regarding art and identity (Museum of Modern Art, 2013). MoMA not only acts as museum, but a learning facility. By using Google Hangout, the museum can provide art education and discussion to a broad audience. Imagine doing the same at your school. You can give families and the community at large the tools they need.

Another widely known video communication tool is Skype, which has a website called "Skype in the classroom." This website allows teachers, authors, and families to create profiles and then create a "subject." A subject is a topic you want to discuss with others. Topics can include gardens, oceans, nutrition, and language. This allows teachers to post their current projects and find people who either are doing the same project or are interested in collaborating. Skype in the classroom also allows you to identify the age group you are working with, so you can target your specific audience. Another similar website is epals.com, which connects classrooms around the world and is similarly topic based.

Technology Tools That Strengthen the Community

An interesting project is the Vegetable Garden by Simonsotherhalf (Skype user name), an Australian teacher. In this project, children grow vegetables in temperate climate regions and then compare them. Teachers throughout North America, Asia, Europe, and South America follow and collaborate on this topic. Skype's free account allows you to have conversations with one person or computer at a time (in the same location) rather than a group of people in different locations.

The Tech for a Global Early Childhood Education website has different stories about how teachers around the world use Skype and other digital tools to create a global learning network. This website features a section called "ideas to action," which provides teachers with tips on how to extend communities beyond the classroom walls.

The Power of Social Media

Social media is changing how we conduct social interactions and allows us to stay connected to people at all times. Two-thirds of the global Internet population is on a social network (Nielsen, 2009). Teachers in early childhood education classroom can use social media as a way to connect with other teachers, families, and the community at large. Social media can also be used as a way to document what happens in your classroom, increase awareness of early childhood practices, build relationships with stakeholders, and increase engagement with the early childhood community. If you want to promote quality early care and education, social media can be the vehicle that will help you achieve that goal. Let's explore some of the most popular social networks among early childhood educators.

Facebook is a great place for schools to have a presence online and build a community. Facebook has three types of pages: *profiles*, which are personal time-lines for noncommercial use, *pages*, which are public, and *groups,* which can be open, closed, or secret. If you have a Facebook *profile*, you will be able to create *pages* and *groups*. Facebook *pages* can act as a central channel of communication in which schools can share the latest news, resources, pictures of school events, and more. Each classroom in the school can have a *group* in which they can share pictures with families privately, have conversations, and create polls. If you have a classroom project, such as a vegetable garden, you can look for Facebook pages or groups on the topic, share pictures of your school garden, ask questions to experts or garden enthusiasts, and even invite them to video-chat with you and your classroom through Facebook.

As part of a course I taught to early childhood teachers, I created a Facebook "closed" group. In this group, I was able to share the files needed for the course, and participants were able to share resources they found. When I started teaching this course, we didn't have a Facebook group, and conversations in the classroom were almost inexistent. Conversations were limited to specific questions, even when we were doing a group exercise. After implementing the Facebook group, teachers started commenting about each other's photos, stories, and work, they gave each other suggestions, and true collaboration was born. Facebook provides a natural way for people to engage in meaning-making conversations.

Google Plus is newer than Facebook and has developed rapidly since it started. One of the most interesting characteristics of Google Plus is that one password fits all. Once you have a Google account, you are able to use all Google applications including Google Plus, Hangouts, YouTube, Google Drive, Picasa, among many others.

Google Plus, like Facebook, allows you to create a page for your school, but instead of *groups*, you have *circles*. These circles help you organize your contacts, and you can create as many circles as you want. Unlike Facebook, it does not have advertisements, which provides user with a clean and easy to use interface.

Google Plus allows you to connect and share with as much ease as any Google related app such as YouTube and Google Hangout. This social network website lends itself to create learning communities. A good example is one of the Google Plus communities, Technology in Education. This community has more than 7,000 members, who share resources and discuss varying topics related to technology and education.

Twitter can be compared to a listserv. Professionals used to sign-up for listservs, a type of email communication list, so they could be aware of what was happening in their field. The only problem is that listservs are one-way communication tools; people sign up and they receive emails or newsletters. In Twitter, users sign up and follow their topics of interest, allowing two-way communication and ongoing support. Twitter gives you access to leaders in the field of early childhood education, allowing you to ask questions and receive resources or the latest research. Besides following people on twitter, you can join twitter chats, a more exciting way to collaborate with people around the world.

Twitter was one of the first social media platforms to support *hashtags,* which is a keyword, prefixed by the symbol "#", that helps to catalogue and organize content online (Facebook and Google Plus now support hashtags). By using a hashtag (#), you can find a group of people with your same interest. Twitter chats use hashtags to contain messages in such groups. A good example of that is #ECETechChat. This chat meets regularly to discuss topics around technology and early childhood education. This chats brings together leaders in the field, practitioners, developers, and families.

Twitter lends itself to true collaboration. What is interesting about Twitter chats is that there are not experts and learners, but everyone contributes equally to the learning process by posting questions and sharing resources. Teachers can create their own accounts or hashtags to share information with families or to advocate for early education. Some education related hashtags you can start following are: #earlyed, #ECE, #ECETech, #ECETechChat, #edchat, #kinderchat, #STEM, and #spedchat. See the EdTech List of Best Education Hashtags in the "Learn More . . ." section at the end of this chapter.

Other social media channels you should explore further are

- *Edmodo:* Even though this social learning platform lends itself better to older students, it can be a great tool for teachers and families to communicate. Edmodo can be accessed by computer and mobile device.
- *Pinterest:* Pinterest provides teachers a way to "pin" great resources and share with families or other teachers. Pinterest can serve as a collection of great resources.

- *LinkedIn:* This professional social network provides a way to connect with people on the field of early childhood education. In this network, you can join groups such as "Digital Literacy for Children," where members share links and information regarding technology and early childhood. These groups also allow for discussions as people can add comments to different posts.
- *Blogs:* This online tool provides teachers and schools with a space to share with families and the community at large best practices in early childhood. Blogs provide a natural way for users to have conversations regarding a topic by commenting on each blog posts. Blogs are easy to produce and maintain: They can be edited by email and through cellphone apps. If you are a new blogger, try blogger.com or tumblr.com as they are user friendly.

Position Statement Alignment

> Modeling the effective use of technology and interactive media for parent communication and family engagement also creates opportunities to help parents themselves become better informed, empowers them to make responsible choices about technology use and screen time at home, engages them as teachers who can extend classroom learning activities into the home, and encourages co-viewing, co-participation, and joint media engagement between parents and their children.
>
> NAEYC & Fred Rogers Center (2012), p. 8

Conclusion

You may have heard the statement that making a community strong is not about the individualism, but a collective effort between people here and there. Digital tools can expand and combine the networks that families, practitioners, policy makers, and universities have to provide a bigger platform for communities to create movements and make informed decisions to better the quality of early education here and there, and to provide access to quality resources and opportunities to our most deserving community members: our children.

Technology puts resources for teachers, families, and children at their fingertips. It is important that early childhood educators use technology to inform families about best practices in early childhood education, so families can become advocates of their children education. Technology is not the only communication tool and it is not the answer to the problems in our community, but it is another medium, another communication channel that might help reach more people in more places; another way to teach, learn, paint, read, and communicate.

Teacher Takeaways

1. *Go from micro to macro:* A child's learning is influenced by all the people in his or her life and the experiences he or she is presented with. Start by providing a classroom environment that allows children and families to connect

with each other, learn from one another, and create a school family. Once this is achieved, collaborate with other classrooms within your school and outside your school. This provides children with skills needed in today's world, such as problem solving, teamwork, and communication.

2. *Deliver instruction through multiple forms of media:* Teachers nowadays have more than books and posters. When learning about a topic in your classroom, explore with your children other resources such as instructional videos, audio clips, animation, and videoconferences.

3. *Encourage collaboration:* It is great to share with families and the community at large what is happening in your classroom, but in order to really engage them and make sure that children's learning does not stop in the classroom, you have to include in your emails and social media post what in marketing is known as a "call to action." A call to action tells your audience what you want them to do next. In education, it can be an activity to do at home, a link to a resource or a volunteer opportunity in your classroom.

4. *Stay connected:* To achieve a meaningful, two-way communication and equitable access to information, resources, and communication with each family in your classroom, it is important to use multiple communication channels such as face-to-face meetings, flyers, journals, newsletters, text messages, emails, websites, blogs, and others. Ask families at the beginning of the year what their preferred mode of communication is. This is used in marketing. Stores email you, text you, bombard you with TV commercials, and mail you coupons just to get your attention. Why not do the same in your classrooms to get families engaged?

5. *Keep informed:* Use social media to share ideas, learn from others, connect with families, collect resources, and ask questions. Start with one social media channel at a time and keep in mind that online profiles are an extension of yourself, so keep them clean and professional.

References

Bruner, J. (1985). Vygotsky: An historical and conceptual perspective. *Culture, communication, and cognition: Vygotskian perspectives* (pp. 21–34). London, UK: Cambridge University Press.

Cox Suarez, S. (2006). Making learning visible through documentation: Creating a culture of inquiry among pre-service teachers. *The New Educator, 2*(1), 33–55.

File, T. (2013). *Computer and Internet use in the United States* (pp. 20–569). Retrieved from www.census.gov/prod/2013pubs/p20–569.pdf

Halgunseth, L., & Peterson, A. (2009). *Family engagement, diverse families, and early childhood education programs: An integrated review of the literature.* National Association for the Education of Young Children, The Pew Charitable Trusts. Retrieved from www.naeyc.org/files/naeyc/file/research/FamEngage.pdf

Henri, F., & Pudelko, B. (2003). Understanding and analyzing activity and learning in virtual communities. *Journal of Computer Assisted Learning,* (19), 474–487. Retrieved from http://hal.archives-ouvertes.fr/docs/00/19/02/67/PDF/Henri-France-2003.pdf

Laughlin, L. (2013). *Who's minding the kids? Child care arrangements: Spring 2011* (pp. 70–135). Retrieved from www.census.gov/prod/2013pubs/p70-135.pdf

MacQueen, K. M., McLellan, E., Metzger, D. S., Kegeles, S., Strauss, R. P., Scotti, R., Blanchard, L., & Trotter, II, R. T. (2001). What is community? An evidence-based definition for participatory public health. *American Journal of Public Health, 91*(12), 1929–1938. Retrieved from www.ncbi.nlm.nih.gov/pmc/articles/PMC1446906/pdf/0911926.pdf

Museum of Modern Art. (2013). *MoMa learning*. Retrieved from https://plus.google.com/u/0/105146531863088524568/posts

National Association for the Education of Young Children, & Fred Rogers Center for Early Learning and Children's Media at Saint Vincent College. (2012). *Technology and interactive media as tools in early childhood programs serving children from birth through age 8*. Washington, DC: NAEYC; Latrobe, PA: Fred Rogers Center for Early Learning and Children's Media at Saint Vincent College.

Nielsen. (2009). Social networking's new global footprint. Retrieved from www.nielsen.com/us/en/newswire/2009/social-networking-new-global-footprint.html

Project Tomorrow. (2011, March). *Evaluation report of the impact of project k-nect on teaching and learning*. Retrieved from www.tomorrow.org/docs/ProjectKNect_Evaluation Report_Mar2011.pdf

Quan-Haase, A., Wellman, B., Witte, J., & Hampton, K. N. (2002). Capitalizing on the Internet: Network capital, participatory capital, and sense of community. In B. Wellman & C. Haythornthwaite (Eds.), *The Internet in everyday life* (pp. 291–324). Oxford, UK: Blackwell.

Reaney, P. (2012, March 27). Most of world interconnected through email and social media. *Reuters*. Retrieved from www.reuters.com/article/2012/03/27/uk-socialmedia-online-poll-idUSLNE82Q02120120327

Smith, A. (2013, June 5). *Smartphone ownership 2013*. Retrieved from http://pewinternet.org/Reports/2013/Smartphone-Ownership-2013.aspx

U.S. Census Bureau. (2010). *Languages spoken at home in the United States and Puerto Rico*. Retrieved October 7, 2013, from www.census.gov.hhes/socdemo/language

Vygotsky, L. (1978). *Mind in society: The development of higher psychological processes*. Cambridge, MA: Harvard University Press

Wellman, B. (2002). Little boxes, glocalization, and networked individualism. *Digital cities II: Computational and sociological approaches*. Second Kyoto Workshop on Digital Cities, Kyoto, Japan, October 18–20, 2001. Revised papers (pp. 10–25). Berlin, Germany: Springer. (Original work published 1991). Retrieved from www.vdebooks.com/digital-cities-ii-computational-and-sociological-approaches-PDF-11294939/

Wenger, E. (2006, June). Communities of practice a brief introduction. Retrieved from www.ewenger.com/theory/

Resources

- Bing Translator, www.bing.com/translator
- Blogger, www.blogger.com/
- Edmodo, www.edmodo.com
- epals.com, www.epals.com
- Facebook, www.facebook.com
- Flickr, www.flickr.com

- Google Drive, https://drive.google.com/
- Google Plus (Google+), www.google.com/+/
- Google Plus Hangouts, www.google.com/+/learnmore/hangouts/
- Google Plus Community: Technology in Education, https://plus.google.com/u/0/communities/106567026492773899034
- Google Translate, http://translate.google.com
- LinkedIn, www.linkedin.com
- Nielsen, www.nielsen.com
- Panorimo.com, www.panoramio.com/
- Picasa, http://picasa.google.com
- Pinterest, www.pinterest.com
- QR Code Generator, www.qrstuff.com/
- Remind101, www.remind101.com
- Skype, www.skype.com/en/
- Skype in the Classroom, https://education.skype.com
- Tumbler, www.tumblr.com
- Twitter, https://twitter.com
- YouTube, www.youtube.com

Learn More ...

- EdTech *Printable EdTech List of Best Education Hashtags,* www.edtechmagazine.com/k12/article/2013/03/printable-list-best-education-hashtags-infographic
- MoMA, Museum of Modern Art, www.moma.org
- Project LinCS 2 Durham (Linking Communities and Scientists), http://lincs2durham.org/index.html
- Project Tomorrow, www.tomorrow.org
- Tech for a Global Early Childhood Education, http://globalearlyed.wordpress.com
- United Way of Miami-Dade, www.unitedwaymiami.org
- United Way Center for Excellence in Early Education, www.unitedwaycfe.org
- Visible Thinking, www.visiblethinkingpz.org/

Access, Content, and Engagement: How Children's Librarians Support Early Learning in the Digital Age

Cen Campbell and Carisa Kluver

Introduction

This chapter is a collaboration between a children's librarian, Cen Campbell, and a former social worker, Carisa Kluver, who met and began developing new media trainings for children's librarians in 2011. Cen is the librarian for the digital children's library at Bookboard.com and the founder at LittleeLit.com, a blog that focuses on developing best practices for the incorporation of new media into early literacy programming. Carisa runs the book app review site Digital-Storytime.com and the Digital Media Diet blog.

When we first began collaborating, our two websites, LittleeLit.com and DigitalMediaDiet.com, were among many independent voices in the blogosphere trying to create and promote informed discourse, resources, and standards around the use of new media with young children. Bringing digital devices into the highly democratic space of public libraries was much more controversial than either of us expected. While creating her evaluation criteria for Digital-Storytime.com, Carisa sought the help of librarians, but she was often encouraged to focus only on print titles for her young son. When Cen began introducing apps into storytime, she was met with some support but also a lot of skepticism about the value and ethics of using "screens" in library settings. In the end, our experiences made us even more committed to creating a new model for how we approach digital content for children in libraries. Our model is built on three key aspects of library services to children—Access, Content, and Engagement (ACE)—and this chapter focuses on how children's librarians can use ACE to support early learning in the digital age.

Understanding the Digital Context for Informal Learning

When the first apps were introduced to a smartphone audience in 2008, it would have been difficult to predict just how much of a revolution would be coming in the way we consume, share, and create content in every sphere of daily life. Not only has the digital age disrupted nearly every industry and occupation, but this change has happened at a lightning fast pace. While it has penetrated deeply into society at every income level, uncertainty remains about the impact on young learners and early literacy.

With an average of more than 8 hours a day of "screen time" for children ages 8–18 (Common Sense Media, 2013), concerns have been raised about the impact on brain development and about how and how much content is being consumed. At the same time, concerns have been raised about who may be left behind: families and communities without access to high-speed Internet and digital devices. Issues of access and connectivity can negatively impact the ability of these children and families to take advantage of the best new media has to offer, including tools for early learning, literacy, communication, and even the ability to have a meaningful political voice.

This leaves professionals in fields that work with children and families struggling over whether children have too much or too little exposure to this new media landscape. The guidance from research and evaluation of the impact of these new tools is too embryonic to shape best practices with the kind of certainty most professionals are seeking, and it will take years, if not decades, to fully understand all the implications of technology, digital media, and interactive touch-screens on young children, parents, families, and communities.

In the meantime, lessons learned from years of research on children's television, media, and earlier technologies will have to make do for understanding how new forms of media consumption may affect developing brains. We can't wait for the research to catch up with the digital realities; many families are already using the latest digital devices and apps with their young children, even in the absence of conclusive and authoritative research. A whole generation of children will grow up while we "wait and see," so creating best practices even as new technologies and digital media emerge is as important as supporting future research.

Luckily, in the case of curation and evaluation of media, we are not starting from scratch. Children's librarians have been curating and evaluating new forms of media for years. While interactive tablet-based and touch-screen media are new and uneven in quality, librarians can act as media mentors in their communities by providing recommendations for age appropriate, high-quality media, alongside modeling of healthy consumption for families with young children. Children's librarians can now serve as media literacy specialists, a role consistent with their expertise.

Growing Young Minds (Institute of Museum and Library Services [IMLS], 2013) was a report funded by the IMLS that outlined 10 ways in which libraries and museums support early learning. The report suggests that libraries can provide leadership and access around the use of digital media with young families by providing access, modeling, and opportunities for engagement with new media. It is important to keep in mind, however, that digital technologies are ubiquitous, and guidance from librarians to families with young children span all of the services that they traditionally provide. Even though specific attention is paid to "linking new digital technologies to learning," guidance around new media and young children also permeates most of the other factors mentioned in this report. For example, "supporting parents as the child's first teacher" includes guidance in the use of new media, as do "high-quality learning experiences, opportunities to explore STEM (science, technology, engineering, and mathematics) concepts, focusing on Common Core standards," and "adding capacity to early learning networks" (IMLS, 2013).

10 Ways Museums and Libraries Support Community Early Learning Efforts

1. Increase high-quality early learning experiences
2. Engage and support families as their child's first teachers
3. Support development of executive function and "deeper learning" skills through literacy and STEM-based experiences
4. Create seamless links across early learning and the early grades
5. Position children for meeting expectations of the Common Core State Standards
6. Address the Summer Slide
7. Link new digital technologies to learning
8. Improve family health and nutrition
9. Leverage community partnerships
10. Add capacity to early learning networks

IMLS (2013)

Position Statement Alignment

> As they do for young children, educators have a responsibility to parents and families to model appropriate, effective, and positive uses of technology, media, methods of communication, and social media that are safe, secure, healthy, acceptable, responsible, and ethical.
>
> National Association for the Education of Young Children [NAEYC] & Fred Rogers Center (2012), pp. 7–8

Why Are Children's Librarians Ideal Media Mentors?

Children's librarians are the ideal media mentors for young children, parents, and educators because they:

- Are experienced in the curation and evaluation of different types of media, including emergent media
- Have expertise in the development of regular, free, ongoing early literacy and early learning programming
- Are dedicated to the core values of promoting a love of reading, providing resources to support lifelong learning and equity of access

- Have access to captive populations within their facilities; parents and care-givers choose to come to the library with their children (unlike schools or child-care centers where children are dropped off)
- Have relationships with numerous community organizations (including other public entities and nonprofit and for-profit organizations) and are ideal partners for collaborative technology-based projects.

Children's Librarians as Media Mentors

ACE—Access

One of the American Library Association's cornerstones of public library ser-vices is *Equity of Access* (ALA, n.d.). This ALA pillar of service has traditionally referred to free and equitable access to information, but also to the technology that enables the transmission of information. Access to databases, computers, Internet, and WiFi are commonplace and uncontested in areas designed for adult use but, with the arrival of commercial and proprietary digital devices (and their associated software), designed specifically for use by children, questions of what constitutes equitable access are not as clear. Public libraries now conduct needs-based assessments to determine what sort of services and programming they can offer in order to effectively bridge the digital divide in their communities, and the answer is not always to provide access to the actual devices.

According to the Commons Sense Media report, *Zero to Eight: Children's Media Use in America* (2013, p. 9), "The percent of children with access to some type of 'smart' mobile device at home (e.g., smartphone, tablet) has jumped from half (52%) to three-quarters (75%) of all children in just two years." And time on the devices tripled between 2011 and 2013. With nearly half of households own-ing a tablet or eReader in the short time since they were introduced, it's likely that by the end of this decade, there will be very few Americans without exposure to apps and e-books on a regular basis (Pew Research Center, 2013).

While the digital divide between lower- and higher-income families may be decreasing due to increased device ownership, the content being selected is still not equal. High-speed Internet access has also stalled, with fewer than half of low-income families logging on to the super-charged information highway in a world where more than 85% of higher-income children have easy on-ramps. In addition, 35% of lower-income parents have downloaded educational apps for their child, while 75% of higher-income parents have done so (Common Sense Media, 2013). Data on how much of the time children actually spend with high-quality content are still lacking, but the early data makes it clear that the digital divide is not going away anytime soon. Given these swiftly changing adoption numbers, librarians are uniquely positioned to provide access to knowledgeable staff, high-quality librarian-selected media, as well as circulating collections of devices and programming that incorporates both traditional and emergent formats.

As with any large paradigm shift, there are barriers to implementation that arise from both the mundane (budget, storage space, upkeep, etc.) and also from environmental, human, organizational, and societal factors. Barriers to access exist for individuals and libraries alike, and new formats and devices offer their own set of considerations when large public institutions begin to deploy services around them, including cost, geographic isolation, digital publishing, and the digital divide.

Luckily, the digital shift has brought the cost of children's digital content so low that high-quality content can now be found for a wide variety of budgets, including free, quality digital libraries that can include hundreds of titles (for example, International Children's Digital Library, Bookflix, Tumblebooks, Over-Drive, Axis 360, and EbscoHost). Many communities in rural areas that have difficulty acquiring physical content can also now use libraries and museums as distribution hubs for various digital formats of information, education, and entertainment.

Another exceptional change in access is for content creators, which is increasingly important for young people growing up in the digital realm. Nowadays, almost anyone, including children, can publish their work for access by the general public. Sifting through this sea of new and self-published content can be a challenge, but it is also the cornerstone of access to not only read, but share ideas with little or no gatekeeping. Librarians are beginning to model the use of content creation for young children in storytime settings, such as recording the children's retelling of a story and using an app like 30 Hands or My Story to produce a digital rendering.

The Common Sense Media report (2013) also identified a new manifestation of the digital divide that relates to tablet technology: the "app gap." Inequality of access to both home and mobile devices, as well as high-speed WiFi, creates disparities between young children who have access to these devices and those who do not. *Giving our Children a Fighting Chance: Poverty, Literacy and the Development of Information Capital*, the report on a 10-year study in two neighborhood libraries in Philadelphia conducted by Susan B. Neuman and Donna Celano (Neuman & Celano, 2012), outlines startling discrepancies in the use of libraries, the most startling of which centered around the use of technology with children. Not only did access to technology not help to bridge the digital divide, it exacerbated it, according to the study. Providing access alone is not enough; libraries must also offer opportunities and modeling for engagement between children and caregivers. Storytime is the ideal setting to offer a solution to the digital divide through providing access to devices, offering recommendations for high-quality content, and modeling engagement between the caregiver and the child.

ACE—Content

One of the biggest challenges for librarians, educators, and parents is finding high-quality, age-appropriate digital content. Two big concerns are the lack of curated content and the need for professional development on the use of new media with young children. Children's librarians are ideally poised to offer both resources and are beginning to provide the same kind of "reader's advisory" recommendations for interactive media as they have traditionally done for print media.

While there are some recommendation resources for interactive media (see "10 Recommended App Review Sites," below), reviewers often have a hard time keeping up with the quantity of new apps, and the marketplace has some idiosyncrasies that make accurate judgments challenging. Internet searches for children's app reviews result in a plethora of websites that look like review sites, but most of them include aggregated data from iTunes or the Google-Play Store, with descriptions that are often written by the developers and are hard to separate from real reviews. More troublesome, however, is the tendency of app review sites, for a variety of practical business reasons, to gloss over problems and provide glowing reviews even when there is a major flaw in the content or technical function of the app (Kluver, 2011). It is vital, therefore to not only evaluate the apps, but also to evaluate the "evaluators." Determining online authority is not always an easy task, however.

Finding Quality Apps—How to Evaluate the Evaluator

When looking at app reviews, you want to know as much as you can about the reviewer and to avoid reviews written by the app creator, or comments posted by rivals for the app you are researching. Use sites that identify and clearly list the following:

- Author of the review
- Date of publication (is the review up-to-date with the latest release of the app?)
- Clear disclosure about priority/expedited reviews, advertising, or other potential conflicts of interest
- Connections with the developers of the products being reviewed

10 Recommended App Review Sites (http:// childrensappreview.blogspot.com/)

- App Friday, www.appfriday.com
- AppShopper, http://appshopper.com
- Children's Technology Review, http://childrenstech.com
- Digital-Storytime, http://digital-storytime.com
- The Horn Book, www.hbook.com/category/choosing-books/app-review-of-the-week/
- The iMums, www.theimum.com
- Kirkus Reviews, www.kirkusreviews.com/book-reviews/ipad/

- Smart Apps for Kids, www.smartappsforkids.com www.facebook.com/smartappsforkids
- TeachersWithApps.com, http://teacherswithapps.com
- School Library Journal, Touch and Go, http://blogs.slj.com/touchandgo/

ACE—Engagement

Engagement can refer to the child's focus and interaction with the apps or other content on a device, but it also refers to the interaction and relationship with a caregiver that takes place when a device is used in a social context. Early research indicates that the tension between engagement and distraction may be one of the most useful places to focus on when looking at effectiveness for educational use (Schugar, Smith, & Schugar, 2013). Interactive and animated elements within an educational or storybook app have the unique opportunity to create meaningful connections either to the narrative or to a specific learning goal. This new medium shows promise for using app design to reinforce concepts and plot and avoid the pitfalls of a distraction or "seductive detail" that takes young readers on a digital wild goose chase instead of directing them to the meaningful message within the narrative.

In addition to the engaging nature of the medium itself, however, is a vitally necessary component: The active engagement of parents, caregivers, or peers in a child's consumption of digital media. Young children learn from relationships and meaningful exchanges with the people in their lives. Libraries have the ideal opportunity, and often a captive audience, to model for parents and caregivers what engagement focused around a digital device should look like, and to show how technology can enhance, not replace, those interactions.

The concept of "Media Mentorship" suggested by Lisa Guernsey, Director of the Early Education Initiative and the Learning Technologies Project at New America (Guernsey, 2013), has become a topic of conversation among early childhood educators, media literacy specialists, researchers, academics, and librarians. Children growing up in our media-rich environment need adults in their lives to guide the quality and content of their interaction with various forms of media. While parents should ideally perform this role for their children, the digital shift has left many parents and educators at a loss for where to find their own guidance and scrambling to improve their own digital media literacy, let alone how to guide subsequent generations. The primary work of LittleeLit.com now focuses almost entirely on positioning children's librarians to act as media mentors in the communities they serve. We feel that children's librarians are the ideal media mentors because of their expertise in two key areas: curating and evaluating high-quality, age-appropriate media and modeling the use of all types of media (which includes print and digital materials) with young children.

One challenge that children's librarians face as media mentors is the common depiction of even very young children interacting on their own, one-on-one, with a tablet device. The result of this modeling (often found in mainstream media outlets) is that many parents assume that tablets are "meant" to be used that way and that tablet technology is so intuitive that their child does not need direction or supervision when using it. Realistically, parents sometimes use mobile media as digital babysitters to keep the child safe, still, or quiet, and while this may not be the best use of the technology, librarians and other informal educators need to approach these uses of these new types of media without judgment, and armed with recommendations for high-quality, age-appropriate media. In storytime, children's librarians have the opportunity to model how you can turn an otherwise solitary medium into a cuddly, book-based, educational, and interactive learning tool to be shared.

Learn More ... Blogs to Read

- ALSC, www.alsc.ala.org/blog/www.alsc.ala.org/blog/
- The Digital Media Diet, http://digitalmediadiet.com
- LittleeLit, http://littleelit.com
- MOMs with apps, http://momswithapps.com

Position Statement Alignment

> Adults have a responsibility to protect and empower children—to protect them in a way that helps them develop the skills they need to ultimately protect themselves as they grow—and to help children learn to ask questions and think critically about the technologies and media they use. Adults have a responsibility to expose children to, and to model, developmentally appropriate and active uses of digital tools, media, and methods of communication and learning in safe, healthy, acceptable, responsible, and socially positive ways.
>
> NAEYC & Fred Rogers Center (2012), p. 10

Storytimes and Technology

The staple of library services and programs to children, in the eyes of the public, are the baby, toddler, and preschool storytimes that take place in almost every one of the 6000 or so public libraries that exist in the United States. While the format and emphasis of storytimes have changed over the years, public expectation for the provision of this vital service has remained largely unchanged.

Until a decade or two ago, the norm for storytime was that children were separated from their parents and reunited with them once the program was over. Now, parents are expected to stay with their children during the program so that they can learn how to support their young child's literacy development through parent education points presented during the course of the storytime. The shift happened when librarians began to realize that the most effective way to get parents to read to their kids (often in at-risk environments) was to show them how. Many librarians will even joke that storytimes are not for the kids at all; they're for the caregivers. Storytime provides parents with a model for how co-reading can happen at home, and with the introduction of new media to even the youngest children; this service is more vital than ever.

A new addition to the storyteller's toolkit is tablet technology, usually in the form of an iPad or Android tablet, and often mirrored onto a TV screen or projected. The children's digital publishing market is rapidly growing, and since libraries provide access to books in all formats, the inclusion of apps and e-books in library services, programming, and collections is a necessary and exciting part of librarianship in the digital age.

Storytimes offer an ideal forum for sharing bite-sized bits of information about choosing high-quality, age-appropriate media, sharing the media experience with children, and making media consumption an engaged, active experience for both the children and their caretakers. In addition to addressing the changing needs of families and their digital reading choices, tablet computers serve as powerful teaching tools for parents and their very young children. Presentation software like Keynote or Google Drive can be used to engage the multiple learning styles of everyone in attendance at storytime. For example, visual cues that indicate movement from one activity to another (like an image of a sleeping child before you come to the lullaby section of your program). Music, sounds, lyrics, and opening and goodbye slides can all contribute to the overall quality of the program. Content can also be easily shared online via Slideshare or through the library's website. Caregivers often want to remember the books, songs, and activities that were shared, so librarians can provide links to all content (digital or otherwise) used during the storytime. This allows parents to access content later, download content for themselves, find out how to access digital resources through the library, or to place holds on physical items.

Engagement Models

There are a number of different models and initiatives that actively support parent-child engagement, usually based around traditional literacy skills. These programs are beginning to extend their reach to digital formats and literacies as well. Two of these well-established storytime resources take into account current research and best practices for presenting early literacy programs that support family literacy. Every Child Ready to Read (ALSC/PLA, n.d.) and Mother Goose on the Loose are beginning to develop techniques for intelligent, intentional, developmentally appropriate use of technology like tablets. The emphasis of both of these programs is on engagement between the parent or caregiver and the child. Any technology that is employed in these programs must first support that mission, and beyond that, be the best tool for conveying whatever information the storyteller wishes to convey.

Tips for Parents, Educators, Librarians, and Other Helping Professionals

1. Model joint media engagement for parents and caregiver
2. Create opportunities for co-viewing and peer/social engagement for children
3. Demonstrate dialogic reading techniques as ways to deepen engagement during media use
4. Focus on the quality of interaction with other people, not on the device or specific content for very young children
5. Provide resources to extend learning to other activities, both on-screen and off
6. Connect storytime experiences and content to transferable knowledge, comprehension goals, and early literacy curriculum and activities

Every Child Ready to Read (ECRR) is a parent education initiative that was developed by the Association of Library Services to Children and the Public Library Association (ALSC/PLA). ECRR was developed to serve the needs of children aged 0–5, but the emphasis of this program is on the development of traditional, print-based literacy. An emphasis on the use of nonfiction and STEM (science, technology, engineering, and math) during storytime and parental education "asides" (learning tips) make this approach slightly different from more traditional storytime models. It provides an excellent framework for developing early literacy programs that support families with young children who are learning to read in a traditional, print-based sense, but they also lend themselves well to programs that introduce new media as material or focus points for caregivers to engage with their young children.

Librarians who have begun using new media (usually apps or e-books) in their storytimes often do so with the intent of reflecting the media marketplace in which today's families exist. They provide recommendations for high-quality digital media (as well as print), while supporting early literacy skills and early learning practices. The most common example of this is using apps that highlight the early learning practices or early literacy skills or that encourage content creation and joint media engagement with a caregiver.

Apps to Use to Exemplify Literacy Supporting Behaviors

- A Present for Milo
- Good Night Moon
- How Rocket Learned to Read
- Mr. Brown Can Moo! Can You?—Dr. Seuss
- Pete the Cat
- Press Here
- Wild about Books

Mother Goose on the Loose is a musical parent-engagement program, created by Dr. Betsy Diamant-Cohen for children 0 to 3. It excels in the seamless integration of technology as an aid to learning. Diamant-Cohen has developed a technology statement in conjunction with LittleeLit.com to guide the use of new media, including a felt-board themed app designed to encourage parent-child engagement using Mother Goose on the Loose images and songs. The core of the technology statement is this:

> Technology handled with careful consideration, in moderation; in ways that fit in with the program's intent and don't overwhelm, that enhance but don't replace, and that encourage parent/child interaction is appropriate for use in a Mother Goose on the Loose program.
>
> Mother Goose on the Loose (Software Smoothie, 2013).

Mother Goose on the Loose programs focus on supporting the parent to be their child's first and best teacher and, in that vein, uses the best storytelling techniques and tools to support a positive learning environment for both the parent and child. Simple use of images, color, sound, music, digital felt boards, and digital books are currently being tested in Mother Goose on the Loose programs all around the country, and the results from this experimentation can be found on LittleeLit.com.

Conclusion

While innovative programs like Mother Goose on the Loose are quickly adapting to the realities of family reading habits by including healthy examples of age-appropriate consumption of digital media with emergent technologies, librarians are simultaneously developing new toolkits for acting as media mentors in their communities. During this transition, it is important to remember that most of the existing ethics, frameworks, and toolkits within the profession are still relevant. In fact, they are even more relevant now, while formats are changing at the speed of light. The foundations of our respective fields can guide our work with tablets and other new media as well as provide us with useful advice to offer parents and the public about healthy (or healthier) ways to integrate our digital diets into the rest of our lives. The heart of the message is that we have to be conscious, thoughtful, and selective about our children's (and hopefully also our own) media use.

By addressing needs within a framework of access, content, and engagement (ACE), we can begin to understand how to integrate digital media into existing library practices, and promote the role of librarians as Media Mentors for parents, families, and educators. We can also begin to build new skills for the unique challenges and opportunities presented by this digital sandbox.

Understanding the issues of access and choosing content is part of any traditional library role, although the details are more complex and harder to research for digital materials. But shifting the focus from the device to the engagement of the users (with each other) is a revolution in the making—a change in the basic question we ask of ourselves as professionals. This revolution may lead us to dramatically different answers in the future; so being active during this digital age transformation is essential for librarians. And what better place can there be, than the 21st-century library to broadcast this message? We hope it will be one that is widely received and carried deeply into the fabric of all our institutions, beginning with the public libraries.

Position Statement Alignment

> Digital citizenship also includes developing judgment regarding appropriate use of digital media; children and adults need to be able to find and choose appropriate and valid sources, resources, tools, and applications for completing a task, seeking information, learning, and entertainment.
>
> NAEYC & Fred Rogers Center (2012), p. 10

Teacher Takeaways

- Attend a new media storytime at your library to observe the storyteller in action.
- Introduce yourself and ask questions after the program.
- If you'd like to bring a group of children in to the library for new media programs, call and ask if that is a service your library offers. If it isn't, see the next point.
- Consider partnering with your local library, especially when seeking grant funding. Collaborative projects between formal and informal learning environments, especially around emergent technologies, are attractive to potential funders.
- Contact your local library and ask for resources you need to support your classroom activities, especially around the use of technology with young children. Your library responds to community needs; if you need something, ask for it!
- Take advantage of what your library can do for you, for example: a child-centric technology petting zoo; a storytime that includes new media; app recommendation lists or information about using technology wisely with young children to send home to parents.

References

American Library Association. (n.d.). *Equity of access.* Retrieved from www.ala.org/advocacy/access/equityofaccess

Association of Library Services for Children, & Public Library Association. (n.d.). Every child ready to read. Retrieved from http://everychildreadytoread.org

Common Sense Media. (2013). *Media and violence: An analysis of current research.* San Francisco, CA: Common Sense Media.

Guernsey, L. (2013, May 1). iPads in the classroom and media mentors [Web log post]. Retrieved from http://earlyed.newamerica.net/blogposts/2013/ipads_in_the_classroom_and_media_mentors-83299

Institute of Museum and Library Services. (2013). *Growing young minds: How museums and libraries create lifelong learning.* Washington, DC: Author.

Kluver, C. (2011, November 1). The dirty little secret about app review sites [Web log post]. Retrieved from http://digitalmediadiet.com/?p=509

National Association for the Education of Young Children, & Fred Rogers Center for Early Learning and Children's Media at Saint Vincent College. (2012). *Technology and interactive media as tools in early childhood programs serving children from birth through age 8.* Washington, DC: NAEYC; Latrobe, PA: Fred Rogers Center for Early Learning and Children's Media at Saint Vincent College.

Neuman, S. B., & Celano, D. (2012). *Giving our children a fighting chance: Poverty, literacy and the development of information capital.* New York, NY: Teachers College Press.

Pew Research Center. (2013, October). *Tablet and e-reader ownership update.* Washington, DC: Pew Research Center's Internet & American Life Project. Retrieved from http://pewinternet.org/Reports/2013/Tablets-and-ereaders.aspx

Schugar, H. R., Smith, C. A., & Schugar J. T. (2013). Teaching with interactive picture e-books in grades K–6. *The Reading Teacher, 66*(8), 615–624. DO—10.1002/trtr.1168

Resources

Apps, Software, Online Resources, and Activities

- *30 Hands*, 30 Hands Learning, Inc., http://30hands.ipresentonline.com/site/index
- App Friday, www.appfriday.com
- AppoLearning, www.appolearning.com/
- AppShopper, http://appshopper.com
- Apple iTunes App Store, https://itunes.apple.com/us/genre/ios/id36
- *A Present for Milo*, Ruckus Media Group, http://ruckusreport.com
- Axis 360 Digital Media Library, http://btol.com/axis360/
- Bookboard.com, http://bookboard.com
- Bookflix, http://auth.grolier.com/login/bookflix/login.php
- Children's Technology Review, http://childrenstech.com
- Common Sense Media, www.commonsensemedia.org www.commonsensemedia.org/
- The Digital Media Diet, http://digitalmediadiet.com
- Digital-Storytime.com, http://digital-storytime.com
- EbscoHost, www.ebscohost.com
- *Goodnight Moon*, Loud Crow Interactive http://loudcrow.com
- Google Drive, https://drive.google.com
- Google Play
- The Horn Book, www.hbook.com/category/choosing-books/app-review-of-the-week/
- *How Rocket Learned to Read*, Random House Kids, www.randomhousekids.com/brand/how-rocket-learned-to-read/
- The iMums, www.theimum.com

- International Children's Digital Library, http://en.childrenslibrary.org/about/foundation.shtml
- iTunes, Apple, www.apple.com/itunes/
- Keynote, Apple, www.apple.com/mac/keynote/
- Kindle, Amazon, https://kindle.amazon.com
- Kirkus Reviews, www.kirkusreviews.com/book-reviews/ipad/
- Little eLit, http://littleelit.com
- Mother Goose on the Loose, www.mgol.net
- *Mr. Brown Can Moo! Can You?—Dr. Seuss*, Oceanhouse Media, www.oceanhousemedia.com
- *My Story—Book Maker for Kids*, Cause Labs, http://mystoryapp.org
- Nook, Barnes & Noble, www.barnesandnoble.com/u/nook/379003208/
- OverDrive, www.overdrive.com
- *Pete the Cat*, Harper Collins Children's Books, www.harpercollinschildrens.com/feature/petethecat/
- *Press Here*, Chronicle Books, www.chroniclebooks.com/presshere
- School Library Journal, Touch and Go, http://blogs.slj.com/touchandgo/
- Slideshare, www.slideshare.net/
- Smart Apps for Kids, www.smartappsforkids.com
- TeachersWithApps.com, http://teacherswithapps.com
- Tumblebooks, www.tumblebooks.com
- Wild About Books, Random House Children's Books, www.rhkidsapps.com/wild-about-books/

Websites

- ALA, American Library Association, www.ala.org/
- Every Child Ready to Read, www.everychildreadytoread.org
- IMLS, Institute of Museum and Library Services, www.imls.gov
- Pew Research Center's Internet and American Life Project, www.pewinternet.org/

Learn More . . .

- ALA, *Equity of Access* Brochure, www.ala.org/aboutala/sites/ala.org.aboutala/files/content/missionhistory/keyactionareas/equityaction/EquityBrochure.pdf
- ALSC, Association of Library Services to Children, www.alsc.ala.org/
- Campaign for Grade-Level Reading, http://gradelevelreading.net
- Center on Media and Human Development at Northwestern University & National Center for Families Learning. (2013). Media, technology, and reading in Hispanic families: A national survey. Retrieved from http://familieslearning.org/PDF/Hispanic FamMediaSurvey_Dec13.pdf
- COPPA, Children's Online Privacy Protection Act, www.ftc.gov/opa/2013/07/coppa.shtm
- Guernsey, L. (n.d.). Screen time: how electronic media-from baby videos to educational software-affects your young child. Retrieved from www.lisaguernsey.com/Screen-Time.htm

- Guernsey, L., Levine, M. H., Chiong, C, & Stevens, M. (2012, December 10). *Pioneering literacy in the digital Wild West: Empowering parents and educators.* Retrieved from www.joanganzcooneycenter.org/publication/pioneering-literacy/
- Herr-Stephenson, Rhoten, Perkel, & Sims. (2011). *Digital media and technology in afterschool programs, libraries, and museums.*
- Institute of Museum and Library Services. (2013). *Growing young minds: How museums and libraries create lifelong learning.* Washington, DC: Author.
- Jackson, S. (n.d.). With digital technologies, can school libraries help transform learning? Retrieved from http://remakelearning.org/blog/2013/01/17/with-digital-technologies-can-school-libraries-help-transform-learning/
- Learning in hand: Ways to evaluate educational apps. (2012, March). Retrieved from http://learninginhand.com/blog/ways-to-evaluate-educational-apps.html
- Miller, C., Zickuhr, K., Rainie, L., & Purcell, K. (2013, May 1). *Parents, children, libraries, and reading.* Retrieved from http://libraries.pewinternet.org/2013/05/01/parents-children-libraries-and-reading/
- Mother Goose on the Loose! (n.d.). *MGOL and Technology.* Retrieved from www.mgol.net/about/mgol-and-technology/
- Neuman, S. B., & Celano, D. C. (2012). *Worlds apart: One city, two libraries, and ten years of watching inequality grow.* Retrieved from www.aft.org/pdfs/americaneducator/fall2012/Neuman.pdf
- Rideout, V. (2014, January 24). *Learning at home: Families' educational media use in America.* Retrieved from www.joanganzcooneycenter.org/publication/learning-at-home/
- UPCLOSE, Center for Learning in Out of School Environments, http://upcloselrdc.wordpress.com
- Zickuhr, K., Rainie, L., & Purcell, K. (2013, January 22). *Library services in the digital age.* Retrieved from http://libraries.pewinternet.org/2013/01/22/library-services/

Connected Educator—Connected Learner: The Evolving Roles of Teachers in the 21st Century and Beyond

Amanda Armstrong

Introduction

The term, *connected educator*, has become more prevalent in blogs, articles, and initiatives as digital tools transform our personal and professional lives. We now have connected educator month or week and create websites dedicated to this topic. *Merriam-Webster* (2013) defines *connected* as "joined or linked together" and "having useful, social, professional, or commercial relationships." These definitions resonate with the philosophies behind being a connected early childhood educator in the 21st century.

Becoming a connected educator refers to "the need for teachers to fully exploit the transformative potential of emerging learning technologies—and to do it within a global framework" (Nussbaum-Beach & Hall, 2012, p. 29). Using online communities or blended learning approaches, a connected educator builds relationships with other professionals and curates resources to support their learning along with others to improve their practice. No longer do educators have to wait to receive a letter, make a phone call, or have an in-person meeting. They can set up a meeting on Google hangout, get real-time feedback from others using Twitter, send a report through email, and confirm appointments using their smartphones.

As early childhood educators are figuring out how to appropriately use technology and interactive media with young children and apply the principles and guidelines of the National Association for the Education of Young Children (NAEYC) and Fred Rogers Center joint position statement (2012) to practice, it is more valuable for than ever for educators to be connected to other professionals and families and to create a community of practice and communities of interest. The position statement reminds us that along with using technology to support young children's holistic growth and development, early childhood educators should also use these tools to support their professional growth and development. Educators now have digital tools that make it easier to communicate with others, test their ideas, and see what's happening in classrooms and informal learning settings around the world. As educators understand and experience of the value of appropriately using digital tools, they can also help young children use technology appropriately as they become active digital and global citizens.

Position Statement Alignment

> For the adults who work with young children, digital literacy includes both knowledge and competence. Educators need the understanding, skills, and ability to use technology and interactive media to access information, communicate with other professionals, and participate in professional development to improve learning and prepare young children for a lifetime of technology use.
>
> National Association for the Education of Young Children [NAEYC] & Fred Rogers Center (2012), p. 9

Connecting With Professionals

With the prevalence of digital tools, early childhood educators can now learn anywhere, anytime, and about almost anything from multiple devices. Educators in this digital world need to be prepared to use digital tools to support their professional growth, as well as learn approaches to using technology appropriately with young children. To build these skills and abilities, educators need to use digital tools to create their own professional learning network (PLN) that includes fellow early childhood professionals working in formal and informal spaces, as well as professionals in other fields. When designed intentionally, a PLN can become a community of practice to focus on a specific area of the educators' work.

A PLN is "a system of interpersonal connections and resources that support informal learning" (Trust, 2012, p. 34). By tapping the resources and information from colleagues in different informal learning spaces, early childhood settings, and teacher educations programs, educators can expand their knowledge and understanding of using digital tools to support early learning along with new ways of using traditional materials. Technology makes it easier to share educators' stories and ideas through online communities, webinars, virtual meetings, and social media. One way this has been applied is through a Facebook group designed to share information about apps for children with specials needs. Members share apps, tips, articles, funding information, and what's working with their clients or their program. Some members also meet offline to have in-person meetings or meet up at conferences. A Facebook group is a resource for members and supports their learning in an interactive, social, and fun way.

While it is valuable to include diverse early childhood professionals in the PLN, educators can also learn from professionals outside the field. These conversations can spark ideas or create a different lens for seeing how best to use a technology tool. To help deepen educators' understanding of technology and digital media, they can also build reciprocal relationships with children's media creators and app developers. Getting their perspective offers a way of understanding the design process as well as helping app developers and children's media creators understand what matters most to support children's healthy growth and development. Educators can connect with them through social media, sending an email, or attending conferences and webinars where these designers share their work, like Dust or Magic. Participating in these types of events gives educators a deeper appreciation and understanding of the work and intentionality that goes into designing quality app for young children.

As global citizens, it's important that educators use technology to connect with professionals in different parts of the world. Through these connections, they can build their own digital literacy and competency through meaningful experiences. Tools such as Skype, Google Plus, email, social media, Adobe Connect, and WebEx can be used to communicate, and Google Drive and Dropbox are tools for sharing and editing documents with others in different locations. Digital connections can be combined with in-person events to help strengthen connections and conversations. Educators need to be open to developing their PLN to help them learn different approaches to using technology and traditional materials with young learners.

Connecting Through a Community of Practice

Early childhood educators can take the connections they gather from their professional learning network to create a community of practice (COP). Unlike the PLN, the COP is "groups of people who share a concern or a passion for something they do and learn how to do it better through interacting with one another" (Helm, 2007, p. 12). To create a COP from a PLN, educators can intentionally select individuals that are committed to enhancing a specific skill, exploring a shared interest, or addressing a common cause. The COP has to include an area of interest, a sense of community, and shared practice (Helm, 2007). For instance, educators can build a community of practice where they focus on finding appropriate ways to use technology to support early literacy skills. Educators can create subgroups on online communities and use a combination of synchronous and asynchronous tools, such as chat messages, online meetings, and emails, to discuss their concerns, desired outcomes, and approaches to improving their practice. With these tools, educators can use photos and videos to share what they're doing in their classrooms and use this community as a place to pose questions, get feedback, and solve problems. By intentionally creating a community of practice, educators can evolve their professional growth and build meaningful relationships with colleagues.

Connecting With Families

Early childhood professionals' work with young children, parents and families are an intricate part of the community. To support this relationship, technology can offer rich and meaningful ways to help families feel connected to the program and informed about their children's experiences. Educators can use technology to build on face-to-face communication and keep parents regularly updated.

Position Statement Alignment

> Technology tools offer new opportunities for educators to build relationships, maintain ongoing communication, and exchange information and share online resources with parents and families.
>
> NAEYC & Fred Rogers Center (2012), p. 7

To keep parents informed, educators can use online tools, like social media, to let parents know the activities the students are working on or expected events. For instance, some classrooms have a Twitter account. Parents can follow the classroom's account to view completed projects and receive tips from educators to support their children's work. Security and confidentiality are always issues to address, so educators can set up secured classroom or school blogs, send families a video or photo through email, or update students' work in a shared and secured cloud-based storage system. The type of tool can be determined by the type of accessibility families have to technology and Internet at home. If there aren't technologies in the home, educators can remind families to use their local libraries as a resource to access online content.

While technology is a way for educators to communicate with families, it also offers opportunities for families to connect with educators and their children's classrooms. Families can send a quick email to educators to build the communication between home and school. If parents or caregivers are away from home due to business or another matter, they can set up online meetings with educators. To bring students' culture and family life into the program, family members can audio record stories to play during story or circle time or capture photos and video from a recent trip for their children to share with the class.

These approaches help build community within the program and provide inspiration for new projects in the classroom. For educators, technology can become a bridge and an invitation for families to share and be connected to a part of their children's classroom community.

Position Statement Alignment

> With technology becoming more prevalent as a means of sharing information and communicating with one another, early childhood educators have an opportunity to build stronger relationships with parents and enhance family engagement. Early childhood educators always have had a responsibility to support parents and families by sharing knowledge about child development and learning.
>
> NAEYC & Fred Rogers Center (2012), p. 7

Developing Young Connecters

As educators build connection to professionals and families, it's important to remember they are helping young children find their way in the connected world safely and appropriately. Educators understand that early childhood builds foundational skills for children, and this includes digital literacy and being a responsible digital citizen. Connected educators have the opportunity to be role models and help young children navigate through digital and online tools and resources to children build digital literacy and become responsible digital citizens.

Position Statement Alignment

> Adults have a responsibility to expose children to, and to model, developmentally appropriate and active uses of digital tools, media, and methods of communication and learning in safe, healthy, acceptable, responsible, and socially positive ways.
>
> NAEYC & Fred Rogers Center (2012), p. 10

By using digital tools to support children's learning and by modeling appropriate use of these tools, educators help children learn the various ways technology tools can be used to support their learning. Connected educators are aware of the affordances of technologies as well as what is developmentally appropriate for their students. Educators can create an atmosphere where children feel open to exploring and learning about these tools to build their curiosity, exploration, and creativity. From having time to explore, children can become familiar with these tools and learn when it's best to use a digital camera, tablet, or music player. Educators become a model for children who watch them use technology appropriately in their program.

Educators can also help children use technology to connect to the world by creating opportunities to connect with other classrooms in their country or other parts of the world. These experiences, when intentionally designed, help young children learn the meaning of being a digital citizen. Educators can use tools, such as Skype in the classroom or video messaging, to build this understanding through a tangible experience. These experiences help children understand how to treat others online and offline, the type of information that is OK to share, and how to find appropriate content to view online. Creating these authentic experiences will help children discover the meaning of being a digital citizen and a young connecter in the 21st century.

Connected Educator↔Connected Learner

The idea of being a connected educator involves creating connected learning opportunities. Technology offers the ability to communicate with families and professionals and share ideas with individuals or groups. Since there are a variety of ways of learning, educators can find the approach that works best for them. For instance, they can subscribe to YouTube videos from an organization that supports the appropriate use of technology with young children, take a course on iTunes U to learn about new topics or best practices, or follow a teacher's blog site to learn what they're doing to support early learning in the classroom.

Educators who aren't comfortable using only online tools can take a blended approach to learning by combining offline and online professional development opportunities. Having online learning experiences coupled with in-person education offers the ability to deepen knowledge and connections and gather resources. Table 17.1 and 17.2 are designed to help educators discover offline and online strategies they can use to support their professional growth. Table 17.1 includes a list of several tools and strategies for getting connected, and Table 17.2 includes approaches to using social media to develop connected learning.

Becoming a Connected Educator

Though the idea of being a connected educator can be enticing, you may feel unsure of your first steps and have some mental hurdles to overcome. Here are

Table 17.1 Tools to Support Your Professional Growth

Tool	Description	Examples
Social Media	Online networks where people can create, share ideas, and exchange information	Facebook, Twitter, Pinterest, LinkedIn
Blog Sites	Informational sites that consist of posts from a single individual, small group, or organization	Edublogs, Fred Rogers Center, Edutopia, Language Castle, LittleeLit
Online Communities	Virtual communities that post content about specific topics and consist of members that engage through chats, comments, subgroups, etc.	Classroom 2.0, edWeb.net, Connected Educators
Webinars	Online presentations, seminars, workshops, or panels that focus on a specific content area	Early Childhood Investigations, TEC Center
Online Meetings/Web conferences	Online services that host virtual meetings that allow people to connect from different locations	WebEx, Google Hangout, GoToMeeting, Skype
Conferences	Formal meetings or discussions that occur in-person or online	NAEYC, ISTE, FETC, K12 online
Workshops	Interactive and hands-on meetings that engage groups in a particular topic	State-led resource centers, professional development programs, education centered nonprofit organizations
Tech Playdates	Gatherings of professionals and/or parents that play with technology tools and share ideas of best practice	PLAYDATE13

Table 17.2 Social Media Approaches to Develop Connected Learning

Social Media Tool	Learning Approach	Examples
Facebook	Create a group that focuses on a specific topic in early learning and/or follow early childhood organizations that provide up-to-date information	**Groups:** iPad Apps and Info for Special Kids, Follow: Exchange Press, Center of Media and Child Health, NAMLE
Twitter	Use hashtag to search or tweet information on a specific topic and/or follow a person or organization that provides relevant content	**Hashtags:** #ecetechchat, #edtech, #kinderchat Follow: @remakelearning, @childtech, @edsurge @TEC_Center
Pinterest	Create a board and pin articles on early childhood topics and/or view other member's boards	**Boards:** Common Sense Media, ALSCblog, PBS Kids, Joan Ganz Cooney Center at Sesame Workshop

some common reasons why educators have trouble initiating their connected learning with advice on how to approach the issue:

- *I don't have time.* It's amazing the amount of information you can learn in 15–30 minutes. Even if you can't join a chat or webinar in real-time, you can catch up on discussions by searching for the hashtag (i.e., #ECETech-Chat) on Twitter, play back a segment of the webinar, or check for updated responses in a learning community discussion forum or chat. Create set times during the week to get in the habit of being part of online conversations and communities.
- *I have nothing to say.* Educators have unique situations, stories, and experiences to bring to any conversation. Most likely one educator's story will resonate with another and help him or her overcome a challenge or inspires a new idea. You can start by discussing a project that is working well for you, which helps you become a resource for others. Over time, you can share activities that did not produce the projected outcome and seek feedback from others with similar experiences and interests.
- *I'm conscious of other people's feedback.* Start by watching a conversation if you don't feel comfortable expressing your thoughts at first. Gradually, you can make participation goals for yourself. For instance, during the first 2 weeks, your goal can be to join a new Twitter hashtag and observe the discussion. During the 3rd week, you make a few responses to people's comments and gradually become a regular participant and contributor to the conversation.

Staying Connected

Once you have moved beyond the initial hesitation, you are ready to experience the benefits of being a connected educator. Here are some ideas to help you continue the momentum and stay connected:

- *Value other's input.* Demonstrate your interests in other people's comments and stories by actively participating in discussions. Ask questions, make suggestions, share a story, or describe a best practice. All of these ways to participate are important contributions that build the learning community.
- *Listen (or read).* You can learn a lot from listening or reading other people's stories. Listen, read, and reflect on these stories and then make thoughtful contributions to the conversation. By showing your interest and that you care, you'll start getting connected and building professional relationships.
- *Share your ideas.* As valuable as it is to listen, it is just as important to share your stories. This makes your PLN stronger and brings in fresh knowledge to others in the COP. You will learn new perspectives as you receive feedback from people in diverse fields and professions. Sharing ideas also gives people within your PLN and COP an idea of your values, experiences, framework, and style.

Teacher's Voice

My strategies for being a "connected educator" involve dedicating a portion of my day (anywhere from 5 minutes to 1.5 hours) to connecting with other educators online. I primarily stay connected by using Twitter, where I'm able to participate in real-time chats that are specific to a grade or topic and can also learn from a broad range of other educators whom I might not interact with otherwise. I also participate in other social media communities, like LinkedIn or Google+, in order to stay up-to-date with new approaches to teaching and learning and using technology tools. These networks give me an opportunity to connect with people beyond borders and time zones and across disciplines and communities. By being connected, I have access to a network of people every day of the year and that network is built on the premise of collaborative exchange and meaningful connections. In order to make those connections meaningful, I strive to actively contribute resources and provide support to other educators as well. One other way that I try to be a connected educator is by maintaining a blog where I can share my learning and reflections on integrating technology in early childhood classrooms. This space provides a place where I can share my ideas and receive feedback from other connected educators and by commenting on their blogs, we can establish a collegial relationship that we can each grow from.

Maggie Powers, Lower School Technology Coordinator, The Episcopal Academy, Philadelphia, PA, and a Technology and Education

Consultant specializing in early childhood education, social media, and global education.

Conclusion

Being a connected educator is an approach to enhancing your professional and personal life. The rewards of being a connected educator include developing rich and close connections with professionals and families, gaining and sharing knowledge about diverse topics, and accessing a multitude of resources to improve your own knowledge and skills. Early childhood professionals understand the value of building relationships with young children, parents, families, and other educators, and using technology tools adds a new dimension to this experience. Technology will continue to change and evolve over time. Being a connected educator, and embracing the philosophy behind this idea, are timeless and will endure through future educational technology trends and the emergence of new technology tools.

Teacher Takeaways

- Use social media to follow or friend organizations and professionals that provide content on early childhood topics and share what's happening in your program to develop a PLN.
- Communicate with parents through social media, blogs, video messages, and/or email to keep the updated about your programs and to bring families into the classroom.
- Model the appropriate and intentional use of technology to support children's digital literacy and create experiences where they connect with others across the world to help them understand how to be digital citizens.
- Create a tech playgroup with other teachers in your program or school to try out new digital tools and apps. Schedule a tech playdate where each person can show and share what technology tools they are using and what they are doing with technology in the classroom as a tool for early learning and as a tool to strengthen the home-school connection.

References

Connected. (2013). In *Merriam-Webster*'s Online Dictionary. Retrieved from www.merriam-webster.com/dictionary/connected

Helm, J. H. (2007). Building communities of practice: Energize your professional development by connecting with a purpose. *Young Children*, *62*(4), 12–17.

National Association for the Education of Young Children, & Fred Rogers Center for Early Learning and Children's Media at Saint Vincent College. (2012). *Technology and Interactive Media as Tools in Early Childhood Programs Serving Children from Birth through Age 8*. Washington, DC: NAEYC; Latrobe, PA: Fred Rogers Center for Early Learning and Children's Media at Saint Vincent College.

Nussbaum-Beach, S., & Hall, L. R. (2012). *The connected educator* [iBooks version]. Retrieved from https://itun.es/us/346gF.1

Trust, T. (2012). Professional learning networks designed for teacher learning. *Journal of Digital Learning in Teacher Education*, 28(4), 133–138.

Resources

Websites, Blogs, and Tools for the Connected Educator

- Adobe Connect, www.adobe.com/products/adobeconnect.html
- ALSC blog, www.alsc.ala.org/blog/
- Center on Media and Child Health, www.cmch.tv
- Children's Technology Review, http://childrenstech.com/
- Classroom 2.0, www.classroom20.com
- Common Sense Media, www.commonsensemedia.org
- Connected Educators, http://connectededucators.org
- Connected Learning, http://connectedlearning.tv
- Dropbox, www.dropbox.com
- Dust or Magic, http://dustormagic.com
- Early Childhood Investigations, www.earlychildhoodwebinars.com
- Early Childhood Technology Network, www.ecetech.net
- Edublogs, http://edublogs.org
- Edudemic, www.edudemic.com
- Edutopia, www.edutopia.org
- EdSurge, www.edsurge.com
- edWeb.net, http://home.edweb.net
- Exchange, www.childcareexchange.com
- Facebook, www.facebook.com
- FETC, http://fetc.org/Events/Educational-Technology-Conference/Home.aspx
- Fred Rogers Center, www.fredrogerscenter.org
- Google Drive, https://drive.google.com/
- Google Hangouts, www.google.com/+/learnmore/hangouts/
- Google Plus, www.google.com/+/
- GoToMeeting, www.gotomeeting.com/online/
- iPad Apps and Info for Special Kids, www.facebook.com/groups/345626498830538/
- ISTE, www.iste.org
- iTunes U, www.apple.com/education/ipad/itunes-u/
- Joan Ganz Cooney Center at Sesame Workshop, www.joanganzcooneycenter.org
- K12, http://k12onlineconference.org/
- Kinderchat, www.kinderchat123.net
- Language Castle LLC, http://languagecastle.com/Language_Castle/LANGUAGE_CASTLE_HOME.html
- LinkedIn, www.linkedin.com
- Little eLit, http://littleelit.com
- NAEYC & Fred Rogers Center Joint Position Statement, www.naeyc.org/content/technology-and-young-children
- NAMLE, http://namle.net
- Pinterest, www.pinterest.com

- PBS Kids, http://pbskids.org
- Pittsburgh Kids + Creativity Network, http://remakelearning.org/
- PLAYDATE 13, https://sites.google.com/site/playdatechicago13/
- Skype, www.skype.com/en/
- Skype in the classroom, https://education.skype.com
- TEC Center at Erikson Institute, http://teccenter.erikson.edu
- Twitter, https://twitter.com
- WebEx, www.webex.com
- YouTube, www.youtube.com

Learn More ...

- 10 tips for becoming a connected educator. (2013, March 21). Teacher Leadership. *Edutopia.* Retrieved from www.edutopia.org/blog/10-tips-become-connected-educator-elana-leoni?utm_source=facebook&utm_medium=post&utm_campaign=blog-becoming-connected-CEM-wrapup-quote
- *Connect and inspire: Online communities of practice in education.* U.S. Department of Education, Office of Educational Technology. Retrieved from http://connectededucators.org/report/files/2011/03/0143_OCOP-Main-report.pdf
- Dabbs, L. M. (2012, August 7). Five tips for new teachers to become connected educators. Retrieved from www.edutopia.org/blog/new-teachers-becoming-connected-educators-lisa-dabbs
- Dunn, J. (21 July, 2013). How to improve your social media skills in 30 minutes a day. Retrieved from www.edudemic.com/how-to-improve-your-social-media-skills-in-30-minutes-a-day/
- How do I get a PLN? (2013, November 18). Education Trends. *Edutopia.* Retrieved from www.edutopia.org/blog/how-do-i-get-a-pln-tom-whitby
- MacMeekin, M. (n.d.). Morphing into a 21st century teacher. Retrieved from http://anethicalisland.wordpress.com/2013/03/30/21st-century-learning/

Subject Index

Name Index

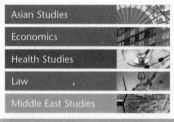